MARY HAYDEN
Irish Historian and Feminist
1862–1942

Mary Hayden
young scholar

Joyce Padbury

MARY HAYDEN
Irish Historian and Feminist
1862–1942

ARLEN
HOUSE

Mary Hayden
Irish Historian and Feminist
1862–1942

is published in 2021 by
ARLEN HOUSE
42 Grange Abbey Road
Baldoyle
Dublin D13 A0F3
Phone: +353 86 8360236
Email: arlenhouse@gmail.com

978–1–85132–263–3, paperback

International distribution by
SYRACUSE UNIVERSITY PRESS
621 Skytop Road, Suite 110
Syracuse
New York
USA 13244–5290
Phone: 315–443–5534/Fax: 315–443–5545
Email: supress@syr.edu
www.syracuseuniversitypress.syr.edu

Typesetting by Arlen House

Cover artwork:
'Mary Hayden' (c. 1935)
by Lily Williams
is reproduced courtesy of the Department of History, UCD

CONTENTS

To the memory of my parents

ACKNOWLEDGEMENTS

The research for and writing of this biography had been completed and left aside, when Art Cosgrove and Fergus D'Arcy urged me to pursue its publication. My special thanks go to them for their encouragement and expert advice. While engaged in the research I benefitted from the suggestions and opinions of many people, historians and others. In particular my gratitude is expressed to those pioneers in the study of women's history, the late Margaret Mac Curtain and Mary Cullen. Also especially helpful were the late Margaret Ó hÓgartaigh, and Clara Cullen who in addition compiled the bibliography. Conan Kennedy provided a wealth of information, both personally and in his edition of the diaries of Mary Hayden.

Various repositories in Dublin were consulted, where the staff were always helpful. In particular I should mention the National Archives of Ireland, the National Library of Ireland, the University College Dublin Library, the University College Dublin Archives, the National University of Ireland Archives, the Dublin Diocesan Archives and Alexandra College Library.

A publication grant awarded by the National University of Ireland is acknowledged with grateful appreciation.

Finally, the expertise, commitment and patience of Alan Hayes and his team at Arlen House made this book possible. I thank them warmly.

CAISM	Central Association of Irish School Mistresses
IAWGCG	Irish Association of Women Graduates and Candidate Graduates
ICWSA	Irish Catholic Women's Suffrage Association
IWFL	Irish Women's Franchise League
IWRL	Irish Women's Reform League
IWSLGA	Irish Women's Suffrage and Local Government Association
IWCLGA	Irish Women's Citizens and Local Government Association
IWSF	Irish Women's Suffrage Federation
IWWU	Irish Women Workers' Union
NCWI	National Council of Women of Ireland
NUWGA	National University Women Graduates' Association
WNHAI	Women's National Health Association of Ireland
WSPU	Women's Social and Political Union

FOREWORD

Donal McCartney

Mary Hayden belonged to that generation of remarkable women of the early twentieth century who contributed significantly to an emerging, independent Ireland. For her special role in that evolution she deserved a full biography which she has now received in this book by Joyce Padbury. Hitherto, much of the biographical work on Hayden's female contemporaries has concentrated, understandably, on those who were politically active and militant. Hayden's chief contribution was as a feminist. Her campaigns were for the equality of rights for women, especially in education and suffrage. Beyond that she had so little interest in the intense nationalism of her time that she could almost be described as apolitical. She was a determined Feminist (capital F); at best, only a low-case nationalist. As her biographer points out, Hayden's feminism took precedence over her nationalism. However, her enthusiastic involvement in the Gaelic League made her a cultural nationalist but without following her close friend, Pearse, and other activists in the language movement into militant nationalism. She disapproved of the 1916 Rising.

Her early life may not have been untypical of that of other middle-class children growing up in Dublin in the second half of the nineteenth century. What made her different from most other girls from comfortable homes was the diary she kept and which has survived. Padbury has made excellent use of this source to depict, scrutinise and comment on the mind and personality of an independent and ambitious feminist in the making. The diary also provides us with some interesting social commentary and observations. Her childhood was secure, but saddened by the death of her mother when Mary was eleven. She had one sibling, John, whose apparent lack of ambition displeased her. She was not happy in the convent schools to which she was sent. It was not until her father agreed to her attendance at Alexandra College that she found a school greatly to her liking and where she was inspired by a couple of her teachers.

Her father was the highly respected Thomas Hayden, Professor of Anatomy and Physiology in the Medical School of the newly established Catholic University, physician in the Mater Hospital and a Vice-President of the Royal College of Physicians. He seems to have often indulged his daughter. He died when she was nineteen and at the start of her successful university career. But, as Padbury argues, the discrimination against women in education which she then encountered sparked her campaigns for the rights of women, beginning in 1902 with the Irish Association of Women Graduates and Candidate Graduates, of which she was a co-founder, activist in the women's suffrage movement, and in her outspoken opposition to the 1937 Constitution because of its articles relating to women.

Under the Irish Universities Act (1908) establishing the National University of Ireland, it was confirmed that:

women shall be eligible equally with men to be members of the University or of any authority of the University, or to hold any office or enjoy any advantage of the University.

Hayden was the only woman appointed to the University's first Senate of 35 members. She was also, with her friend Agnes O'Farrelly, appointed to the Governing Body of University College Dublin. Successful in her application for the Lectureship in Modern Irish History in 1909, she became the first Professor of that subject when its status was raised in 1911. Padbury devotes a couple of well-researched chapters to her role as an academic presence until her retirement in 1938. Among her former students Hayden's reputation was that of a formidable, competent and effective teacher. This was during the early decades in UCD when teaching took preference over research. According to the Statutes by which the College was governed, a professor was required 'to devote himself to research and the advancement of knowledge' only 'so far as is compatible with the duties of his chair'. (One wonders what Hayden would have thought of the gender bias in that statement!)

Hayden's reputation as a researcher has to be judged in the light of the circumstances that her research and publications were done before modern historical scientific methods became the norm in Irish academic circles. A bibliography of Hayden's writings is provided which will enable anyone interested to judge for themselves. She is best known to later generations of secondary and third level students for her *Short History of the Irish People* (1921) which she co-authored with George Moonan. As Padbury states, Professor Hayden did not allow her feminism to interfere with her historical writing. Readers of the *Short History of the Irish People* today will find it surprising that the only reference to the Ladies' Land League is that it was founded mainly by Michael Davitt. The Parnell sisters are not mentioned; nor is there any reference to the women's organisations of Hayden's own time. Padbury offers a reasonable explanation for the absence of women from Hayden's historical work; and she also implies that the harsher dismissal of her work by some living academics is hardly warranted.

Mary Hayden, feminist and academic, comes alive in the pages of this objective, precise, balanced and well-written biography.

MARY HAYDEN

Irish Historian and Feminist
1862–1942

INTRODUCTION

The name of Mary Hayden turns up, briefly, in various accounts of the events of the twentieth century, but she is still a relatively unknown person. She features briefly in the *Dictionary of Irish Biography*, in an entry by Diarmaid Ferriter, in the *Oxford Dictionary of National Biography*, in an entry by Senia Pašeta, and her contribution to women's opportunities and roles in higher education has been the subject of a recent article by Judith Harford.[1] However, to date there has been no full biography. Consequently, this present book aims to reconstruct her life, in order to discover the Victorian child and follow her rocky path to feminist campaigner and university professor. She was an active participant in feminist campaigns until her death in 1942 and was also one of the earliest women university professors. However, the widely-used history textbook of which she was co-author seemed to be her main claim to fame.[2] Little is known about this woman, who led a busy life of teaching, writing and activism in educational and feminist causes.

The long life of Mary Hayden began with a conventional, comfortable upbringing in mid-Victorian

Dublin and ended eighty years later during the Second World War in a Dublin vastly different from the city and the society into which she had been born. Though not involved in party politics, she participated in many events, organisations and groups which made lasting changes to that society. An account of her life is a graphic record of the changes affecting women between the mid points of the nineteenth and the twentieth centuries.

Her early life gives us a fascinating picture of a girl and young woman growing up in middle-class Victorian Dublin. Her background was relatively sheltered, but not excessively restricted. She found the conventions of life for a middle-class woman to be increasingly unacceptable, and flouted them in small and then greater ways, as she developed her independent character and began to apply her critical faculties to the anomalies of life for a woman. The comfort in which she spent her childhood and early adult years allowed her the opportunity for study and travel. Gradually she came to her understanding of feminism, which she dated from about the turn of the century.

It is particularly fortunate that Hayden's diaries are available, covering about twenty-five years from the age of fifteen, in which there is vivid detail about her early life, her interests, her personality, her studies and her friendships. If she kept diaries in later life they have not survived, but it is clear from other sources that the strong-minded woman of the early years continued to take an outspoken and independent stance on the issues she considered important. Her name is particularly associated with women's struggles for admission to the university, for the parliamentary franchise, and in opposition to the 1937 constitution. Her entire life exhibits a consistent concern for the equality of women as human beings and in their role in society. The two areas where she saw most need for equal opportunity for women were in education and in employment, a reflection of her own middle-class position. That is not to suggest that she ignored the lives of the majority of Irish women, circumscribed as they were by limited education, domestic duties and the conditions of low-level labour. Convinced that education was the key to a better life, she engaged in social work which was usually of an educational nature, and she was involved in some early moves to encourage women workers to form trade unions.

In feminist terms, Mary Hayden can be seen as a telling link between the pioneering women of late nineteenth-century Ireland and their feminist successors of the early twentieth century. Organised action in Ireland for the emancipation of women is traced from the 1860s, and to the efforts of Anna Haslam and Isabella Tod in campaigns for specific rights and educational opportunities for women.[3] When Hayden was born in 1862, women were considered to be subordinate to men in rights, roles and opportunities in a patriarchal society. Hayden's determination to pursue her education led her in the course of time to see the possibilities of emancipation and to become an avowed feminist. As she later wrote, the earliest significant influences on her were Anna Haslam, Alice Oldham and Isabella Mulvany,[4] the latter two her teachers in Alexandra College, the former her lifelong inspiration, and all advocates of the advancement of the role of women. Hayden outlived these three women, and herself became a mentor for feminists of the early twentieth century.

The involvement in reform and philanthropy of the earliest of these three, Anna Haslam (born in 1829), has been described as 'a classic case of the evolution of a feminist'.[5] Hayden had some involvement in philanthropic work, but her main early interest was in education and then in suffrage, an equally recognisable route for the evolution of a feminist. Though the opportunities open to women were limited mostly to the private sphere, Hayden was personally ambitious for a publicly recognisable role, which she eventually obtained as a professor of the new National University of Ireland. The origins of her feminism were rooted in her own strivings to escape from the conventional life expected of a young middle-class woman in late nineteenth-century Dublin. Her engagement, and that of some other contemporary women, with various matters relating to women's lives from the late nineteenth century onwards is an element of the development of feminism in Ireland. In education she was a leader, an achiever and a teacher. In public life, she was an example and a voice proclaiming women's role. The history of Irish feminism must include an appreciation of the relevance of Mary Hayden.

Though advanced in her thinking and courageous in her public actions, she was neither extreme nor militant. Not specifically interested in party politics, she became a believer in Home Rule, contented with the new Irish State of the 1920s and 1930s but critical of much of the legislation of those decades which she saw as detrimental to the position of women.

Mary Hayden's working life was spent in teaching, and she became the first holder of the professorship of Modern Irish History in University College Dublin, a chair which she held for twenty-seven years. The textbook, *A Short History of the Irish People* (1921), of which she was co-author with George A Moonan (in fact she wrote most of it from the sixteenth century onwards), was in use in Irish secondary schools into the 1960s. In her time she was regarded as a significant scholar, who had surmounted the nineteenth century obstacles to women's higher education and advanced to a senior position in the new National University of Ireland where she had a few, but not many, women colleagues.

Probably the best known women in early twentieth-century Irish history are Maud Gonne MacBride, Constance Markievicz and Hanna Sheehy Skeffington,[6] who were all Hayden's contemporaries. They came from varied backgrounds, but all four had been reared in comfort, with no personal experience of hardship or poverty. In adulthood, Hayden was very different from the other three in not being involved in republican nationalist organisations and not sharing their republican aspirations, which may perhaps explain the neglect of her somewhat different life story. At the same time, she was a lifelong friend of Hanna Sheehy Skeffington and was closely associated with her in a succession of campaigns for women's rights.

Not untypical of the many intelligent, independent-minded protagonists of women's emancipation of the period, such as Louie Bennett or Jennie Wyse Power,[7] Hayden was a prominent and admired feminist of her day, whose life provides an illuminating commentary on aspects of Irish history which deserve to be more widely known. Her life is important as an illustration of one woman's experience in late Victorian and early twentieth-century Ireland. Many other, and some better known, women had different experiences, in circumstances which differed from hers – such as poverty or misfortune, political action, imprisonment, national acclaim or literary fame. Hayden's life is no less significant in telling us so much about her progress from protected Victorian girlhood to university professorship and twentieth-century feminist. Her efforts and achievements, her failures and disappointments, introduce us to a less well-known strand of women's experience in Ireland.

Hayden's biography tells us how this woman of almost Unionist sympathy, from questioning her own prospects, grew to challenge accepted perceptions of women's opportunities and women's role, to embrace the national heritage, to adopt the concept of Home Rule, and to welcome the Irish Free State but participate in feminist opposition to some of its legislation. At different times and in various issues, she was working beside Unionists, or constitutional nationalists, or republicans, or militants. Her life story is remarkable for the route she travelled which, in retrospect, shows her consistent development of the understanding of women's autonomy.

The principal source for Mary Hayden's early life is her diary. Why did the young girl commence a diary and continue to keep it for about twenty-five years? The diary was a place to which she could retreat, where she could speak to herself, discover her individuality, and contemplate her relationships. As one scholar has commented, the diary was 'used by women to sort their own lives'; it was 'a way of bringing meaning to disorder'.[8] For the biographer, Mary Hayden's diary is a record of her doings, her hopes and her fears, revealing in its immediacy, though the many excisions suggest some later discretion or reconsideration of the material. Hayden's diary enables us to reconstruct her early life in more detail than would otherwise be possible. Her reactions to the joys and sorrows of her daily life offer an insight on a bright young girl with a growing sense of self as she moved into adulthood. Circumstances, family and financial, contributed to the evolution of the independent character which Mary Hayden's childhood personality had longed to be. The yearnings of the introspective child were unspecified, undefined, but in time became an ambition for intellectual pursuits and learning, for independence and dignity, and for an autonomous role in a society of equal citizens.

For her later life there are practically no personal papers. We are dependent on her published articles, her letters to newspapers, and reports of her speeches and attendance at meetings, to help us reconstruct her life. The records of the

National University Women Graduates' Association provide valuable information. The Minutes of the Governing Body of University College Dublin and of the Senate of the National University of Ireland tell us something about her membership of those bodies. There is also her historical writing – articles and book reviews published in journals, and the textbook co-authored with George A Moonan. A small number of letters from Hayden are in the Eoin MacNeill, Hanna Sheehy Skeffington, Patrick Pearse and R. Dudley Edwards papers, but few letters to her survive.

Mary Hayden's diaries, written in small notebooks, span the years 1878 to 1903, but there are gaps where volumes seem to be missing, and in several instances she records that she has lost a volume. There are many excisions from the diaries. Pages have been both cut out and torn out, which suggests they were removed at different times. The excisions seem to be of two kinds – references to herself which are too personal to be revealed, and comments on others which may be severely critical. It seems likely that the excisions were the work of Hayden herself, rather than of her relative, Fr Cyril Crean (grandson of Michael Crean) who deposited the diaries in the National Library of Ireland in about 1972. Hayden preserved these diaries for sixty or so years, through numerous house moves, which presumably means she thought them of some value, but was it for her own interest or for posterity? Did she, in her late seventies, with her lifelong interest in the lives of women and children in earlier periods, think of these diaries of her girlhood and young adulthood as source material for the study of women's experiences in the nineteenth and twentieth centuries? Did she hope or expect that the significance of women's role, both in contemporary life and in history, would gradually begin to be understood? And was she offering herself to posterity as an example of that significant role? In that hope, some personal record of her later life would surely also have been left, since those were the years of feminist campaigning and of her professional achievement. As personal letters were not kept, the survival of the diaries may be no more than a fortunate accident, a relic of her early years held on to as a personal treasure. Perhaps as her life became more fulfilling, she felt less need to give vent to her thoughts and doings in the private medium of a diary. The absence of diaries for these later years is our misfortune. The volumes we have comprise a fascinating introduction to the life of an early feminist. Since the research for this work was carried out, the diaries of Mary Hayden have been published which makes them more accessible.[9] The editor, Conan Kennedy, has included informative annotation and appendices.

Her public life spanned the second half of her eighty years. A professor of the new National University of Ireland, she took part in the campaign for women's suffrage, in protests against discriminatory legislation and regulations of the Irish Free State, and in a campaign against the Irish Constitution of 1937. These events have been recounted elsewhere, but Mary Hayden's part in them is not well known. From her published writings and her reported speeches, it is clear that she was a prominent and respected activist, while at the same time fulfilling her role as a university professor. This book describes these various events by concentrating on Hayden's participation in them. It is a tale worth telling, whether she herself so intended, and it is a significant source for the history of Irish feminism.

NOTES

1   Diarmaid Ferriter, 'Mary Hayden', *Dictionary of Irish Biography* (Cambridge, 2009), Vol. 4, pp 531–2; Senia Pašeta, 'Mary Teresa Hayden', *Oxford Dictionary of National Biography* (Oxford, 2004), vol. 28, pp 5–6; J. Harford, 'The Historiography of the Professoriate: Reflections on the Role and Legacy of Professor

Mary Hayden (1862–1942)', *Paedagogica Historica* (2019), https://doi.org/10.1080/00309230.2019.1669681.

2   Mary Hayden and G.A. Moonan, *A Short History of the Irish People* (Dublin, 1921).

3   Mary Cullen, 'Women, Emancipation and Politics, 1860–1984' in J.R. Hill (ed.), *A New History of Ireland*, Vol. VII (Oxford, 2003), pp 832–33. Anna Haslam (1829–1922), Quaker, activist in the cause of rights for women, founder of the Irish Women's Suffrage and Local Government Association. Isabella Tod (1836–1896), Scottish-born resident of Belfast, campaigner and writer on women's rights, notably in education and suffrage.

4   Alice Oldham (1850–1907), teacher, advocate of the higher education of women, first President of Irish Association of Women Graduates and Candidate Graduates. Isabella Mulvany, headmistress of Alexandra School, one of first nine women graduates (1884) of the Royal University of Ireland.

5   Carmel Quinlan, *Genteel Revolutionaries* (Cork, 2002), p. x.

6   Maud Gonne MacBride (1866–1953), English-born Irish nationalist and republican, founder of Inghinidhe na hÉireann. Constance Markievicz (1868–1927), born into the Anglo-Irish ascendancy Gore-Booth family, revolutionary and labour activist, first woman elected to the British House of Commons (1918), but did not take her seat. Hanna Sheehy Skeffington (1877–1946), teacher, suffragist, republican, journalist.

7   Louie Bennett (1870–1956), suffragist, trade unionist, pacifist. Jennie Wyse Power (1858–1941), nationalist, feminist, business woman, active member of the Ladies' Land League, Cumann na mBan, Sinn Féin and later Senator.

8   Joanne E. Cooper. 'Shaping Meaning: Women's Diaries, Journals and Letters – The Old and the New' in Dale Spender (ed.), *Personal Chronicles: Women's Autobiographical Writings* (New York, 1987). See also Suzanne L. Bunkers, '"Faithful Friend": Nineteenth-Century Midwestern American Women's Unpublished Diaries' in Spender (ed.), *Personal Chronicles*.

9   *The Diaries of Mary Hayden 1878–1903* (Killala, 2005), Vols. I–V, edited and annotated by Conan Kennedy.

I

A VICTORIAN CHILDHOOD
1862–85

Family Background and Early Life

Mary Teresa Hayden was born on 19 May 1862 at 30 Harcourt Street, Dublin, the home of her parents Thomas and Mary Ann (née Ryan). Both parents were of Tipperary origin. Thomas was a medical practitioner, and Professor of Anatomy and Physiology at the Catholic University School of Medicine. He was born in 1823 in Parsons Hill, Co. Tipperary of a Protestant father and Catholic mother, and there is a suggestion that Thomas's own father, who died in 1828 while his children were very young, attempted to disinherit his children should they be reared as Catholic but, according to the same source, the Protestant clergyman cousin, Edward Hayden who then benefited from the will, restored the inheritance to the children.[1] The Protestant grandfather, John Hayden, had owned property in Tipperary and in Kilkenny, and Mary's reference to her grandfather as only a small gentleman farmer seems to refer to him rather than to her maternal lineage.[2] Her father's brother John now lived at Parsons Hill. Thomas Hayden, the eldest of the family, received his medical education in Dublin at the Peter Street School of Medicine and the Meath Hospital. He gained the College of Surgeons licentiate in 1850, its fellowship two years later, and was lecturer in Anatomy at the Peter Street School of Medicine until the establishment of the Catholic University School of Medicine in 1855. Also appointed physician in the new Mater Misericordiae Hospital in 1861, he authored articles in medical journals and a medical textbook. He was associated with *Atlantis*, a literary and scientific journal founded by John Henry Newman to publish the work of professors of the Catholic University of Ireland, of which Newman was Rector.[3] Hayden was later a Vice-President of the Royal College of Physicians (1876–77). Mary recalled how he brought her to see the table laid for some grand banquet at the College; '…the table decorated with flowers and the shining of the light through the red glasses which left stains like that of spilt claret on the white cloth'.[4] For the year prior to his death in 1881 Dr Hayden was a member of the first Senate of the Royal University of Ireland. Thomas Hayden was clearly a man of distinction in Dublin professional life. Considered very polite, he was known as 'gentle Thomas'.[5] On his deathbed, he told his children he had had a hard life and had worked his way to the top.[6]

Less is known about Mary Ann Ryan (also referred to as Marianne), a daughter of Patrick Ryan of Raffane near Thurles.[7] Of her mother, Mary recalled that she 'could say sharp clever things at times' and was interested in politics. Some old letters from Mary Ann to Thomas displayed her clearheadedness, business capacity and energy, but of 'Mama's real abilities' her daughter had no idea. Mary also noted that letters from her mother to her father before their marriage were 'not gushing', and added that 'we must have inherited our aversion to gush from her'.[8] Mary regretted remembering so little about her mother who died in 1873. The most vivid recollection was being brought at the age of eleven to her dying mother's bedside, and howling.[9] Mary recorded the death in 1895 in a convent near Leeds of the elderly nun, Aunt Kate, her mother's last surviving sister, whom Mary had visited several times and had described as 'practical, like Mama'.[10]

Mary was the second of two Hayden children, the elder being her brother John born in 1858. Their childhood was comfortable and happy, though blighted by the early loss of their mother. The Hayden's housekeeper, Mrs Cox, became and remained an important figure in the lives of Mary and her brother, but the principal female influence on Mary, after her mother's death, was Mrs Emma Crean, wife of Michael Crean, a cousin of Thomas Hayden. Mrs Crean had a care for Mary's welfare and included her in much activity with her own daughters, Mary, Emma and Eleanor.

Ireland in the second half of the nineteenth century was a predominantly rural country with a declining population and widespread poverty, both rural and urban; but growing numbers began to live in towns which became centres of activity. The large towns were Dublin and Cork, where commercial and administrative occupations predominated, and Belfast, a centre of industry.[11] There was a growing middle class, as Catholics in particular advanced themselves in commerce and in the professions. For instance, Macardle's brewery was established in Dundalk in 1862,[12] and Boland's Flour Mills commenced in Dublin in 1874.[13] Mary Hayden's father was a distinguished physician and his cousin, Michael Crean was a barrister whose wife Emma was of the Dunn family who owned Morrison's Hotel on Dawson Street.

For a family like the Haydens, Dublin in the late nineteenth century was a pleasant city in which to live, still retaining 'the beautiful buildings, monuments, parks, streets and squares ... inherited from the Anglo-Irish Ascendancy'.[14] Some few years after his wife's death, Dr Hayden and his family moved to 18 Merrion Square, an even better address than Harcourt Street. Dublin's best residences were in the areas around Mountjoy Square, north of the river Liffey and, on the south, around St Stephen's Green and Merrion Square. But close to these fine houses, back lanes contained some of Europe's worst slum housing, with 'inhuman poverty ... on a massive scale'.[15] Mary, as she grew to adulthood, would become familiar with the slums, engaging in charitable work, visiting the homes of the poor and helping to clothe their children.

Dr Hayden employed a number of servants, and the family entertained and visited. At a young age Mary had a pony named Bess, and later a horse named Alice, and she remained a keen horsewoman well into her adult life. Her reminiscences of life in Merrion Square describe sitting with her father in his study in the evenings:

How cosy the room looked in the winter evenings ... The wide fireplace, the two sideboards, the big gasolier, the marble clock on the mantlepiece, the chairs covered in dark leather and the big square table – Papa in his grey dressing gown in an armchair at one side of the fire, I at the table close beside him, pouring over Virgil or Caesar, or Smith and Hull ...[16]

There were Sunday walks with her father to Sandymount, Donnybrook and Ballsbridge, visits with him to view the pictures at the Hibernian Academy,[17] and his dinner parties which, until old enough to attend, she would observe from upstairs. In summer Dr Hayden would rent a house outside the city, in for instance Monkstown or Howth, where Mary enjoyed swimming and climbing. Swimming was 'grand fun', especially in deep water.[18] The newly-developed railways to Bray and Howth enabled Dublin residents to holiday outside the city during the summer.[19] Mary became a constant user of these trains.

The Crean cousins, Mary Hayden's closest relatives in Dublin, were her family for many years. She was very friendly with the elder Crean girls, but as she grew older her interest in scholarship meant that they had less in common and they at times called her a blue stocking.[20] She proved good at entertaining the younger children, especially telling them stories or teaching them lessons, and she recalled one as Johnnie, 'a tiny little fellow in tunics and a broad straw hat, coming out with me on Saturday to buy sugar-sticks, and fish in the Dodder'.[21]

There is no evidence of severity of discipline in the Hayden family, but Dr Hayden's authority was respected and obeyed until his death. In her grief then Mary regretted the trouble she had caused him, which one may presume referred to her somewhat unconventional character, while as yet aged only nineteen. He had rebuked her for 'disliking the refinements of female society' when she complained that ladies at his dinner parties spoiled things with their 'stupid conversation' about weddings and balls.[22] On another occasion she regretted the ending of cricket, climbing and the 'general liberty of action' denied to grown ladies.[23] She recognised in later years that she had been 'allowed to lead a somewhat *gamin* life' in contrast to the ladylike upbringing of her cousin Eleanor Crean.[24] In 1881 Dr Hayden told his daughter that she should enjoy things like other people, when she felt that she preferred school and games to parties and tennis.[25]

Hayden's early education had been in a variety of schools. From 1873, for two or three years, she was a boarder at the Ursuline Convent in Thurles, Co. Tipperary, where her mother's sister Margaret was a nun. She was unhappy at boarding school, probably distressed by her absence from home and family following so soon after the death of her mother. Despite her later poor opinion of convent schools and her assertion that she never learned anything until she was fifteen,[26] she was awarded prizes and distinctions at the Ursulines for History, Christian Doctrine, Geography and application.[27] Hayden's name was enrolled at Mount Anville, Co. Dublin in September 1875 where she remained only two months, transferring then to the new day school of the same Sacred Heart Order at Harcourt Street, where she attended until 1877.

When she started to keep her diary in January 1878 Hayden was about to commence attendance for a few months at Miss Cantwell's school in Mountjoy Square, which from its curriculum of drawing, arithmetic and French verbs, seems to have been a finishing school for young ladies. Hayden's own reading at home at this time on the history of Turkey, the life of Schiller, and Byron's *Childe Harold* was more stimulating. Precocious in her reading, she dismissed *Pride and Prejudice* as a case of 'much ado about nothing'.[28] One may speculate that the widowed Dr Hayden did not know what best to do for his independent-minded young daughter whom he reprimanded on receipt of an unsatisfactory report from Miss Cantwell.[29] In late August 1878 Dr Hayden was advised to go to the south of France for health reasons. He brought his daughter as far as Paris where she was to board in a convent until his return. She spent about a month at the convent with ninety other girls staying for the holidays. The daily routine, which she later recalled as monotonous and dull,[30] consisted of prayers, meals, walks in the Luxembourg Gardens, and visits to the principal sights. She feared she might be left at school in the convent, but this fear proved groundless. On her father's return at the end of September they moved to the Hotel Tronche, near the Madeleine, and spent two days enjoying themselves.[31]

Dr Hayden's indulgence of his daughter had included travel, sometimes as his companion to meetings of the British Medical Association. Though he thought to please her by bringing her to such events she dreaded the soirées and garden parties, where, as she wrote, 'I do not know what to say or do'.[32] They attended one such meeting in Cambridge where she coped better with the social events than on a previous occasion in Cork, somewhat overpowering events for an unsophisticated eighteen year old girl. However the Cambridge colleges attracted her greatly, though she thought life at Girton would not match the enjoyment offered by the men's colleges.[33] Father and daughter then spent a week doing the sights in London, but Hayden failed to persuade her father to continue as far as Oberammergau to see the passion play. In the following year 1881 they were at the British Medical Association meeting on the Isle of Wight, and to Hayden's delight he afterwards brought her to Germany and Switzerland. She was excited to be in Germany 'a country I have often wished to see'. 'For the first time, I saw the Rhine ... a grand river truly, but muddy, something the colour of cough mixture'. She described their journey, until they finally stayed at St Moritz which she found to be 'horridly fashionable' but a glorious place for climbing.[34] This was their last holiday together, only months before her father died. His illness and death from pneumonia on 30 October 1881 is recounted in some detail in Hayden's diary. She grieved for him as the only one in the world who 'really loved me', who had always indulged her, 'proud of whatever success I might achieve'.[35]

The death of Dr Hayden meant many changes to the lives of his two children. They moved from Merrion Square to 42 Moyne Road, Rathmines, which Hayden called a 'sardine box of a house'[36] though she was to become fond of her cosy home there. In fact these houses were substantial family homes in the expanding fashionable southern suburbs. This was the last residence where Mary and John would be the sole occupants. In later homes, they appear to have been sub-tenants or lodgers. Dr Hayden's will divided his estate leaving to Mary capital of £3000, to John £500 and the proceeds of the sale of the house and furniture; in John's case the capital was not to be his unless he married and otherwise was on his death to be divided among the children of Thomas Hayden's brother, John.[37] Probate of the estate took nearly three years to obtain, during which time Mary and John were dependent upon the trustees, Michael Crean and their uncle, John Hayden, for the release of dividends on the invested capital. At times they were short of ready cash, which worried Mary greatly, but they nevertheless were both able to continue their lives in their reduced circumstances. They brought one servant, Lizzie, from the Merrion Square house. John, who had been advised by his father on his deathbed to think of a profession, decided to read for the English bar at Gray's Inn, London. Mary had not much confidence in this plan, recognising that her 'provokingly dreamy' brother[38] had nothing like her own determined energy. They quarrelled frequently, though she sometimes admitted to her diary that it was partly her fault. For her own part, she threw herself into her studies for the matriculation examination, classes and grinds, and a constant round of activities which included frequent trips to Bray where her friend Josephine McGauran lived. Torn between learning and enjoyment, she admitted that 'my old quiet life of study has gone to pieces'[39] and on one occasion she got a 'well merited lecture' from John about her frequent expeditions to Bray.[40]

Political Background

In public affairs the 1870s saw many of the Irish members of parliament at Westminster beginning to act as a group, independent of the English political parties, recognising the value of working together on Irish issues like land reform and education. The failure of the Fenian insurrection of 1867 helped to turn attention to constitutional methods of redressing the Irish question, with increasing concentration on the cause of home rule in some form. Charles Stewart Parnell, first elected in 1875, had within a few years become the leader of a reasonably disciplined Irish party, supported by a mass movement, the Land League, in the New Departure which united revolutionary aspirations with demands for land reform and for home rule in the party's efforts at Westminster. Neither the land agitation throughout the country nor the parliamentary activity seemed to impinge to any extent on young Mary's life in Dublin. She regularly heard the land question discussed by her father and his dining companions, to no useful purpose as it seemed to her in September 1881, which was shortly after Gladstone's Land Act of 1881 and while the Land War still continued.[41]

There is a brief reference in her diary to the 'astounding news' that the Chief Secretary Cavendish and the Under Secretary Burke had been assassinated.[42] The Hayden family belonged to a Catholic bourgeoisie which saw no compelling reason to quarrel with the established political situation of union with Britain. The efforts of the Irish members at Westminster encouraged interest in constitutional nationalism and in the possibility of achieving a measure of home rule. This anticipation raised the need for the middle class and its sons to prepare for the political, social and economic advancement and the leadership opportunities which would accompany the return of a parliament to Dublin, a need provided for by increasing numbers of secondary schools opened by religious orders of priests, brothers and nuns, and in due course by government recognition of the demand with the establishment of the Intermediate Education Board (1878) and the Royal University of Ireland (1880). The call was for education for the sons of this growing Catholic middle class. And before the end of the century, Catholic men were entering the professions in increasing numbers.[43]

Women's Education

Secondary education for girls was limited, and in general women's education did not call for serious work. The lack of university educated women teachers and the tradition that secondary education for girls should differ from that of boys meant that when available it was more concerned with feminine accomplishments than with intellectual attainments, and standards were low.[44] Middle-class women were destined for marriage or for the convent, lives for which convent schools prepared them. Hayden recalled that at Mount Anville 'really useful things [like] Latin and Greek were entirely omitted'.[45] She had a poor opinion of contemporary convent education which she described as giving girls a smattering only of various subjects, a little French, no mathematics or real introduction to literature in either English or French.[46] But, from the mid-nineteenth century onwards, there had been sustained efforts to improve the quality of education available to women, as was also happening in England. The Cambridge and Oxford Local Examinations were opened to girls, and schools and colleges for women were being established in England from the middle of the century.[47] In Ireland, the growth of middle-class, commercial and manufacturing families in cities and towns like Belfast, Dublin and Cork, led to demand for education for their daughters.[48]

The aim was to prepare women for employment and release them from dependency. In 1859 Margaret Byers founded a school for girls, later called Victoria College, in Belfast. She desired for girls 'the same opportunities for sound scholarship' as given to their brothers in the best boys' schools. In 1866 Alexandra College in Dublin was established through the efforts of Anne Jellicoe. Alexandra offered to girls both a secondary education and a university-style liberal education to fit them for careers as teachers.[49] In 1867 Isabella Tod founded the Ladies'

Institute, Belfast. These women held pioneering views on women's education, and served as role models for Protestant women.[50] They, and others such as Anna Haslam, by petitions, meetings, lobbying and other campaigning, secured the inclusion of women in the provisions of the legislation in the late 1870s on secondary and university education. For Catholic girls, convent schools conducted by the Dominican, Loreto, Ursuline, Sacred Heart and other orders of nuns increased in number, while adhering until the later years of the century to the traditional ideas on women's education. As yet, there were few strong role models for Catholic women.

The Intermediate Act 1878, which established a system of public examinations with scholarships and prizes open equally to girls and boys, was an important development in the provision of secondary education in Ireland, and particularly for women's education; for instance Latin and mathematics became part of the normal curriculum for girls taking examinations and competing for prizes. The number of convent schools presenting pupils for the Intermediate Examinations increased from twenty-nine in 1893 to forty-five in 1898.[51] Better secondary education opened up employment opportunities for women as clerical workers in the post office and civil service, and as teachers, careers of some dignity, and the possibility of university degrees for women was to follow. But many parents and churchmen did not yet approve of or see any need for an academic type secondary education for girls. Hayden considered that her cousin Eleanor Crean who had been 'taken from school' at the age of fifteen, was 'half-educated'.[52]

Alexandra College

Hayden was fortunate to have an understanding father who allowed his determined daughter to continue her education beyond the elementary level, and her move at the age of sixteen to the Protestant Alexandra College may have been an acceptance by her father of her scholarly bent. Hayden has recorded no comment about her attendance at a Protestant school, and her father's partly Protestant background may have helped his decision. That decision was to have significant effect on his daughter's life, encouraging her questing nature and leading her towards the company of Protestant and non-conformist women. The experience of attendance at Alexandra was influential in the development of the feminist movement in Ireland. Leading feminists such as Mary Hayden, Louie Bennett, Kathleen Lynn, the Gifford sisters and Dorothy Macardle all passed some of their formative years at Alexandra.

In October 1878 Hayden started at Alexandra College where she was extremely happy.[53] She enjoyed the company, got into scrapes (for instance for climbing through a window),[54] and was taught Latin and English by Isabella Mulvany, later to become a lifelong friend. Her frequent references to Isabella as 'the Chief' were never less than complimentary, 'a wonderful woman, I never met anyone like her'.[55] Isabella Mulvany became something of a role model for Hayden. In 1880 Mulvany became headmistress of Alexandra School at the age of twenty-six, and upon the establishment of the Royal University of Ireland she availed of the first opportunity (1884) for women to take a degree. Mulvany and another teacher at Alexandra, Alice Oldham, both advocates of the higher education of women, made a deep impression on Hayden.[56]

Since 1870 Trinity College had held two examinations at junior and senior level for the women students at Alexandra,[57] and there were now also open to women the examinations of the new Intermediate Board. Academically Hayden was good, though not outstanding. At the Trinity examination in 1880 she took history, geography, arithmetic, French, Latin, mathematics, zoology, botany, and was placed 16 of 62.[58] The examination was taken in Trinity, giving her a taste for the College and an envy of life there which she continued to experience on every visit. In the Intermediate Middle Grade examination the same year, she achieved a much better place than expected.[59] In 1881 she took the second Trinity and the Senior Intermediate examinations. She thought that 'Papa did not seem satisfied with my success' in getting third place on the scholarship list at Trinity, though her brother John considered it very good.[60] She was dismayed that Dr Hayden thought her schooling should now end. During their visit to her Aunt Margaret, her mother's sister, at her convent in Thurles, Archbishop Croke, also visiting, commented on Hayden's Senior Intermediate Examination and supposed her schooling was now finished. Dr Hayden agreed and when afterwards questioned by his daughter told her she had studied enough. She cried in bed, thinking it unfair that her brother was permitted further years of study, a typical unhappy experience of many middle-class young women.[61] Hayden became very melancholy at the thought of leaving school; though now aged nineteen, she still felt that 'school is everything to me, society, amusement, work'.[62]

Among the friends Hayden made at Alexandra were the Conan girls, whose religious background was also mixed. In the Conan family, mother and daughters were Protestant, father and sons Catholic, an arrangement which then was not unusual, known as the Palatine Pact. There was a similar arrangement in the Gifford family.[63] The compromise called for no comment from Hayden. Nor did she experience any awkwardness as a Catholic in the school. While there were many Protestants among Hayden's friends of the Alexandra and university years, she also maintained her earlier friendships among

Catholics. In this Hayden was somewhat unusual, unlike for instance Louie Bennett, a Protestant, who was more conscious of the divide between Protestant and Catholic families,[64] or C.S. Andrews, a Catholic, who thought Protestants were remote and different.[65] Hayden's commitment to her own religion, and her apparent indifference to prejudice about those of other faiths, is an early pointer to the balance which she would display in later life on various issues. Hayden became very friendly with the (Protestant) Mulvany family; later she 'got into a fine row' at confession about going to the wedding of Mary Mulvany in a Protestant church.[66] Hayden herself was and remained a committed, practising Catholic, and never referred to the fact of her Protestant paternal grandfather. Her lack of sectarian consciousness may owe something to that inheritance. There were several nuns on her mother's side, and she often commented on the confinements of convent life which were alien to her own venturesome spirit.

The Position of Women

An early manifestation of women's political action, the Ladies' Land League (1881) and its most prominent member Anna Parnell, apparently aroused no interest in the young Mary Hayden. The Ladies' Land League was a significant organised contribution by women to a national cause, but specifically women's rights were not part of its programme. Hayden as yet showed little interest in national issues.

In general, women were seen as 'subordinate to men and subject to male authority in decisions about their lives'.[67] Women were not permitted to vote, be members of public bodies or enter the professions; nor were middle-class women expected to earn their own living. The movement for the emancipation of women, rooted in the belief in a common rational human nature and in the

39

equality of the individual, led to questioning of the anomalies existing in women's lives. Feminist movements began by addressing themselves to women's economic dependency and consequent exploitation.[68] The word 'feminism' was not in use until the 1890s, but organised feminist action in Ireland is traced to the 1860s, with claims by small numbers of women for property rights for married women, for repeal of the Contagious Diseases Acts (for the regulation of prostitution and which applied only to women), for improvements in women's education and employment opportunities, and for women's suffrage,[69] and by the second half of the century these issues were receiving attention in Ireland from a few women, of whom the most remarkable were Anna Haslam and Isabella Tod.[70]

How aware the young Mary Hayden was of these issues we cannot tell, except that she enthusiastically availed of the new educational opportunities for women. As her diary shows she was conscious of the patriarchal nature of her society. Her continued association with Alexandra College, and meeting Anna Haslam, certainly encouraged and influenced her development of a female consciousness with fundamental implications for her attitude to the role of women. Haslam lived until 1922 and saw the achievement of the parliamentary franchise for women. Tod died in 1896, having fought successfully for many improvements in women's lives, notably in the area of education. Hayden may not have met Tod though she knew of her significance,[71] but she certainly knew and admired Haslam, whom she probably met before the end of the century in Alexandra, which Haslam used to visit.

Undergraduate Years
The Royal University of Ireland established under the University Education (Ireland) Act of 1879, was an attempt to provide acceptable higher education for Irish Catholics.

Here again, through the efforts of women like Tod and Haslam, women were included in the provisions as eligible to present, on an equal basis with men, for the examinations and degrees of the new university. The Royal was an examining and degree awarding university, but provided no teaching. The Royal University was immediately availed of, as a means of attaining degrees, by the students, all male, attending the University College on St Stephen's Green conducted by the Jesuits. The Catholic University of Ireland, established by the Irish bishops in 1854 without regular endowment and without the power to grant degrees, had not prospered, apart from its Medical School in Cecilia Street, whose students could qualify by taking the licentiate of the Royal College of Surgeons. In 1882 the institution on St Stephen's Green was re-organised as University College, and in 1883 its management was given to the Jesuits. 'This marked the end of the Catholic University as a teaching institution, though it continued to have a nominal existence.'[72] The Jesuit managed University College was its virtual successor.

The Royal University offered the first opportunity in Ireland for women to take degrees, which they began to do in small but increasing numbers from the first nine women graduates in 1884. Similarly the University of London which was not a teaching institution admitted women from 1878 to the same examinations as men.[73] Not admitted to University College, women had to find teaching in various ways,[74] with Protestant schools in Dublin and Belfast in the lead,[75] but once women began to present for public examinations, and in order to discourage Catholic women from attendance at Protestant institutions, Catholic schools and colleges were established with the encouragement of Archbishop William Walsh of Dublin and the increasing interest of Catholic parents. The Dominican sisters commenced university classes in 1886 leading to their establishment of St Mary's College in 1893, which was followed the next year by the Loreto Institute and by the Ursuline St Angela's in Cork. Hayden had completed her undergraduate studies before these colleges were established, but she later became particularly associated with St Mary's as a teacher and a champion.

The exciting prospect offered by the Royal University immediately appealed to Hayden and a friend at Alexandra, Annie Patterson.[76] When Hayden first heard that 'ladies would be eligible for degrees in the new University', she wrote 'perhaps DV I may try for one some time'.[77] Hayden felt she dare not mention the idea to her father, but thought if she prepared for the matriculation examination he might let her try it. But in order to enter for the examination she would have to apply to her father for evidence of her age, which she was reluctant to do.[78] The difficulty was resolved in a most unexpected way. Thomas Hayden became ill and in a month was dead. In fact, Thomas Hayden was a member of the Senate of the new University, and it is likely that he would have yielded to his daughter's wish to proceed with her studies.

She passed the Matriculation Examination in late 1882 and the following January she won the three year scholarship of the Royal University, which provided £50 a year and the title of Scholar. The first woman to win this award, she was overwhelmed with congratulations when she called to Alexandra College.[79] A sub-leader in the *Freeman's Journal* on recent scholarship awards by the Royal University was especially glad to note the second scholarship in Modern Literature 'obtained by the daughter of the late eminent and lamented Dr Hayden, Miss Mary Hayden, a gifted young lady educated at the Alexandra College'.[80] This was achievement and public recognition of the sort normally reserved to men, and Hayden was delighted to figure in that context.

Commencing her university courses in 1882, Hayden attended classes for the Royal University examinations conducted at 11 South Frederick Street by Henry McIntosh, who had taught her at Alexandra. McIntosh was also a teacher in several Dublin colleges; he later taught in the Methodist College, Belfast, where Hayden visited him in 1894, and where he became headmaster. She had a high regard for him, his character and ability, and was pleased that he 'seems to treat women as if they were on a footing of perfect equality'.[81] Her choice of words suggests her own lack of conviction at that stage on the subject of women's equality. She also liked his brothers Mod and Louis and his sister Effie, all members of her wide circle of friends.

In October 1883 the women Royal University students held a meeting in Alexandra College to request teaching by the University Fellows, who were appointed only to men's colleges, but Hayden who was present was not optimistic.[82] Some months earlier the Royal University Senate had turned down a similar appeal from the Central Association of Irish School Mistresses (CAISM).[83] The CAISM had been formed in 1882 to advance the higher education of women in Ireland at both intermediate and university level; its driving force was Alice Oldham, of Alexandra. The CAISM was largely composed of Protestant teachers campaigning for the admission of women to Trinity College; it later organised women's submissions to the Robertson Commission on University Education and the foundation of the Irish Association of Women Graduates and Candidate Graduates (IAWGCG), in which Hayden would be prominently involved. However, in November 1883 two members of University College, Fr Thomas Finlay and Abbé G. Polin, commenced classes in Logic and French respectively for women students, apparently at the request of Alexandra College. Hayden attended these classes and recorded going to

Alexandra to pay for them. Fr Finlay, she noted, 'seems a capital teacher'.[84] She considered the attendance of a Mrs Hayes as matron at the Abbé's French class to be 'a little unnecessary' considering the age, appearance and profession of the teacher.[85] The arrangement for a matron apparently did not continue, but it was not exceptional. In the early years of the women's colleges at Cambridge, chaperones were expected to attend women's classes when a man was lecturing.[86]

Hayden passed at the first and second year Royal University examinations in 1883 and 1884 quite comfortably, but without the distinction for which she had hoped. In 1883 she considered her marks 'very bad indeed', but in fact she gained honours in English, Latin and French, all low seconds in her own words, and an exhibition prize of £15 coming last on the exhibition list.[87] The following year she was even more disappointed, gaining no prize and though again second honours in three subjects, her low result in English, her best subject, disappointed both herself and her teacher McIntosh. Examination honours and distinctions were not announced until the conferring ceremony which in October 1884 was the first occasion on which women were among the graduates. Hayden's disappointment with her second year result, though real, was swamped somewhat by the excitement surrounding the nine women graduates, the first women to achieve university degrees, who were greeted with a burst of applause, one Isabella Mulvany taking 'off her cap to us'.[88] Mulvany and four other Alexandra teachers were among these nine women graduates.[89]

While staying in regular contact with her Crean relations, Hayden's wider circle of school and university friends tended to be those who were taking the Royal University examinations, the young women and men of the Conan, McIntosh and Mulvany families. Included in social occasions and expeditions were Trinity students, such as friends of Arthur Conan, who proceeded to Trinity on completion of his Royal University MA in 1886. There were frequent forays to Trinity for sports and social occasions, which always made Hayden long to be a student there. Her brother John, after some years at the Catholic University, had been permitted by their father to enter Trinity but apart from keeping his name on the books for a while does not seem to have attended. John's interests, like his sister's, were literary. At the Catholic University he was prominent in the Literary and Historical debating society. He was secretary of the Society in 1878–79, and won a medal there in 1880.[90] He tried writing poems and stories which Hayden did not rate very highly though some were accepted for publication. Later he persevered with poetry and had his work published regularly from 1893 to 1926, mostly in the *Irish Monthly*, a Jesuit produced journal, one of several with which Fr Tom Finlay was associated. A brief fragment of diary by John confirms Hayden's portrayal of him as an avid purchaser of books, for which he was often in debt. He recorded that he used his sister's watch as security to retrieve his clothes from pawn, and he seemed to be in the habit of borrowing money from her.[91]

Shortage of ready cash was a constant worry for Hayden. Once lacking the full train fare from Bray to Dublin, she walked laden with books eight miles to Carrickmines where she could afford to board the train.[92] Moyne Road was proving too expensive and she arranged to take lodgings with Mrs Cox, their former family housekeeper, who had taken a house at 10 Russell Street, north of the Liffey. After some haggling with Mrs Cox about the rent, Hayden, her furniture and possessions moved to Russell Street on 26 November 1884.[93] The move was also the occasion of a blazing row with John, who wanted to keep their own house and was of no help to her in the practicalities of their lives. Since their father's death, Hayden exercised an authority which society did not accord to her as the younger and the female. For some women, the perhaps unexpected need to assume such a role or to support themselves came as a positive experience,[94] and this was true of Hayden. She was protective of her brother who was a more selfish character; while genuinely fond of him, Hayden was frequently provoked by his behaviour. John left for London to continue his legal studies, but regularly came back to their home in Russell Street. Hayden disliked moving to the north side of the city, but in time settled contentedly in what was to be her home for over fourteen years. She had accommodation there for herself and John, room to entertain visitors, and for the occasional dinner or tea party. Around the same time the Crean family moved nearby to 'a splendid house as big as a barracks' in Eccles Street[95] where she was a frequent caller, giving lessons to the boys and included in many family events.

Now in her final year of study for the BA degree, Hayden was attending German classes at Alexandra College and thinking of a possible sojourn in Germany. A surprising new responsibility arrived in 1884 when she agreed, somewhat reluctantly, to become the guardian of a hitherto unknown relative, a fifteen year old orphan cousin, Annie Ryan. Annie was a first cousin of Hayden's on her mother's side. Following the death of the previous guardian and a legal contest about a new appointment, Counsel instructed by Thomas V. Ryan, a solicitor, applied for the appointment of Miss Hayden, 'a lady of independent means' and a 'distinguished graduate of the Royal University'. This solicitor was possibly the same Ryan who had been Dr Hayden's solicitor and was dealing with his estate. The Lord Chancellor, before whom the case was heard, appointed Hayden as most eminently suited to be the guardian. The appointment, reported in the newspapers, caused interest and mild amusement among Hayden's friends. It was however a recognition of her standing as a responsible individual, in preference to the men seeking the appointment.

Annie, with an annuity of £340 and capital of £2000, was not a financial burden on Hayden, who wrote of keeping off the 'fortune hunters', and vowed that she would honestly spend on Annie the allowance provided for her.[96] Hayden realised that she had taken on 'a pretty heavy responsibility' which seems to have been thrust upon her by the solicitor, Ryan. She placed Annie in a convent school at Isleworth outside London, but she visited her at school and looked after her during school holidays, having the young girl to live with her at Russell Street, with some of the holiday responsibility shared by a relative of her former guardian. Hayden brought Annie to Paris in 1886 on a sightseeing trip which did not greatly interest the young girl and she regularly bought Annie whatever outfits she wanted. The two had little in common. Annie's stay of six weeks in summer 1886 was 'more than I can bear', and when John then arrived, the situation became 'rather trying'.[97] But Hayden, though she often found her young charge aggravating, seems to have looked after her with patience, care and kindness. John Hayden was less tolerant of the young girl, causing Mary to worry that the two got on so badly.[98]

The story was to end sadly. After a year in Nantes at a sister convent of the order, the Faithful Companions of Jesus, with which she had been at school, Annie decided that she wished to enter the order. Hayden was not altogether surprised by the decision though she found it hard to understand. Bringing Annie to the convent for the last time, Hayden observed that her guardianship had now ended after 'a stormy six years'.[99] Mary and John attended Annie's formal reception as a novice in May 1891.[100] About a year after her final profession in July 1893 Annie, now

Mother Anastasia, moved to Australia where at the age of twenty-four she died in 1895. On her decision to enter the convent, Annie's land had been bought by Uncle John Ryan whose will in 1895 leaving his property to his agent, Walsh, was to prove such a disappointment to his relatives.[101]

As planned, Hayden spent the early summer months of 1885 in Bonn at the home of the Bischof family studying for the BA examination, concentrating principally on her German. Travel was becoming an acceptable component of the final phase of a girl's education, and the study of languages would prepare girls for work as teachers or to do translations, both acceptable occupations for women.[102] This was the beginning of a long friendship with the family of Dr Bischof. Hayden enjoyed life in this lively home and many family outings in Bonn and the surrounding countryside. Though at times critical of the children's behaviour, she thought their mother was too hard on the boys, 'showing more her severity than her affection'.[103]

Returning to Dublin in August 1885, Hayden spent the next two months attending various tutors for lessons in the three subjects for her degree, German, English and French. She feared that her head was so full of works and authors she might 'forget who wrote *Paradise Lost*'.[104] The examination began on 1 October with English in which she felt she did not do well;[105] German and French were on the succeeding days. She was notified on 19 October that she had passed but further details were not announced until the conferring ceremony held on 27 October. In Modern Literature, Hayden, Josephine Conan, Annie Haslett and Alice Lyster[106] were all awarded second class honours. Agnes Conan passed, and another member of the Conan family, Arthur, got first class honours and first place in classics. For the conferring day Hayden had her hair curled at Prost's, the Dublin hairdressers, and wore a new dress, hat and gloves to the Royal University where the graduates donned cap and gown, signed the register and went in procession to the hall for the ceremony and the announcement of the awards. In modern languages the only first honours went to a man, Joseph Ball. Mary Hayden came first of the second class honours with a scholarship of £25, followed by Alice Lyster who received a similar prize. Hayden had hoped for an award, and recorded her delight with the comment, 'What an unexpected windfall, what grand luck'.[107]

The Young Adult

Pondering, with her friend Josephine McGauran, on the effects of an absence of maternal authority, Hayden concluded that it left girls more reserved, more self-reliant and independent, less prone to unreasoning obedience, and with fewer feminine virtues.[108] This is, in fact, a description of how she saw herself at the age of twenty. It is also her appreciation of the freedom not to conform, allowed to her through the absence of a mother against whose influence as a role model she might find herself rebelling.[109] But a mother might well have eased Hayden's feelings of inadequacy when she saw putting up her hair and wearing long dresses as unattractive aspects of growing up. Her reaction to these superficial rites of passage into Victorian womanhood were similarly experienced by many of her contemporaries who saw these conventions as restrictions imposed on adult womanhood.[110] Hayden would in time acquire confidence through her academic achievements.

The encumbrance of voluminous female clothing, such as 'lumbering old petticoats and skirts',[111] Hayden found an impediment to some of her favourite pastimes, walking, climbing and swimming. Her impatience with restrictions interfering with her preferred activities suggests a foretaste of her later reaction to more fundamental constraints on women's independence. Nevertheless, as a young woman she was not uninterested in her clothes, often described in her diaries, her dress for a party or her outfit for a walking expedition, and she regretted when she could not afford to buy something new. Dressing up for parties with the Crean girls and for amateur theatricals was great fun. But her attire was not of major importance to her and was not permitted to intrude on her fairly busy life.[112] Yet Hayden was a competent seamstress, mending her own garments and John's socks, and occasionally making a blouse or jacket for herself.[113] In 1893–94 Hayden attended dressmaking classes in the technical school where she learned how to draw patterns, and made a grey jacket.[114] Around the same time she also took up knitting. Clearly, she was not averse to exercising some conventional feminine skills.

In her young days she sometimes thought herself ugly, but photographs from the mid 1880s onwards show a pleasant face with regular features. She was of no more than average height. Her short haircut is frequently mentioned. Tired of struggles with her long plait, she first had her hair cut short in 1883,[115] an unconventional act at the time which she recounted merely as one of convenience. Some contemporary women likewise found long hair and hair pins fiendishly difficult.[116] Hayden kept her hair short for the rest of her life, though this did not prevent her going to Prost's to have it curled for special occasions.

Josephine McGauran, who lived in Bray, was one of Hayden's closest friends, of whom she was very fond. Josephine was a more flighty character than the sober-minded Hayden, who disapproved of Josephine's use of cosmetics and her fast life, but she continued to feel affection for her childhood friend.[117] Josephine later married Frank Kelly after a courtship conducted sometimes in the Moyne Road house, where Hayden worried about leaving them together, 'the flesh (especially among the male persuasion) is weak'.[118] Victorian respectability did not countenance a young woman spending too long alone with a male companion. Yet, in another instance, Hayden herself would ridicule the 'absurd rule' that her cousin Mary Crean and her fiancé were never to be left alone together. 'Do they think he'd eat her'?[119]

The early loss of her mother from whom her strong personality was probably inherited, and the male household in which Hayden grew up, all contributed to the formation of a self-reliant woman of independent character.[120] As a child, she was something of a tomboy; she retained her preference for more energetic pastimes – climbing, horse riding, swimming. While growing up, she saw a man's role as more attractive than her own; her teacher, McIntosh's equal treatment of his women students 'flattered my vanity, for to "feel a boy" was ever my delight'.[121] Similarly, 'many women's autobiographies record moments of wishing that they had not been born female'.[122]

Hayden admired her father's professional standing, without expecting an opportunity to emulate it, and she respected her brother John for his seniority and learning, while realising he was unlikely to achieve very much. She envied the possibilities in education and in eventual adult life available to her brother, and to men in general, without much anticipation that her own life would differ in any degree from the confined role of her middle-class women contemporaries. She was a classic example of the effect that a male-dominated social structure had on women's sense of themselves.[123] Though the private, domestic role did not appeal to Hayden, she did not at that stage foresee much alternative or the prospect of women in professional and public life. She genuinely liked studying, learning, and the challenge offered by competitive examinations, without having in mind a defined personal goal. But at the age of nineteen, mountain climbing in Switzerland had provoked her thoughts on ambition, the 'natural ... desire to be among the first, or among the few' as the motive for great actions.[124] The belief in separate spheres, public and private, for men and women, meant that a public role was a male role.[125] The young Hayden's sometimes expressed wish to be a man, and her pursuit of the education available to men was her way of protesting against the inadequacy of the role assigned to her. Then, meeting women like Oldham and Mulvany, her teachers at Alexandra, and later Anna Haslam, showed her that she was by no means alone in her hunger for something more. The realisation that these women believed in the advancement of women as a valid aim encouraged the young Hayden to take a more optimistic view of what women's lives could be.

NOTES

1   NLI MacIomaire papers, Ms 24043.
2   Hayden Diary, 9 November 1888.
3   Donal McCartney, *UCD A National Idea: The History of University College Dublin* (Dublin, 1999), p. 5.
4   Hayden Diary, 19 June 1883.
5   F.O.C. Meenan, *Cecilia Street: The Catholic University School of Medicine 1855–1931* (Dublin, 1987), pp 11–12; Charles A. Cameron, *History of the Royal College of Surgeons in Ireland and of the Irish Schools of Medicine* (Dublin, 1916), pp 750–51.
6   Hayden Diary, 30 September 1881.
7   Hayden Diary, 18 March 1895.
8   Hayden Diary, 12 October 1885.
9   Hayden Diary, 6 November 1891.
10 Hayden Diary, 20 November 1890.
11 K. Theodore Hoppen, *Ireland Since 1800: Conflict and Conformity* (London, 1989), pp 104–5; R.F. Foster, *Modern Ireland 1600–1972* (London, 1989), pp 344, 385.
12 Nadia Clare Smith, *Dorothy Macardle: A Life* (Dublin, 2007), p. 6.
13 John P. Boland, KSG, *Some Memories* (Dublin, 1928).
14 C.S. Andrews, *Dublin Made Me* (Dublin, 1979), p. 9.

15 Jacinta Prunty, 'Margaret Louisa Aylward' in Mary Cullen and Maria Luddy (eds), *Women, Power and Consciousness in 19th Century Ireland* (Dublin, 1995), pp 60–61.

16 Hayden Diary, 28 October 1888.

17 Hayden Diary, 14 May 1881.

18 Hayden Diary, 30 July 1881.

19 James Killen, 'Transport in Dublin: Past, Present and Future' in F.H.A. Aalen and Kevin Whelan (eds), *Dublin City and County: From Prehistory to Present* (Dublin, 1992), p. 306.

20 Hayden Diary, 3 April 1881.

21 Hayden Diary, 24 September 1888.

22 Hayden Diary, 14 March 1880.

23 Hayden Diary, 19 May 1880.

24 Hayden Diary, 13 July 1886.

25 Hayden Diary, 28 January, 1 February 1881.

26 Hayden Diary, 28 January 1891.

27 Mercedes Lillis, 'The Ursulines in Thurles: The First Hundred Years 1787–1887' in William Corbett and William Nolan (eds), *Thurles: The Cathedral Town* (Dublin, 1989), p. 208. The Ursuline records have Hayden there in 1876 though she was evidently at Mount Anville in 1875.

28 Hayden Diary, 16 March 1880.

29 Hayden Diary, 25 June 1878.

30 Hayden Diary, 20 July 1880.

31 Hayden Diary, 27 September 1878.

32 Hayden Diary, 7 July 1880.

33 Hayden Diary, 9 and 13 August 1880.

34 Hayden Diary, 18–28 August 1881.

35 Hayden Diary, 20 December 1881.

36 Hayden Diary, 13 April 1882.

37 Hayden Diary, 3 November 1881.

38 Hayden Diary, 1 March 1882.

39 Hayden Diary, 1 August 1882.

40 Hayden Diary, 29 December 1882.

41 Hayden Diary, 9 September 1881. Donal McCartney, 'Parnell, Davitt and the Land Question' in Carla King (ed.), *Famine, Land and Culture in Ireland* (Dublin, 2000), p. 79.

42 Hayden Diary, 7 May 1882.

43 Senia Pašeta, *Before the Revolution: Nationalism, Social Change and Ireland's Catholic Elite, 1879–1922* (Cork, 1999), p. 82.

44 Maria Luddy, 'Isabella Tod 1836–1896', in Cullen and Luddy, *op cit*, p. 201; Mary Cullen, 'Women, Emancipation and Politics:

1860–1984' in J.R. Hill (ed.), *A New History of Ireland,* Vol VII (Oxford, 2003), pp 835–36.

45   Hayden Diary, 15 September 1880.

46   Hayden Diary, 20 September 1883.

47   Deirdre Raftery, 'The Higher Education of Women in Ireland, 1860–1904' in Susan Parkes (ed.), *A Danger to the Men? A History of Women in Trinity College Dublin 1904–2004* (Dublin, 2004), p. 6.

48   Susan M. Parkes, 'Intermediate Education for Girls' in Deirdre Raftery and Susan M. Parkes, *Female Education in Ireland 1700–1900* (Dublin, 2007), p. 70.

49   *Ibid*, p. 73.

50   Eibhlin Breathnach, 'Charting New Waters; Women's Experiences in Higher Education, 1879–1908' in Mary Cullen (ed.), *Girls Don't Do Honours: Irish Women in Education in the 19th and 20th Centuries* (Dublin, 1987), p. 56; Rosemary Cullen Owens, *Louie Bennett* (Cork, 2001), p. 7.

51   Anne O'Connor, 'The Revolution in Girls' Secondary Education in Ireland 1860–1910' in Cullen, *op cit*, p. 48.

52   Hayden Diary, 19 May 1886.

53   Hayden Diary, 8 July 1880.

54   Hayden Diary, 12 May 1880.

55   Hayden Diary, 6 July 1889.

56   Mary Hayden, 'Three Notable Irishwomen'. Unpublished paper possibly read to the Women Graduates Association, NLI Hayden papers, Ms 24007 Box 14.

57   Anne V. O'Connor, 'Anne Jellicoe 1823–1880' in Cullen and Luddy, *op cit*, pp 144, 145.

58   Hayden Diary, May 1880.

59   Hayden Diary, 14 October 1880.

60   Hayden Diary, 24 May 1881.

61   Carol Dyhouse, *Feminism and the Family in England 1880–1939* (Oxford, 1989), p. 16.

62   Hayden Diary, 25 June 1881 *et seq.*

63   Marie O'Neill, *Grace Gifford Plunkett and Irish Freedom* (Dublin, 2000), p. 4.

64   Owens, *Louie Bennett*, p. 4.

65   Andrews, *op cit*, p. 9.

66   Hayden Diary, 31 December 1884, 17 January 1885. The bride who became Mrs Murphy was the grandmother of the poet Richard Murphy who has recorded his memories of her sister, the teacher Isabella his great aunt Bella, in his memoir *The Kick*.

67   Cullen and Luddy, *op cit*, 'Introduction', p. 15.

68 Richard J. Evans, *The Feminists: Women's Emancipation Movements in Europe, America and Australasia 1840–1920* (London, 1977), p. 25.

69 Cullen, *op cit*, pp 832–36; Rosemary Cullen Owens, *A Social History of Women in Ireland 1870–1970* (Dublin, 2005), Chapter 1.

70 Cullen, *op cit*, pp 832–33.

71 Mary Hayden, 'Three Notable Irishwomen', NLI, Mary Hayden papers, Ms 24007 (14).

72 Donal McCartney, *UCD A National Idea: The History of University College, Dublin* (Dublin, 1999), pp 16–18.

73 Martha Vicinus, *Independent Women: Work and Community for Single Women 1850–1920* (Chicago, 1988), p. 125.

74 Eibhlin Breathnach, 'Charting New Waters: Women's Experience in Higher Education 1879–1908' in Cullen, *op cit*, p. 59.

75 Susan Parkes and Judith Harford, 'Women and Higher Education in Ireland' in Raftery and Parkes, *op cit*, p. 110.

76 Annie Patterson (1889–1934) became a music teacher, a founder of the Feis Ceoil and a lecturer in UCC.

77 Hayden Diary, 25 January 1880.

78 Hayden Diary, 29 September 1881.

79 Hayden Diary, 1 February 1883.

80 *Freeman's Journal*, 1 February 1883.

81 Hayden Diary, 3 December 1883.

82 Hayden Diary, 12 October 1883.

83 Eibhlin Breathnach, 'Women and Higher Education in Ireland (1879–1914)', *The Crane Bag* 4, 1980, pp 47–54.

84 Hayden Diary, 19 November 1883.

85 Hayden Diary, 21 November 1883.

86 June Purvis, *A History of Women's Education in England* (Milton Keynes, 1991), p. 115.

87 Hayden Diary, 17 October 1883.

88 Hayden Diary, 22, 23, 24 October 1884.

89 Anne V. O'Connor and Susan M. Parkes, *Gladly Learn and Gladly Teach: Alexandra College and School 1866–1966* (Dublin, 1984), p. 44.

90 Hayden Diary, 8, 10 December 1880; James Meenan (ed.), *Centenary History of the Literary and Historical Society 1855–1955* (Dublin 2005, 2nd ed.), p. 262.

91 'The Diary of John J. Hayden' 25 April–15 June 1878, in Conan Kennedy (ed.), *The Diaries of Mary Hayden* (Killala, 2005), Vol. V, pp 2351–2362.

92 Hayden Diary, 21 August 1883.

93 Hayden Diary, 26 November 1884.

94 Dyhouse, *op cit*, p. 33.

95 Hayden Diary, 29 November 1884.

96 *Freeman's Journal*, 15 December 1884; Hayden Diary, 8, 10, 11, 13, 15 December 1884.

97 Hayden Diary, 12, 18 July 1886.

98 Hayden Diary, 2 August 1888.

99 Hayden Diary, 6 December 1890.

100 Hayden Diary, 6 May 1891.

101 Hayden Diary, 8 August 1895.

102 Michelle Perrot 'Stepping Out' in Genevieve Fraise and Michelle Perrot (eds), *A History of Women in the West, IV: Emerging Feminism from Revolution to World War* (Harvard, 1993), p. 468.

103 Hayden Diary, 27 April 1885.

104 Hayden Diary, 16 September 1885.

105 Hayden Diary, 1 October 1885.

106 Alice Lyster became a teacher and school principal in England. She was a sister of Thomas Lyster, Chief Librarian of the National Library of Ireland. Kennedy, *op cit*, Vol V, p. 2308.

107 Hayden Diary, 27 October 1885.

108 Hayden Diary, 24 May 1882.

109 Dyhouse, *op cit*, p. 27.

110 *Ibid*, pp 21–22.

111 Hayden Diary, 17 January 1885.

112 Hayden Diary, 23 July 1896.

113 Hayden Diary, 14 October 1895.

114 Hayden Diary, 14 February 1894.

115 Hayden Diary, 7 August 1881 and 30 March 1883.

116 Dyhouse, *op cit*, p. 22.

117 Hayden Diary, 29 October 1884, 6 June 1886.

118 Hayden Diary, 8 February 1883.

119 Hayden Diary, 24 March 1883, 26 April 1883.

120 Hayden Diary, 18 January 1881.

121 Hayden Diary, 3 December 1883.

122 Dyhouse, *op cit*, p. 21.

123 Phyllis Rose, *Woman of Letters: A Life of Virginia Woolf* (London, 1978), p. 65.

124 Hayden Diary, 26 August 1881.

125 Vicinus, *op cit*, pp 1–2.

II

THE YOUNG SCHOLAR
1886–1895

Hayden continued with her studies, and began to teach and write. She led an agreeable social life in Dublin and abroad, and became involved in the lively cultural scene of the Celtic revival. But there were personal problems, with her brother, her friends, and her own purpose in life as an independent woman.

Satisfied with her BA result, Hayden had no hesitation about proceeding for a further two years to the MA degree, with no more defined purpose to her plans than that she wished to continue learning. She wanted for her life something other than the traditional family and domestic role now being undertaken by various girl friends as they married. For herself she saw marriage as an abandonment of independence and a narrowing of her horizons. While marriage was a recognition of adulthood, in fact by confirming women's dependent status, it continued to deny them the status of an adult.[1]

Though money worries were never far from her mind, she and John were fortunate to have an income from the investment of their inheritance from their father, adequate for their modest support as they pursued their immediate goals. By now, a life in teaching would seem to be the predictable outcome for Hayden, and some teaching work started to come her way. For the MA she was again attending classes at 11 Frederick Street and also had lessons on English literature from Henry McIntosh at his home on Haddington Road. She was enrolled as a student at Alexandra College,[2] and private study, to which she applied herself with ease, was a regular part of her life. Hayden commenced some teaching at Alexandra College in autumn 1886 when she was asked to take over a first university class during the absence of McIntosh who was ill.[3]

An Independent Woman

Though she was a seriously-minded young woman, Hayden's life was by no means all work. She was gregarious and lively, and disliked being introduced as 'the BA' which made her feel self-conscious.[4] She was a bridesmaid for the marriage on 5 July 1886 of her cousin, Emmie Crean to Stephen Quinn of Limerick. Her account of the wedding, including getting her bridesmaid's dress at Slynes (the Grafton Street shop which survived until the mid-twentieth century), the marriage at St Joseph's, Berkeley Road, and the breakfast at the Crean home in Eccles Street, gives an entertaining picture of a family event in middle-class Dublin. The ceremony, conducted by Dr Donnelly,[5] a Dublin bishop and family friend, was short. Back at Eccles St:

> the breakfast was duly consumed ... There were speeches of course, not particularly original. James Quinn proposed the health of the bridesmaids and Father Moore replied in their

name – any one of them could have done it as well, I dare say – only they were officially supposed to be too timid.[6]

Hayden's impatience with contemporary conventions for women is obvious. The wedding was one of many occasions when Hayden commented on 'the awful ordeal of taking a man for better or worse' and of a woman's loss of independence in marriage. She thought it unlikely that she would ever marry, 'I should want a great deal and I have nothing much to give in return'.[7] Moreover a husband might 'get in my way, and rule me and use me' according to his moods.[8] She desired for herself a professional life with her own income and status. Such aspirations by unmarried middle-class women were one source of the developing feminist movement.[9] In her middle age and established with an independent life, Hayden would feel some desire for the companionship of a husband, but her emotions then were focused on the impending death of the man she might have married. On the whole, the young Hayden did not envisage marriage as an element of the life she wished to lead.

Social life in Dublin included events in Trinity College like the College Races, after which ladies might be invited to tea in gentlemen's rooms. Visits to Trinity invariably aroused Hayden's envy, she felt she could study sixteen hours a day in such quarters.[10] Walking around St Stephen's Green, down Grafton Street, or from Trinity College to the Royal Dublin Society and the National Library, 'people constantly met one another' and knew each other in the city's small middle-class society.[11] The National Library, established by legislation in 1877, was by 1890 located in a new building beside Leinster House, the home of the Royal Dublin Society.[12]

Hayden was a regular walker, encountering friends and acquaintances on her daily rounds. Despite her genuine application to serious study, she disliked being alone for too long. Her activities included speaking at meetings of societies in Alexandra College, and not infrequent dances which she enjoyed or not depending on the partners she encountered. Hayden had a wide circle of friends, and added new acquaintances fairly easily. She welcomed company, but also recorded her criticism of those she did not care for. A dancing partner danced abominably and evidently believed that 'no flattery is too gross to be swallowed by a woman'.[13] At another dance, one partner smelt of smoke and the next of scented hair oil, 'the former odour was greatly preferable to the latter'.[14] She had little time for those, either men or women, whom she found lacking in intelligence or with no pretensions to culture. Small talk was not one of her talents. Compliments from young men upset her, and flirting, which she often referred to as the 'eternal he and she', earned her disapproval. On her own admission she had a sharp tongue, recorded at times with regret, 'when I think of an appropriate taunt, or a nicely rounded rude sentence ... [I] cannot avoid saying it'[15] – what Elizabeth Bennet acknowledged as 'the misfortune of speaking with bitterness'.[16]

Nor was her wide circle of friends and acquaintances influenced by religious denomination. The young Hayden was an observant Catholic, as is clear from the frequent diary records of attending Mass and confession, but the piety of her ward Annie Ryan she found off-putting.[17] She worried about the validity of an after-life, finding 'infinity and eternity so unknowable'[18] and she wished for a lay man who could persuade her of the truth of what she wanted to believe.[19] Her religion in her young adulthood was more a matter of commitment than of strong conviction. In spite of her doubts, she never considered abandoning her religion, finding it a comfort that 'my own creed is not over firm, but it is a creed at least'.[20] Inevitably, from her Alexandra and Royal University years there were Protestants among her friends, the subject of comment by a busybody in 1889. She heard a rumour that she was to marry one of the (Protestant) McIntosh family – 'who troubles to invent all these fictions?' and another kind lady was interested in 'my spiritual welfare, as I was always with Protestants' but as 'I had been seen at Gardiner St.' (presumably the Jesuit Church there), her spiritual wellbeing was doubtless secure.[21] While it did not inhibit Hayden or loom large in her mind, the attitude to Protestants was often one of prejudice or suspicion, influenced by hostility from the Catholic Church and an increasing identification of Catholicism and nationalism. Furthermore, with improving educational and employment opportunities for Irish women, Catholic women co-operating with Protestant women and sympathising with modern feminist ideas were seen as West Britons, which to some degree Hayden was in her early years. And professional Catholics tended to associate with Protestants.[22] Hayden, somewhat caustically and perhaps snobbishly, came to the conclusion that the cultural tone in Dublin Protestant homes was more admirable than in Catholic families – conversation about works of art or Greek scenery rather than dress, babies and balls[23] – a bias owing something to her associations with Alexandra. In Bonn she had noted with disapproval that the women talked about cooking, 'the faults of their servants [and] the price of meat'.[24] Reminiscent of her childhood complaints about the ladies at her father's dinner parties, these comments hint at the attitude of superiority which she was occasionally to reveal later in life when referring to married women or to professional careers. Hayden's criticisms were not uncharacteristic of an educated woman. The feminist Emily Davies had in 1864 made a similar complaint about the topics of women's conversation, which she attributed to their 'almost complete mental blankness'.[25]

There were frequent congenial gatherings in the McIntosh home, and also in the Mulvany home, where Isabella the teacher lived. Likewise, the Conan family were cultured, entertaining and hospitable; Josephine, Agnes and Arthur all took Royal University degrees with Hayden. The walking expeditions in the Dublin and Wicklow mountains, which she thoroughly enjoyed, were often organised by the Conans. On one such expedition in June 1888 Arthur Conan proposed marriage to Hayden. The proposal came as an unwelcome shock to her. Prior to that date her diary contains much favourable comment about Conan, his intellect, his character, his company and his attention to her, all of which she enjoyed. This is a point where a considerable amount has been removed from the diary but it is clear from what remains that the idea of marriage to Conan was not in her mind, and that she was disturbed by the proposal. He evidently asked her to take time to think about it, which she did without coming to a decision. She wrote that 'it is not in me to care very much for any man, I fear, perhaps because I can like so many tolerably and be good friends with them'.[26] The problem was temporarily postponed by Conan's illness, probably the onset of consumption, and his departure, on doctor's orders, to spend the winter in a warmer climate. Conan would continue to figure in Hayden's life until his death in 1903.

The young Mary Hayden had no interest in Irish politics (as she commented in 1886),[27] the Land League or the fortunes of the Irish parliamentary members at Westminster. In 1890, Charles Stewart Parnell was cited in a divorce case taken by Captain Willie O'Shea and subsequently married O'Shea's former wife Katherine, with whom he had been living for some years. A split developed in the Parliamentary Party, the majority unable to accept Parnell's continued leadership. When Stephen Quinn, husband of her cousin Emmie, was persuaded by the local parish priest, Dr Molony, not to vote for the Parnellite candidate in Limerick in 1891, Hayden's reflection 'if a priest tried that game with me, I'd soon give him an answer'[28] expressed her objection to such clerical direction rather than a particular enthusiasm for Parnell. Later in 1891 Hayden was in Athens when news came of the death of Parnell. Acknowledging his distinction, she thought he had done both 'good and harm'; disparagingly, she predicted quarrelling now among the Irish MPs in one of the few references in her diary to contemporary politics.[29] But parliamentary politics was of course a man's world and she had not yet come to the view that women might penetrate that world. As subordinate beings in a patriarchal society, women were naturally excluded from the body politic.[30] The early feminists disputed the idea of male superiority, and the Victorian notion of woman's role confined to the private sphere.[31] But these were radical ideas in Hayden's young days. Her dissatisfied feelings about women's position in the world did not as yet anticipate any major change in society's perception of women. In time, she would come to the conclusion of many in the developing women's movement that for equality women needed education, remunerative employment and the vote, whereby they could influence changes in the law.[32]

On her way back from Paris in August 1886 Hayden was delayed in London by John's appearance in Lambeth Court on a charge that a watch he had attempted to pawn had been stolen; the case was later dismissed. Hayden recorded that John was enraged by the incident, which she called 'John's scrape' and for which he wanted her to pay his costs.[33] She was fond of John in spite of his irritating ways. He was a hypochondriac, which she humoured; in financial matters he was impractical, and he dithered about his comings and goings to their home in Dublin. Like his sister he was a well read, bookish person, and she valued his good opinion. She worried about his future, recognising that though clever he had 'no push, no energy'.[34] John completed his examinations at Gray's Inn in 1887, and was called to the bar but, as Hayden predicted, obtained few if any briefs and did not practise. His inheritance from his father must have been adequate for his support, supplemented by small fees for his published work and recourse to his sister when short.

In November 1886 Hayden set off for an extended stay in Bonn. She lodged again with the Bischof family, where the father was now a widower, took lessons in French and German, did a little tutoring in English, and applied herself to study for the MA degree. This visit lasted until July 1887. The change from her own solitary life appealed to her, and she wished that she 'had half a dozen brothers and a father'; 'I prefer a masculine household where there are no girls to sit round the table'.[35] The role of the only woman in male company was one she enjoyed, perhaps as an entry to the wider world of men.

The Academic Woman

Writing in her old age, Hayden recalled from her youth how the woman graduate was supposed to be plain, ill-dressed, 'pedantic and unattractive, probably also no longer very young – the "left-overs" of the marriage market ...'[36] Even into the next century 'the intellectual life of women was still largely irrelevant to most middle-class families'.[37] The pursuit of learning at a higher level was a choice which not many women were in a position to make, whether for educational, financial or family reasons. Though constantly worried about money in these years, Hayden usually managed to finance study and travel as she wished, and she had the freedom to embark on a chosen course of action without recourse to authority. Education had the effect of emphasising the limited opportunities open to women. The removal of women's disabilities was a definition of female emancipation for many.[38] But more fundamentally, women like Hayden yearned to do meaningful work, for which they would be recognised and publicly respected.[39]

Back in Dublin, she prepared for the MA examination in October 1887, for which there were five women candidates. Hayden was satisfied with her English literature paper and was 'rather proud' of her German essay; but she found the English language paper 'awfully hard' and was not over pleased with her performance in French.[40] When notified that she had passed, as had all the girls, she wrote, 'I hardly expected to be stuck, so was not much elated'. What she wanted was the prize, for which she had 'worked for nearly two years'.[41] This time she was to be disappointed. For the conferring on 27 October she got her hair curled and went to the Royal University where she noted that lady graduates, of whom there were nineteen including the five MAs, were still 'rather a novelty'. The studentship in modern literature was won by Emma Mary Story, whom Hayden considered 'so clever she doesn't need to stick to her books'.[42] Hayden came next, also with first-class honours, but received neither medal nor prize. She lamented what she might have done with the money – no trip abroad, no new dresses, or no new overcoat for John – and started looking for pupils to grind. In reality the financial consequences may not have been too serious, and life for herself and her brother continued much as before. The real wound might have been to her pride, since academically her first class honours was better than her BA result. This is one of the many places in her diary where pages have been removed.

She made preliminary enquiries about the D.Litt. degree (awarded on an examination),[43] started to study Spanish, taught some private pupils, and appeared in print for the first time when her article on 'Religious Poetry' was published in The Lyceum for March 1888. The article was a book review which the editor, Fr Tom Finlay, had invited her to write. The subject did not appeal to her, but her article is a well written survey with references to a wide range of literature, and is fairly dismissive of the book under review. She was delighted to find her article published, commenting 'here was fame in a small way'.[44] (*The Lyceum* (1887–1891) was a monthly literary magazine founded by Fr Tom Finlay which published much material by members and former students of University College. It was replaced by the *New Ireland Review* and later by *Studies*).[45] Finlay was a person to whom she occasionally turned for advice, and he may have been her confessor. He was rector of Belvedere College, the secondary school for boys, and a professor of mental and moral science at University College. (Finlay later was closely associated with Sir Horace Plunkett in the Irish co-operative movement, and he became one of the first professors 1909–1930 in the new UCD).[46] Finlay, who believed in encouraging young writers,[47] gave Hayden another book to review, a work on comparative philology entitled *Biographies of Words*, and included her article in the April issue of *The Lyceum*.[48]

She decided to learn Greek, ancient classics being a requirement for the D.Litt. degree,[49] in the hope that she might be ready for the examination in three or four years,[50] applying herself determinedly to the study of classical Greek and later in Athens to Modern Greek. She appears to have kept the D.Litt. in mind for a few years, but did not proceed with it. She went with Arthur Conan, who was a postgraduate student in Trinity, to hear several lectures there by Professor Stokes on medieval Irish history which she found very interesting.[51] However, when she and her friend, Lilian Green, began lessons in Greek from a young student in Trinity, the arrangement was quickly ended by a direction from the Dean to the tutor that he was 'strictly forbidden to instruct young ladies in his rooms'.[52] Though the circumstances were quite different, this was another instance of the Victorian respectability which Hayden had noted in regard to her women friends and their male companions; and of course, women were not yet admitted as students at Trinity. Grinds in Latin and Greek were later arranged with William Starkie, 'a queer specimen, but a splendid teacher',[53] for whom Hayden developed an intellectual respect. Starkie, a classical scholar, later became Resident Commissioner of National Education and a member of the Robertson Commission on University Education. When Starkie married, Hayden was on visiting terms with him and his young wife at their Killiney home.[54] (One of their children was Enid Starkie, later an Oxford don).

Hayden had the inclination to write, urged at least in part by her need to earn some money, and she had been encouraged by Finlay who gave her some hints on composition.[55] She was delighted to receive £5 from the *Irish Catholic* for a story[56] and had stories published in the *Irish Monthly* and the *Irish Weekly Independent*. The stories were simple tales, elegantly written, and inclined to point a moral. An article which she submitted to the *Dublin Review* was described by its editor as 'an able historical article'.[57] Published in the July 1890 issue of the journal, it was a scholarly, informed, consideration of the evolution and significance of the medieval *chanson de geste*, and earned her £5.4.6.[58] Attempts to write lighter magazine articles were less successful; several of her efforts were rejected, for instance by *Harpers,* an American periodical which sometimes published writing by college women.[59] She taught classes and pupils as the opportunities arose, with her academic ambitions still a major, if ill-defined, purpose of her activity. Her determination to progress with her Greek studies, and her keen interest in foreign travel, brought her to Athens in September 1889 for a stay of eleven months. Here, as well as her classical studies, she learned Modern Greek, explored the classical sites, gave some English lessons, and made friends with members of the English colony. She had a two-part article titled 'Modern Athens' published in *The Lyceum* in January and February 1891. The £2 payment received did not impress the Creans, provoking Hayden's comment that few women 'understand the pride of making money for themselves'.[60] Economic independence was central to Victorian feminism.[61] *The Lyceum* issue of May 1892 contained another of Hayden's scholarly writings, 'The Song of Dermot and the Earl', a review article on an edition of the medieval poem with literal translation by G.H. Orpen. On the general theme of the *chanson de geste* on which she had written previously, her article gave a descriptive commentary on the poem, which she considered a valuable authority on the Norman invasion. Yet another article by Hayden on the *chanson de geste* was to appear, as had the first, in the *Dublin Review* in April 1894.

These long absences abroad interrupted Hayden's teaching work which she was able to pick up again each time she returned, despite her fear of possible displeasure from Henrietta White, the Principal of Alexandra College, at her abandonment of the Second Arts class there in November 1892.[62] In summer 1892 the Royal University appointed her as a superintendent for the Matriculation Examination for three days at £1 per day, which she considered to be well earned after collecting, sorting and tying up the papers. She was glad to have this work again in subsequent years. In 1894 she reminded Dr McGrath (the Registrar) 'of my existence in view of the coming examinations', and was appointed to superintend in Belfast which she welcomed as fun and money too.[63]

New Friendships and the Old Flame

On Arthur Conan's return to Dublin in 1889 Hayden told him that her feelings for him were no more than those of very good friendship.[64] He was still prepared to wait, was attentive and friendly, and sent her a present of a gold cross. This time it was Hayden who was to winter abroad, in Athens. They corresponded fairly regularly; he sent her an occasional newspaper and told her he planned to work for a Trinity College fellowship. She was no more inclined towards him on her return to Dublin[65] having in the meantime had a somewhat emotional friendship with a young student from Constantinople staying in her lodgings in Athens. This was Markos, a handsome eighteen year old to whom she gave English lessons. They shared a mutual interest in French literature and found each other the most congenial of the lodgers. Markos told her she was the first feminine friend he ever had and was probably experiencing a calf love for this well-read, lively woman who enjoyed his company. She for her part analysed her affection for him as maternal, sisterly and something more, using the word *amante,* probably in its sense of 'sweetheart'.[66] She was definitely smitten by Markos; the whole feeling was new to her, and she wondered why Markos rather than Conan occupied her mind. She had some scruples about their emotional parting, which she felt obliged to mention in confession and was duly reprimanded. Hayden and Markos kept in touch for some years, and met again on a subsequent visit to Athens; in spite of the attraction she continued to feel for him she never regarded him as a marriage prospect.[67]

About 1886 Hayden had become friendly with Lilian Green,[68] some seven years her junior. Green was also a student of the classics, though yet to take the BA degree. She was clever, talented and lively, but their personalities often clashed. Hayden admired her ability and enjoyed her company, and was introduced by her to the Turkish bath,

'... an indecent business ...'[69] Hayden's second and third visits to Greece (September 1891–January 1892 and November 1892–June 1893) were accompanied by Green. The first of these two visits produced an article, published in the *Girl's Own Paper* over the two names, Mary Hayden M.A. and Lilian Green. But Hayden referred to it as 'my article' and may have had a mild dispute about its authorship with Green who, according to Hayden, 'only suggested a few changes'. Hayden received payment of £2.2. and did not record sharing the sum with Green.[70] The *Girl's Own Paper* was an English publication aimed at educated middle-class young women. The article, 'Greek Peasant Girls, and How They Live', was a fanciful, romantic description of the life of a Greek girl. Its points of reference were English – 'our country lasses in England', 'at home in England', and its tone was somewhat patronising. But the theme was an expression of Hayden's interest, which would develop, in the lives of women.[71]

Starting their second visit in November 1892, the two women paused for ten days in Rome, where they met Alfred Webb and his wife. Webb was an Irish MP and a Quaker nationalist whose comment on the two women gives us an insight on their personalities:

> Lilly Green ... and Mary Hayden joined us for a time – the one a Quaker and like a Catholic – the other a Catholic and Quaker-like in manner. Their company added much to the interest of our stay.[72]

Green, as portrayed in Hayden's diary, was a somewhat capricious young woman, whom Hayden both admired for her animation and criticised for her lack of decorum. On both visits to Athens, they lodged in the boarding house where Hayden had spent her first visit, and became friendly with the landlady and her other lodgers. Spending six and eight months in close proximity tested the friendship of the two women, Green's liveliness and popularity, her 'enormous personality',[73] provoking in

Hayden a sense of being overshadowed. At times Hayden felt inadequate in competition with other women in a social scene, while increasingly confident of her own academic distinction. A principal cause of tension between the two women was a young Englishman, Frank Humphries, whom they met in Palestine.

Towards the end of March 1893 Hayden and Green set off from Athens for Egypt, visiting Cairo, the Nile and the Suez Canal, then proceeded by uncomfortable sea and train journeys to Palestine where they joined a party of twenty for a tour of the Holy Land. Hayden's descriptions of the individuals in this group were characteristically sharp. Most members were pleasant and good natured, but she also recorded their defects: a 'plain little dried up woman, given to tears', a 'meddlesome, fussy little man', a 'fat vulgar man … dropped his hs'. One woman was 'insignificant', and another 'much done up'. There was an American clergyman, three of the party were Irish in addition to Hayden and Green; the others were all English. She and Green found two congenial companions among the English in Frank Humphries, a medical doctor aged about thirty, and his father.[74]

The tour, which lasted about two weeks, was on horseback. Hayden and Green revelled in the adventure, the company and the unconventionality. Not having bathing costumes they wore their night dresses to bathe in a brook near Jericho, and on another occasion they were lent by young Humphries two of his colourful pyjama suits, both miles too large.[75]

Hayden found Frank Humphries to be 'a cultivated scholar, of wide reading and apparently great ability' with whom she had many satisfying conversations; she was flattered by his attention. She saw him as a mixture of literary scholar, 'young medico … and the London "swell"'.[76] He seemed to be something of an attractive rogue, he drank too much and according to his own candid accounts had had some unsavoury adventures of which Hayden did not approve. Nevertheless she was fascinated; he was unlike any man she had met before. Green annoyed Hayden by 'a most outlandish conjecture that [Mary] was "gone on" Dr Humphries'.[77]

In Hayden's life there was still Arthur Conan to whom she now wrote a 'long and serious letter'.[78] He had been ill again in Dublin in 1891, which worried her but made her no more positive about her feelings for him. She noted that one cannot marry and 'live on air', and she did not want a formal engagement.[79] Conan had now gained academic distinction in Trinity College, was doing some teaching in Dublin and in 1891 applied to the Royal University for an appointment;[80] but his indecision about his future, and his talk of going to Australia did not please her.[81] On an expedition to Poulaphouca in September 1892 she may have given him some sort of commitment. While Conan 'talked of his future prospects and mine', she listened in a sort of dream, hardly believing. 'I have been so long accustomed to stand on my own feet that it seems incredible I should cease to do so'.[82] Before she set off in November for Athens, they had exchanged tokens. She gave him a locket, thinking this was like 'taking a final plunge', and he gave her a little gold brooch, leaving her with the feeling of his affection so true, reliable and unchanging.[83] Now in June 1893 Conan was in South Africa, and she wished he had a situation fixed, yet moveable, 'to live a few years in one place and a few in another would be just my ideal'.[84] Their correspondence continued over the next two years.

Nevertheless, Hayden was delighted to learn that 'the great Frank Humphries' was coming to Dublin in August 1893 and wanted to see her. She again enjoyed his company, and again had a dispute with Green 'as we mostly have when Frank Humphries comes into the question'. Annoyed to be teased by those who could not understand an 'equal friendship between man and woman',[85] she was unable to admit, even to herself, the sexual element of the attraction she felt towards Humphries. She looked forward to his letters, and on several visits to London to see friends or read in the British Museum she was delighted that he called on her and escorted her on various outings.

Conan, with whom Hayden had what she thought of as a 'kind of bargain',[86] was due home in the summer of 1895, a prospect to which she did not look forward, feeling that she cared for him 'not a scrap – to my shame'. She knew that he was honourable and straight, but life with him might be too dull, 'bourgeois domesticity say in Rathmines I could not stand'. She told Arthur the truth in an interview on which she afterwards reflected unhappily, contrasting his goodness with her own 'atrocious nastiness'. Abroad she had had a taste of what seemed to her a more bohemian life, represented by Frank Humphries. She thought she was like him in shrinking from 'thought of marriage and babies of my own' and that she, like him, was 'radically selfish'.[87] Even before she had met Humphries, she had felt:

> a kind of horror to think that I might settle down in such a [nice little] house to wait for the return of a husband to a quotidian tête-a-tête – but *what* – do I want? My life of the last nine years had made me I fear a thorough Bohemian and the only establishment that would suit me now would be a gypsie's [sic] caravan.[88]

In her distaste for dull domesticity Hayden was not unique. Mary Maguire (later Colum), supposing that she would eventually marry somebody, thought of 'the role of some of the dreary married women I knew, with the monotonous domesticity, the dreary commonplaces, and often loneliness of their lives'.[89] A later associate of Hayden's in the university and suffrage campaigns, Hanna Sheehy Skeffington, also disliked domesticity; though financially she and her husband were not well off, she employed a live-in servant to do the housework.[90] Household chores were an unwelcome distraction, or an obstacle to achievement[91] for some women as they experienced the liberating stimulus of education, or developed interest in women's suffrage. Years earlier Hayden, pondering on her friends' marriages, had concluded 'the only kind of marriage that would be tolerable would be where the husband and wife both worked'.[92] Though she did not elaborate, some recognition of independence for the wife was, to her mind, desirable, as it was for many feminists who intended their married lifestyle to differ from that of their parents.[93] Hayden had only the vaguest childhood memories of the married life of her own parents, but she was critically observant of the marriages of friends and relations. But Hayden's ambivalent feelings about Arthur Conan would continue. She felt sorry to see him leaving again for Africa, especially now that she 'had made things clear to him'.[94]

Academic Advancement and Dublin Cultural Life
The establishment of the Royal University of Ireland had been a fillip in the development of women's education. Women were beginning to present for the examinations of the Royal University, and improved provision for the education of Catholic women became essential to match what was available to Protestants.[95] The Dominican sisters who, since 1886, had been providing classes for women preparing for the Royal University examinations, established their college, St Mary's, in 1893 located successively at Merrion Square, Muckross (Donnybrook) and Eccles Street. Hayden had a long chat about the new college with Mother Patrick Shiel who asked her to be on the tutorial committee.[96] Hayden hoped also for some teaching there, 'money being scarce'. She was teaching a pass matriculation class at Alexandra College, ten shillings

a week 'not very much but something'[97] and commenced some work at the new Dominican College where she is recorded as on the professional staff of St Mary's, 1893–95 and 1900–1909, and also teaching senior classes in the Eccles Street secondary school.[98] Another conversation with Mother Patrick gives the first indication in Hayden's diary that she was thinking of the junior fellowship examination of the Royal University, which would be another step up the academic ladder, and a further penetration into the territory of men. Mother Patrick told her that 'a lot of men are going in for the English Fellowship' to which Hayden added the comment 'alas'.[99] In deciding to compete for the higher academic awards, Hayden and other women did not doubt their own academic ability and capacity for dedicated study but, as in Hayden's case here, they lacked confidence in the system which only slowly and grudgingly was accepting women, and as unequal participants. In later years, Hayden recalled the poor opinion some university authorities had of women students.[100] In preparation for the fellowship examination she attended some lectures at St Mary's College.[101] She did not feel very confident, but her studies were helped by Fr Joseph Darlington, a Royal University fellow in English at the Jesuit University College, who gave her a regular plan of work and greatly relieved her mind with the information 'that history would only be required in its bearing on literature'.[102] Her scholarly interests were still primarily in literature and language. During the next decade she would begin to regard history as a serious subject of study, being influenced no doubt by the growing appreciation of the native past stemming from the literary revival.

Increasingly as the nineteenth century advanced, scholars had been revealing evidence of a past whose language, literature and antiquities were rich in cultural significance.[103] John O'Donovan (1809–61), George Petrie

(1789–1866) and Eugene O'Curry (1796–1862) were but some of the many names associated with these studies; and another at a later stage was Eoin MacNeill who would become a friend and university colleague of Hayden's. This trove of ancient culture became the inspiration towards the end of the century for contemporary writers and artists, encouraging them to find in the native heritage subjects on which to engage their creative talents.[104] W.B. Yeats, Douglas Hyde, Augusta Gregory, and the young Patrick Pearse are some who figured in this literary renaissance.

Hayden encountered many of those associated with the Irish literary revival, notably George Sigerson and W.B. Yeats. She often dined at the Sigerson home in Clare Street, where the younger daughter Hester had become a valued friend, and where Yeats was another regular guest. Sigerson was a prominent medical practitioner and a Celtic scholar who translated and published Irish poetry. A Royal University fellow in Natural Science, he later became a professor in UCD, a member of its Governing Body and of the Senate of the National University of Ireland.

Hayden was an early member of the National Literary Society founded by Yeats and Hyde, having attended a meeting in the Wicklow Hotel in May 1892 to discuss its foundation, a meeting which she thought rather dull, though Yeats 'improves on acquaintance'.[105] However when she subsequently found herself the only female present with seven men at a committee meeting of the new society it was 'rather amusing'; the opportunity to join with men in their intellectual pursuits was a novel and satisfying experience for her. At another committee meeting Hayden met Sir Charles Gavan Duffy.[106] Gavan Duffy had been a Young Irelander, a founder of *The Nation* newspaper (1842) who subsequently had a distinguished life in Australia for which he received a knighthood. Now an elderly man living in Nice, his interest in the literary revival as a possible recovery of the patriotic legacy of Young Ireland[107] often brought him back to Dublin. The National Literary Society sought to recover the native past, its language and customs, and thereby to encourage a modern literature, Irish in inspiration, though written in English. Prevailed upon to read a paper to the society, Hayden rehashed her review article, published in 1892, on Orpen's edition of the Song of Dermot, and read it at a meeting in January 1894.[108] Over the next thirty years, Hayden read papers to the Society on various subjects including Giraldus Cambrensis and Maria Edgeworth.[109] She continued as a member of the Council of the National Literary Society, holding the office of Librarian, 1901–06, and was then added to the list of the Society's Vice-Presidents 'in consideration of her long connection with the Society and her devoted service to Irish literature'.[110]

Interest in the supernatural, the occult, mysticism and the doctrine of theosophy, was another aspect of cultural life in Dublin. Yeats, who believed in second sight, was strongly influenced by these theories. 'Spiritualist experiments became the rage in Dublin, [and Yeats's] friends hilariously recalled his enthusiasm for them'.[111] Hayden was one who did not take them seriously. On one occasion she was present for Yeats's 'mystic performances of looking through the crystal'. She thought he became cross and 'painfully absurd', but nevertheless she walked home with him.[112] Another time when dining at the Sigerson home, Yeats made 'a queer hypnotic experiment' on her, and walking home with her he talked mysticism and she 'felt half inclined to laugh and half sorry for him'.[113] Yeats was a poet with a growing reputation,[114] and Hayden found him interesting to talk to, though 'over fond of big words'.[115] Though not in sympathy with his spiritualism, Hayden seemed to like Yeats, and when he told her that Maud Gonne was ill, she felt 'sorry for the poor fellow'.[116] Maud Gonne received only rare mention in Hayden's diary, though they moved in the same revivalist circles. They were both appointed to the Library Committee of the National Literary Society in 1892.[117] But Gonne in these years was spending considerable time abroad, nor had she many women friends in Dublin, apart from Sarah Purser, the artist.[118]

Hayden enjoyed the stimulus of the debates, discussions and readings in societies and homes around the city, though a debate on politics was not of great interest.[119] The subject of women's rights was coming to her attention. In May 1892 she was present at a debate on the subject, attended by only six women and eight men but it became very hot; 'I threw myself into the fray and fought valiantly'.[120] She read up the subject of women's suffrage in preparation for a debate at the students' union in Alexandra on 20 October 1893. Though the speeches, including one from Miss Oldham, were good, she thought the debate too one-sided. Her own contribution was only a few words and she does not appear to have felt very strongly, commenting a few weeks later after a discussion at the Contemporary Club on the position of women that she was 'getting dreadfully tired' of the subject.[121] The Contemporary Club, another of the many cultural societies of the time, was founded by Charles Oldham (then of TCD and later a professor in UCD) for the exchange of opinion on social, political and literary issues, and was 'open to all shades of opinion'.[122] Membership was limited by number and confined to men; but women were permitted to attend on occasion, and did so as recorded for instance by Hayden, Mary Macken and Maud Gonne.[123] The exclusion of women members is not mentioned by Hayden; it was typical of so much of her experience that it aroused no particular reaction, and the meetings provided opportunities to meet friends among the membership such as Sigerson and Hyde. Another regular attender was

Thomas Haslam.[124] He and his wife Anna were campaigners for women's emancipation with whom Hayden would be closely associated as she became committed to women's suffrage. Hayden's former teacher, Alice Oldham, sister of Charles, was an effective speaker on ladies' night at the Club.[125] This impression of Alice Oldham is confirmed in Hayden's description of a meeting of the club which she thoroughly enjoyed:

> First we had tea and chatted over it, then the debate began, it was not a set debate, but a kind of conversation on the subject set forth – the influence of Literature on Society – only one person spoke at a time, but there were no regular speeches. Several ladies spoke but only Miss Oldham kept well to the point in her remarks.[126]

Hayden's appointment by the Royal University in 1895 – after several unsuccessful applications[127] – as an assistant examiner in French was encouraging, including the pay of £40 which would finance a good trip somewhere.[128] She received both matriculation and first year university papers to mark. Later the same year, there came her significant achievement in winning a junior fellowship in English. The examination, written and oral, lasted four days and left her feeling discouraged.[129] Her delight was all the greater to learn that she had won and, typically, her first thought was of a possible trip to India. She noted that she had beaten Fr George O'Neill by two marks, a fact which was to receive subsequent mention and even to be recorded, as we shall see, in the proceedings of the Robertson Commission in 1903.

At the conferring ceremony on 25 October 1895, places of honour were given to three new junior fellows of whom two were the first women to win this distinction. Hayden was awarded a junior fellowship in English and History, and Katherine Murphy, an MA graduate of 1892, a junior fellowship in Modern Languages.[130] Hayden wondered with amusement what the ladies in the audience would think of the 'blue stockings', now enjoying the description to which she had once objected. The junior fellowship provided payment of £200 a year for four years. Junior fellows had examining duties which included attendance at examiners' meetings and setting examination papers, as well as reading scripts and conducting oral examinations. Hayden enjoyed the contact with colleagues of the University, though the marking of scripts she found quite onerous. On the MA oral examination, she noted 'It was my first experience of questioning a man and I felt rather nervous'.[131] But another of a fellow's duties did not come her way as she was not appointed to teach for the University. Appointments of Royal University fellows in Dublin had so far been made only to University College managed by the Jesuits, where students and staff were entirely male. Hayden continued to teach some classes in Alexandra College and St Mary's where the distinction of her fellowship contributed to the prestige of the institutions. After the expiration of the award, she was regularly described in the two women's colleges as MA, ex-Junior Fellow of the Royal University of Ireland.

Some months after the award of the junior fellowships, there was talk of a senior fellowship for Fr George O'Neill, the candidate narrowly beaten by Hayden in the competition for the junior award.[132] Senior fellows were appointed not on examination results, but on selection by the University Senate; and as Hayden later recalled 'no woman ever attained one'.[133] A correspondent to the *Daily Express* (Dublin) on the subject of the fellows of the Royal University referred specifically to Hayden, her junior fellowship award and the recent appointment of one of the unsuccessful candidates at that examination to a senior fellowship.[134] Hayden ruefully noted that O'Neill had done better by being beaten for the junior award, and Alice Oldham shared her annoyance on the issue. However, when it emerged that O'Neill had not at that time been appointed, the speculation was that the fuss had dissuaded his advocates.[135] The success of Hayden and Katherine Murphy was a significant demonstration of women's ability to compete with men for the higher academic awards. Their achievement was an encouragement to women as to what they might aim for. Alice Oldham had for some years been campaigning for the admission of women to Trinity College.[136] And the increasing consciousness of women that their inferior status in the provision of higher education was unacceptable, would in a few more years result in an organised effort to end this discrimination. Hayden was delighted with her own award, and with the distinction it brought her. For the time being, the O'Neill affair was an irritant, which would become more serious at the end of the century when the two were again in competition.

NOTES

1   Philippa Levine, *Feminist Lives in Victorian England: Private Roles and Public Commitment* (Oxford, 1990), p. 42.
2   Hayden Diary, 28 June 1886.
3   Hayden Diary, September 1886.
4   Hayden Diary, 7 July 1886.
5   Nicholas Donnelly (1837–1920), uncle and guardian of the Boland family, and a coadjutor (i.e. assistant) bishop. He was a noted historian of Catholic Dublin, for which information I am grateful to Professor Fergus D'Arcy.
6   Hayden Diary, 5 July 1886.
7   Hayden Diary, 5 July 1886.
8   Hayden Diary, 10 April 1883.
9   Richard J. Evans, *The Feminists: Women's Emancipation Movements in Europe, America and Australasia* (London, 1977), p. 24.
10 Hayden Diary, 9 June 1886.
11 R.F. Foster, *W.B. Yeats: A Life. 1. The Apprentice Mage 1865–1914* (Oxford, 1997), p. 29.
12 Joseph Brady, 'Dublin at the Turn of the Century' in Joseph Brady and Anngret Simms (eds), *Dublin Through Space and Time*

(Dublin, 2001), pp 229–32. Hayden Diary, 16 January 1883, 1 September 1890.

13   Hayden Diary, 20 October 1885.

14   Hayden Diary, 22 September 1881.

15   Hayden Diary, 27 March 1882.

16   Jane Austen, *Pride and Prejudice* (Nelson Classics), p. 200.

17   Hayden Diary, 3 December 1890.

18   Hayden Diary, 24 February 1888.

19   Hayden Diary, June 1903.

20   Hayden Diary, 24 July 1887.

21   Hayden Diary, 15 February 1889.

22   Senia Pašeta, *Before the Revolution: Nationalism, Social Change and Ireland's Catholic Elite 1879–1922* (Cork, 1999), pp 81, 140.

23   Hayden Diary, 1 April 1892.

24   Hayden Diary, 19 November 1886.

25   June Purvis, *A History of Women's Education in England* (Milton Keynes, 1991), p. 73.

26   Hayden Diary, 3 October 1888.

27   Hayden Diary, 18 December 1886.

28   Hayden Diary, 9 July 1891.

29   Hayden Diary, 8 October 1891.

30   Maria Luddy, 'Women and Politics in Nineteenth Century Ireland' in Maryann Valiulis and Mary O'Dowd (eds), *Women and Irish History* (Dublin, 1997), p. 98.

31   Mary Cullen, 'Women, Emancipation and Politics, 1860–1984' in J.R. Hill (ed.), *A New History of Ireland*, Vol. VII (Oxford, 2003), p. 827; Carmel Quinlan, *Genteel Revolutionaries* (Cork, 2002), p. 109.

32   Deirdre Raftery, 'Francis Power Cobbe (1822–1904)' in Mary Cullen and Maria Luddy (eds), *Women, Power and Consciousness in 19th Century Ireland* (Dublin, 1995), p. 90.

33   Hayden Diary, 6, 7, 18 September 1886.

34   Hayden Diary, 10 April 1881,

35   Hayden Diary, 17 April 1887, 21 May 1887.

36   Mary Hayden, 'A Few Thoughts on Women in Universities and on University Women', *The National Student*, June 1935, p. 70.

37   Martha Vicinus, *Independent Women: Work and Community for Single Women 1850–1920* (Chicago, 1988), pp 123–24, 138.

38   Evans, *op cit*, p. 20.

39   Vicinus, *op cit*, pp 1–2.

40   Hayden Diary, 4–10 October 1887.

41   Hayden Diary, 27 October 1887.

42   Hayden Diary, 13 May 1887.
43   *Royal University of Ireland, Calendar* (Dublin, 1888), p. 78.
44   Hayden Diary, 2 March 1888.
45   Donal McCartney, *UCD A National Idea: The History of University College, Dublin.* p. 23.
46   Thomas J. Morrissey SJ, *Thomas A. Finlay SJ, 1848–1940* (Dublin, 2004).
47   *Ibid*, p. 45.
48   Hayden Diary, Easter Saturday 1888.
49   *Royal University of Ireland, Calendar* (Dublin, 1888), p. 78.
50   Hayden Diary, 30 April 1888.
51   Hayden Diary, 28 February, 8 March, 11 March 1888.
52   Hayden Diary, 28 January 1891.
53   Hayden Diary, 17 April, 22 June 1891.
54   Hayden Diary, 16 November 1893.
55   Hayden Diary, 25, 26 October 1885.
56   Hayden Diary, 5 January 1889.
57   Hayden Diary, 16 March 1889.
58   Hayden Diary, 9 August 1890.
59   Barbara Miller Solomon, *In the Company of Educated Women: A History of Women and Higher Education in America* (Yale, 1985), p. 129. Hayden Diary, 18, 28 July, 1 September 1891.
60   Hayden Diary, 26 January 1891. See Carol Dyhouse, *Feminism and the Family in England 1880–1939* (Oxford, 1989), p. 33.
61   Dyhouse, *ibid.*, p. 54.
62   Hayden Diary, 24 October 1892.
63   Hayden Diary, 31 May, 8 June 1894.
64   Hayden Diary, 8 June 1889.
65   Hayden Diary, 19 April 1890.
66   Hayden Diary, 15 April 1890.
67   *Ibid.*, and also 12 July 1890.
68   Lilian Green (1870–1950), daughter of a Quaker businessman. Student at Alexandra and Royal University. Conan Kennedy (ed), *The Diaries of Mary Hayden,* Vol V, Appendices, p. 2300.
69   Hayden Diary, 23 February 1889.
70   Hayden Diary, 16 June, 16 September, 7 October 1892.
71   Mary Hayden, M.A. and Lilian Green, 'Greek Peasant Girls, and How They Live', *Girl's Own Paper,* 4 June 1892.
72   Alfred Webb, *The Autobiography of a Quaker Nationalist,* edited by Marie-Louise Legg (Cork, 1999), p. 66.
73   Hayden Diary, 6 April 1893.
74   Hayden Diary, 3 April 1893.

75   Hayden Diary, 18 April 1893.
76   Hayden Diary, 6 April, 2 May 1893.
77   Hayden Diary, 7 May 1893.
78   Hayden Diary, 3 June 1893.
79   Hayden Diary, 11 February 1891.
80   Arthur Conan letter, 12 April 1891, in possession of Conan family.
81   Hayden Diary, 24 July 1892.
82   Hayden Diary, 24 September 1892.
83   Hayden Diary, 13 October 1892, 1 November 1892.
84   Hayden Diary, 3 June 1893.
85   Hayden Diary, 14–29 August 1893.
86   Hayden Diary, 30 August 1894.
87   Hayden Diary, 17–30 July 1895.
88   Hayden Diary, 22 March 1891.
89   Mary Colum, *Life and the Dream* (Dublin, 1966, rev. ed.), p. 151.
90   Margaret Ward, *Hanna Sheehy Skeffington: A Life* (Cork, 1997), p. 29.
91   Dyhouse, *op cit*, p. 46.
92   Hayden Diary, 17 November 1883.
93   Dyhouse, *op cit*, p. 39.
94   Hayden Diary, 21 November 1895.
95   Susan M. Parkes and Judith Harford, 'Women and Higher Education in Ireland' in Deirdre Raftery and Susan M. Parkes (eds), *Female Education in Ireland 1700–1900: Minerva or Madonna* (Dublin, 2007), pp 112–13.
96   Hayden Diary, 13 May 1893.
97   Hayden Diary, 13 August, 27 September 1893.
98   'A Tribute to Professor Mary Hayden, D.Litt.', *The Lanthorn, Yearbook of the Dominican College, Eccles Street, Dublin, Christmas 1942* (Dublin, 1942), pp 349–351.
99   Hayden Diary, 19 July 1894.
100   Mary Hayden, 'A Few Thoughts on Women in Universities and on University Women', *The National Student,* June 1935, p. 70.
101   *Royal Commission on University Education in Ireland,* Third Report (Appendix), (1902), pp 357–59.
102   Hayden Diary, 15 November 1894. Fr Darlington appears as Fr Butt in Joyce's *Portrait of the Artist as a Young Man.*
103   F.S.L. Lyons, *Ireland since the Famine* (Glasgow, 1973, rev. ed.), p. 225.
104   *Ibid.*, p. 228.
105   Hayden Diary, 24 May 1892.

106 Hayden Diary, 14, 30 July 1892.

107 Lyons, *op cit*, pp 237–239.

108 Hayden Diary, 25 January 1894.

109 George Sigerson, Testimonial included with Hayden's application (1909) to the Dublin Commissioners. National University of Ireland Archives.

110 National Literary Society, Minute Book 1907–08, NLI Ms 646.

111 R.F. Foster, *W.B. Yeats: A Life. I. The Apprentice Mage 1865–1914* (Oxford, 1997), p. 51.

112 Hayden Diary, 10 August 1892.

113 Hayden Diary, 15 October 1893.

114 Foster, *W.B. Yeats*, p. 90.

115 Hayden Diary, 4 August 1892.

116 Hayden Diary, 18 September 1892.

117 National Literary Society, Minute Book, NLI, Ms 645.

118 Margaret Ward, *Maud Gonne: Ireland's Joan of Arc* (London, 1990), pp 42–3, 52.

119 Hayden Diary, 1 October 1892.

120 Hayden Diary, 23 May 1892.

121 Hayden Diary, 4 November 1893.

122 Mary Macken, 'W.B. Yeats, John O'Leary and the Contemporary Club', *Studies* (March 1939), p. 137.

123 Macken, *ibid.*, pp 136–42.

124 Carmel Quinlan, *Genteel Revolutionaries: Anna and Thomas Haslam and the Irish Women's Movement* (Cork, 2002), p. 144.

125 Macken, *ibid.*, p. 139.

126 Hayden Diary, 1 November 1890.

127 Hayden Diary, 18 October 1892, 21 February 1893.

128 Hayden Diary, 2 February 1895.

129 Hayden Diary, 7–11 October 1895.

130 *Royal University of Ireland, Calendar* (Dublin, 1896), p. 23.

131 Hayden Diary, 5 October 1897.

132 Hayden Diary, 13 and 16 March 1896.

133 Mary Hayden, 'A Few Thoughts on Women in Universities and on University Women', p. 70.

134 Letter from Ramsay Colles, *Daily Express*, 16 March 1896. In 1900 Ramsay Colles, editor of the *Irish Figaro*, printed an attack on Maud Gonne, for which he was physically attacked by Arthur Griffith. Colles was subsequently the unsuccessful defendant in a libel case taken by Maud Gonne. Donal P. McCracken, *The Irish Pro-Boers* (Johannesburg, 1989), pp 83, 86.

135 Hayden Diary, 13, 19, 26 March 1896.

136 Lucinda Thompson, 'The Campaign for Admission, 1870–1904' in Susan M. Parkes (ed.), *A Danger to the Men: A History of Women in Trinity College Dublin, 1904–2004* (Dublin, 2004), p. 29.

Mary Hayden, 1900

III

FROM JUNIOR FELLOW TO EMERGENT FEMINIST
1896–1903

With her junior fellowship, Hayden had gained a sense of security and status. She travelled extensively. She got to know the Haslams, Anna and Thomas, and became increasingly conscious of the possibilities of rights for women. Her social conscience also encouraged her participation in philanthropic activity. Occupied with scholarship and teaching, she nevertheless led a lively life in Dublin, interspersed with further foreign travel.

More Travelling
In April-May 1896 Hayden was again in Athens, where she joined in celebrating the success of an Irish friend, John Pius Boland who won two gold medals in the tennis championships at the Olympic Games. Boland had just completed a law degree at Oxford; he later became an Irish Party MP at Westminster (1900) and a member of the Dublin Commission appointed to implement the provisions of the Irish Universities Act 1908 establishing

the National University of Ireland. Hayden was on visiting terms with the Boland family, whom she met also in the Crean home. She recorded great excitement in 1888 about Boland's Flour Mills' new Joint Stock Company, in which 'everyone [was] applying for shares'. Her application for £200 worth was unsuccessful, but 'I did not sensibly grieve, never do over such matters'.[1] It was an assertion of her economic independence and a display of the business acumen she had attributed to her mother.

There were further enjoyable encounters with Frank Humphries, in Brussels, and in Dublin in September 1896 when he was again working at the Rotunda Hospital. He was much in Hayden's company, got on well with her brother John, and often called at their home in the evening. They enjoyed each other's company and talked a great deal, exchanging some confidences but it does not seem from Hayden's diary that they ever discussed a future together. After an emotional farewell, when he kissed her – 'such long, hard kisses' – she felt that he would soon forget her, who had 'just enlivened a little his three weeks here … he goes back to gaiety and dances and flirtations at Brussels, will he even write?'[2]

She then set off with Lilian Green for the long dreamed of visit to India where they spent Christmas 1896, not returning to Dublin until Easter 1897. Voyaging through the Mediterranean and the Suez Canal, they reached Bombay, whence they covered much ground to Delhi, Colombo and places in between, with many contacts and expatriates to call on. Travel was principally by train, and on occasions by elephant, horse, or local conveyance. One night, stranded at a railway station, 'we established ourselves in the inner waiting room where there were two couches on which we spread our bedding and a very nice civil ayah waited on us'. The Taj Mahal exceeded Hayden's expectations, and they made a return visit to it by moonlight:

> It was a lovely night, the dust in the moonlight looked like
> snow ... Across the garden the building looked lovely; it
> seemed to swim in the air and had a certain ghostly look.

Hayden wrote at length of the sights, which were enthralling, the splendid temples, 'the golden east, how fond I am of it'. The exotic appealed to her, in contrast to the humdrum of life at home. 'It was the India of which I had dreamed, the India that Clive and Warren Hastings knew',[3] a sentence that suggests the contemporary English admiration for the achievements of colonial conquest. When home again in Dublin, she attended a lecture on India where grievances of Indian speakers were noted, but Hayden's comment that according to everyone who knew them, the 'natives cannot be trusted',[4] expressed the then conventional colonial attitude which she and others would soon modify as the events of the Boer War unfolded.

Green wrote an account of the later part of their visit to India, which seems to have been prepared for delivery as a talk. She too was enthralled by the sights and the experience. There are no references to Hayden, beyond telling us that in spite of dire warnings of dishonesty and 'hatred of the English' before they left home:

> we were never better served ... and for over two months of
> our visit we were just two girls without the protecting shadow
> of one of the stronger sex, during which time we visited
> numbers of Indian towns whether native or in British
> occupation ... and never did we encounter a single unfriendly
> look nor receive a rude or discourteous reply.

Green approved of Britain's presence in India, which she referred to as 'our rule'.[5]

As a traveller, sometimes alone, sometimes in a group, Hayden was a tourist, curious, adventurous, revelling in new experiences. Journeys were slow and tiring, but she travelled in reasonable comfort, possible with the advent of mass travel. The firm of Thomas Cook and Son, which she mentions, had been organising travel and tours since the mid nineteenth century, including tours to Egypt and the Holy Land, which may well have been how Hayden and Green had visited these places in 1893.[6] Others undertaking these journeys were mostly English people, with whom Hayden was happy to mix, enjoying the dual identity of being either Irish or English.[7] Green as quoted above, considered herself English when abroad.

In her travels, Hayden was not driven by missionary zeal to bring education or other advantages to local inhabitants. Apart from her two-part article on 'Modern Athens' in *The Lyceum* in 1891, and the article on Greek girls in the *Girl's Own Paper*, there are no published accounts of her travels. She travelled for enjoyment and for cultural experience in the manner of the 'grand tour', which by the late nineteenth century it was possible for an independent-minded woman to do without the accompaniment of a chaperone or a husband. Travel was an adventurous escape from boredom and monotony. Tourism offered well-to-do women an opportunity to get out and see the world, which was certainly its appeal for Hayden.[8] Some years earlier, tales by a cousin of his experiences abroad had aroused her 'old stifled feeling ... a longing to move on, a sense of the size of the world'.[9] By travel, women attempted to break out of their assigned spaces and roles; it took conviction and a spirit of discovery. And, significantly for a woman like Hayden, these journeys were a demonstration of independence and competence. Her desire to travel was constrained only by time and money.

In summer 1898 Hayden took a ship to Spain and the Mediterranean, visiting Lisbon, Gibraltar, Malaga, Tangier and Cadiz. There were only a few passengers, who left the ship at different ports until Hayden was the only woman remaining; she enjoyed being served first at table and having quarters to herself, and felt that she got on well with the young male passengers. She found their chummy intimacy agreeable and undemanding. While the ship was anchored off Malaga, she took a late night bathe, plunging from the ship and swimming about thirty yards.[10] On a similar trip in 1901, with a group which included Henry McIntosh and his wife, Hayden again 'bathed off the ship … I am sure the rest thought it awful'.[11] The temptation to flout convention was irresistible.

In 1896 she had learnt to cycle,[12] thereby acquiring great freedom. She relished the convenience of the bicycle and described riding home at night 'through the deserted streets my lamp burning before me'.[13] The advent of the bicycle and the enthusiasm with which women took to cycling are of immense social significance.[14] The bicycle was an instrument of liberation, as Hayden described. Elizabeth, Countess of Fingall, and her women friends were pleased with their bicycles, 'new and strange sights in the Irish countryside' and their outfits specially designed for cycling.[15] In 1897 Hayden and Effie McIntosh toured Connemara by bicycle, getting thoroughly drenched on some days. Hayden had also many cycling outings to the Dublin mountains with Hester Sigerson and her future husband Donn Piatt. In Hayden's view, Hester was lucky to have such a pleasant, amiable man friend, in contrast to her own unattached life. In spite of her many friendships, she sometimes had the feeling of being an outsider,[16] a position which in a sense she had herself cultivated by her preferred pursuit of her own ambitions. There were also cycling parties from Dublin with the Sigersons[17] and the Starkies.[18]

Philanthropy

From her early adult years Hayden had participated intermittently in charitable work, possibly through the example of Mrs Emma Crean and her daughters. Philanthropy was an area where middle- and upper-class women in nineteenth century Ireland might exercise their abilities outside the home and engage in benevolent work in the spheres of poverty, children, education, temperance, prostitution and visiting homes and institutions. Through charitable work, women expanded their social role, making social work a legitimate occupation and leading some among them ultimately to claim political rights.[19] Nineteenth-century philanthropy was both benevolent, in seeking to alleviate poverty, and reformist in striving for legislative change to improve the circumstances of life for the poor.[20] Reformist concerns often became feminist demands; and the need for social change began to be associated with the acquisition of the vote. Hayden was one whose awakening feminism would in time progress from benevolent deeds to conviction that legislative and other reforms would be necessary in order to improve conditions for women and children. The election of women as poor law guardians and rural district councillors before the end of the century was to be an early manifestation of women's participation as effective administrators and reformers.[21]

Prostitution was a considerable problem in Irish society, and in Dublin there were up to eighteen asylums for the rescue and reclamation of 'fallen women', some of which were named Magdalen Asylums, recalling the repentance of the biblical Mary Magdalen.[22] At the age of twenty Hayden, with the Creans, had visited the Magdalen Asylum (High Park) in Drumcondra. She found the house to be clean and cold, but had no conversation with any of the one hundred women penitents (her word, and the title given to women who entered these asylums).[23] Hayden reflected on the 'sad waste of human life' when 'the weaker and (generally) the more ignorant of the two sharers' in a sin is condemned 'to shame and to a bitter ... expiation', while for the other culprit the sin is applauded as 'gallantry' or at most is condemned as a 'peccadillo'.[24] This is an instance of the awakening of Hayden's social conscience, and a portent of her concerns in later years. Feminists like Anna Haslam, campaigning for repeal of the Contagious Diseases Acts, had objected to the different standards applied to the conduct of men and women. These Acts, passed in the 1860s and finally repealed in 1886, provided for the compulsory medical examination of alleged prostitutes for evidence of venereal disease, as an attempt to control the spread of the disease among the military; but men were not subjected to examination.[25] Anna's husband Thomas had published a pamphlet (1870) as part of the campaign, in which he blamed men for prostitution and the seduction of young girls.[26]

Hayden also recorded a visit to the Hospital for Incurables in Dublin (now a hospice) and another to the workhouse in Clonmel (where a brother of Michael Crean was a doctor),[27] and occasionally accompanied Mrs Emma Crean on her charitable visitations. By 1899 Hayden had cases of her own to visit on behalf of the Children's Clothing Society,[28] a development of her earlier charitable occupation of sewing clothes for poor children, first mentioned when she helped the Crean girls to make a white dress for a child's confirmation.[29] On another occasion, she noted her fingers were sore from 'cutting out charity frocks'.[30] She evidently continued this form of social work for many years. In 1885 she had started to teach a Sunday catechism class for very young uneducated children, work which also she was to continue at a Sacred Heart Home, though she found it 'very difficult to realise the mental state of little children, so as to be able to teach them'.[31]

There were various attempts in the late nineteenth century to improve the housing situation for the Dublin poor, including some efforts by philanthropic bodies such as the Iveagh Trust, established in the 1890s. The Alexandra College Guild of past pupils, founded in 1898 to engage in socially useful work in the city, was one body which, on the suggestion of one of its members, Dr Kathleen Maguire, adopted the idea of buying and renovating existing tenements in which accommodation was then let at modest rents to tenants to be trained in 'cleanliness and neatness'.[32] Despite attempts before the end of the century at slum clearance and at minimal improvements in the living conditions of the city's poor, 'a stout stomach' was still needed by 'anyone venturing into the worst of the city's courtyard cottages and tenement rooms'.[33] In the early years of the twentieth century, Lady Aberdeen, wife of the Viceroy, found a lamentable lack of houses for the working classes, with over 22% of the population of Dublin living in one-room tenements, often families with as many as six occupants.[34] There were also, in the yards behind large houses, many small, dark, insanitary dwellings, which were in fact slums.[35] Hayden, as her diary records, met these conditions on her visitations.

Poor housing gave rise to other needs. Popular philanthropy, in both Protestant and Catholic circles, showed concern 'for the moral and spiritual degeneracy of the lower orders particularly in the growing commercial and industrial towns and cities'.[36] In late nineteenth century Dublin there were various clubs, both Catholic and Protestant, for working girls to provide recreation and instruction, and to act as an alternative to dangerous temptations. In some instances the clubs also provided accommodation and assistance in obtaining employment.[37] Hayden was one of a large council of the Alexandra Guild which acquired and sought funds for a house in Castlewood Avenue, Rathmines, to be used as a hostel 'for working girls of the poorer class' (1912).[38] The Guild held an annual conference on educational and social issues relating to women, at which Hayden was often a speaker.

Though genuinely concerned to make some practical efforts towards the alleviation of distress, Hayden could experience intolerance for 'the lower orders'[39] and occasionally revealed her disdain for the behaviour of her perceived social inferiors:[40]

heavy fathers and their over-dressed wives and roast-beef faced sons, and limpid haired daughters … how very interesting to a philanthropist, not at all picturesque.[41]

Admitting her prejudice, she acknowledged that 'I dislike shop girls and their giggling ways'.[42] Commenting on the ill-behaved students at conferring, she called them 'a common lot' and 'awful specimens of country bumpkins'.[43] On a Gaelic League excursion to Glendalough in 1902, she found most of the group, the girls especially, to be 'common' and 'vulgarians'.[44] When visiting a relative in Tipperary whose 'appearance gave me a shock' – she was badly dressed and 'the house was that of a peasant' – Hayden admitted that she had to repress her 'snobbish feelings' and remember that Miss Ryan was a relation.[45] Her recognition of her own snobbery is an instance of honest self-criticism. She could be at times condescending, but she was not arrogant.

Hayden's feeling of superiority was shared by other women of her class.[46] While Hayden's attitude was patronising, in the long run it strengthened her belief in the importance of education. She was conscious of the contrast between her comfortable, educated life and the poor, miserable existence of many other children.[47] Recognising poverty as a problem, she pondered whether a smaller population might offer some alleviation (without specifying how to 'diminish the pressure of population'), and could not see why 'all good Christians seem to hold up their hands in horror at that idea'.[48] More particularly she noted, about a cousin expecting her fifth child, 'I don't really think it is right, considering how shockingly overpopulated the world is already'. Some years later, when visiting a family in one room where, she wrote, 'the smell nearly made me sick', she added they 'ought not to have so many children'.[49] Apart from these stray thoughts, there is no evidence of Hayden having any considered view on population control or contraception, but she is here expressing the response of contemporary middle-class reformers to the social problems of the poor.[50] She did not echo the Haslams' advocacy of birth control;[51] it was not a subject for public discussion by women, more particularly single women.[52]

Academic Ambitions

Hayden's principal purpose was her scholarly life. The rivalry with George O'Neill, whom she had vanquished in the junior fellowship examination, surfaced again in 1899–1900. Not surprisingly she decided to try for a senior fellowship, since her junior award was coming to an end. Her academic experience now included an article 'Medieval Etiquette' published in the *New Ireland Review*, October 1896, a paper on 'Maria Edgeworth' read to the National Literary Society,[53] and her appointment as an examiner by the Intermediate Examination Board.[54] On Edgeworth, Hayden wrote a detailed perusal of her literary works with a description of the author's life. Hayden judged Edgeworth to be talented, though a little prim and pedantic, and charitable particularly during the famine years of the 1840s. This paper on a literary subject had a historical content in both its subject Edgeworth, and her literary output. Hayden was here writing in the then established genre of women biographers. Her scholarly interests continued to be wide-ranging and she was pleased to be asked by Clement Shorter, husband of Dora Sigerson, to write an article on J.B. Bury for *The Sphere*, the English illustrated weekly journal of contemporary affairs. Hayden's gracefully written article, 'A Distinguished Historian of Trinity College' occasioned by the publication of the seventh volume of Bury's edition of *The Decline and Fall of the Roman Empire* by Edward Gibbon, is laudatory on Bury and knowledgeable about his subject, agreeing with him that the classics of Greece and Rome continue to be the 'groundwork of a liberal education'.[55]

To gain sufficient support for a senior fellowship appointment, she realised that lobbying would be essential. Those on whom she called to exercise what influence they could included the principals of the two colleges where she taught, Mother Patrick Shiel of St Mary's Dominican College and Miss Henrietta White of Alexandra.[56] She wrote many letters, though she detested trying to influence people in this matter and felt it was 'labour in vain'.[57] Her long letter to the Catholic coadjutor bishop, Dr Nicholas Donnelly, elicited a 'nice' reply.[58] Donnelly, who dined occasionally in the Crean home (where she had failed to talk to him about the fellowship), was the uncle and guardian of the Boland family. However, Hayden also received information that the Catholic Archbishop (i.e. Dr William Walsh) would not 'interfere in the matter of the Fellowship'.[59] Walsh had resigned from the Royal University Senate many years previously following a disagreement about the award of a fellowship (though the reason was probably not known to Hayden).[60] The first news that her application had been unsuccessful came from the Registrar of the Royal University, Dr Joseph McGrath, who let her know that she would not be appointed as there were strong claims on the awards from the colleges to which the fellows were usually appointed[61] (which in Dublin was mainly University College managed by the Jesuits). Dr William Delany,[62] President of that College, was later to claim that he felt precluded from appointing a woman to teach men in a Catholic College.[63]

The fellowship went to George O'Neill who, if the earlier gossip was correct, had been waiting for the senior appointment. William Starkie later observed that the gentleman defeated by a lady for the junior fellowship was afterwards appointed over her head to a senior fellowship where he would examine in the examination in which he had himself been unsuccessful.[64] Hayden's disappointment included concern about the loss of the stipend and regret at the reduction in her status at the Royal University, where she continued to obtain some examination work. 'Now I was merely a sort of underling' and 'probably the taking down was good for me morally'[65] – another instance of her self-criticism. O'Neill held his fellowship until the dissolution of the Royal University in 1908 and was then appointed Professor of English Literature in the new UCD.

After much pondering on the subject, John Hayden had left in November 1898 for an extended stay in North America, his sister thinking immediately of a trip there to visit him. She undertook the journey in the winter of 1899–1900, spending Christmas and the New Year in Canada at Yorkton with the Harper family where John was lodging. Hayden had a good time, with skating, dancing and family life, but she observed that the women there were 'toiling all the time at housework and get very little fun'.[66] Though it had not deterred her from making the journey to Canada, she was again worrying about money with the ending of her four-year junior fellowship. The disappointing, though not really unexpected, information about the senior fellowship reached her soon after her return from Canada. Since January 1899 she had moved her lodgings to Stamer Street, off the South Circular Road, (a nice, cheerful house with a 'good bathroom')[67] but now thought of seeking cheaper lodgings; in a fit of loneliness she recorded her woes which included her lack of a position.[68]

In November 1900 encouraged by Agnes O'Farrelly, Hayden applied again for another vacancy as senior fellow in English. Agnes O'Farrelly, a graduate of the Royal University, was a teacher of Irish, a member of the Gaelic League and would later, like Hayden, be appointed to the foundation staff of UCD and to its first Governing Body. Though not very hopeful, Hayden felt it important to put her name forward and started lobbying again.[69] She was discouraged by the general view that the choice this time would be with Delany. Confirmation to this effect came in a letter from Delany (whom, with her fondness for nicknames, she called ironically 'Sweet William') in which he told her that the Statutes excluded women. Hayden knew this was incorrect having previously examined the Statutes, and she now hunted through the parliamentary papers in the National Library to convince herself that there was no such excluding statute.[70] This particular senior fellowship being intended for University College, and Delany's feeling that he could not introduce 'so strange a novelty in a Catholic University College' as a lady lecturing to men, meant that Hayden's name, although she had applied, was not put before the Senate.[71] The only candidate proposed to the Senate, John W. Bacon, was elected unanimously to the senior fellowship. Bacon, who was Delany's nephew, was far less qualified than Hayden, as subsequently pointed out by Henrietta White in her evidence to the Robertson Commission.[72] Hayden's own comment on Bacon's appointment was 'relative force'; she thought the appointment 'a perfect scandal'.[73] She consulted Judge James Shaw, a member of the University Senate, about Delany's letter and received his opinion that the exclusion of women from senior fellowships was not a statutory requirement,[74] nor did Delany claim it as such when giving evidence to the Robertson Commission the following year (when he would base his argument on his belief in separate education for women). A later (1930) Jesuit record of the fellowship affair, while acknowledging Hayden's distinction, maintained that 'the time had not come when women could be included in the College Staff'. O'Neill's career was described as 'marked by versatility', and Bacon was noted as having 'done good work as Tutor in Latin, English and French'.[75]

Hayden continued to feel aggrieved, and wrote to the *Independent* in November 1901,[76] but the letter does not appear to have been published. She avoided meeting Delany, though it was 'not right nor Christian to hate him as I do'; 'if he had fought fair' she could have pardoned him.[77] When she saw Bacon she felt 'bitter anger' at the injustice.[78] She and the other woman junior fellow, Katherine Hogan (née Murphy), went on a deputation to Fr Joseph Darlington SJ, fellow of the Royal University in the Jesuit College, who had previously advised Hayden on her preparation for the junior fellowship examination. This time she did not like the meeting; she felt distrust for Darlington and that he thinks women 'rather fools and easily flattered'.[79] Though she gives us no more explanation, she may have sensed a patronising attitude towards the academic aims of women like herself. Later in life, she recalled the poor opinion some university authorities had of women students. 'Another commonly held view was that university courses were too hard for women ...' and she wrote of 'the most unequal terms' on which women students were obliged to compete with men.[80] In her evidence to the Royal Commission in 1902, Hayden would avail of the opportunity to speak of the senior fellowship episode.

Personal Relationships: Suitors: Children

On her return from India, Hayden was surprised to have no letter from Humphries.[81] He had met them briefly in Brussels on their outward journey, which was to be the last time she saw him. She had written then in her diary:

> Oh Frank, I wish I lived nearer you that I could see you once a month even. Now you are establishing yourself so far away that I shall perhaps not see you once in two years.[82]

She wrote to Humphries for his birthday, but as the correspondence tailed off, she felt she was losing a friend of whom she was very fond.[83] She then learned of his marriage. She thought of him on his wedding night[84] and recurrently for several years.[85] He wrote, some months after his marriage which he did not mention but assumed that Mary knew of it. Addressed 'My dear Mary' and signed 'Your affectionate friend Frank', the letter, though of some comfort, was accepted as the final parting.[86] During the following weeks, she recalled her strong affection for Humphries and wrote, revealingly:

> True I never, had I been foolish enough to marry him, could have made him happy, but not because I did not care for him enough.[87]

She cared a lot, valued his friendship, and experienced an attraction more than she felt for Arthur Conan. She was beginning to feel a need for a personal commitment, though still averse to a settled life of domesticity. Part of the charm of Humphries was the possibility of a varied, interesting and less conventional life. He had sought her out both in London and in Dublin as an entertaining companion, but for his part had, it seems, shown no sign of more permanent thoughts on their relationship. Humphries remained in Hayden's thoughts, which she realised 'was silly of course and unprofitable',[88] while, in her realistic manner, she got on with her busy life of teaching, literary pursuits, friends and travelling.

Conan, now in Cape Colony, was ill. Hayden began to fear that he was dying and, noting the letters arriving from him, she felt that she cared for him more now when she might never see him again.[89] The departure of Humphries from her life may have helped to concentrate her mind. Despite her fondness for travel, she did not accept the suggestion that she might accompany Conan's sister Jeannie to visit him in Africa in autumn 1900.[90] Hayden was in low spirits, short of money, sore about the fellowship, and constantly expecting news of Conan's death. Her acknowledgement that 'he has been as it were my future for so very many years',[91] her remembrance of 'the odd soft sound of his voice as he talked to me ...'[92] and other brief comments expressed her recognition of happiness forfeited. She was, to say the least, lonely. In the last extant volume of her diary, she asked why does God not 'give Arthur and me a little happiness ... two or three years'[93] and envied Hester whose husband Donn was strong and well and with her, while Arthur was dying and she (Mary) 'must trudge along through the twilight and into the darkness alone'.[94] This is the final entry in Hayden's diary. Less than two weeks later, Conan died on 13 August 1903 in Cradock, Cape Province, South Africa, where he is buried. She may in her sorrow have had no inclination to continue a diary, and as far as we know there are no more volumes.

At this point, after she had turned 40, Hayden seemed not averse to the idea of a life with Arthur Conan, had he been in Ireland and in reasonable health. However on the subject of marriage in general, she was still satisfied that its earlier lack of attraction for her had not changed. On a visit in 1903 to a Mrs O'Carroll, where the thought came to her that 'I might have been mistress of this house', she wrote also 'I have never regretted that refusal nor the others'.[95] On another visit to O'Carroll, Hayden noted her two younger children, 'a great nuisance ... evidently spoiled', and added that these infants 'might have been my own', though 'much as I like children' she did not wish them hers.[96] It seems that her hostess's husband was the O'Carroll who, as a young doctor, helped in October 1881 to tend the dying Thomas Hayden, watching over him at night. Young O'Carroll was known to the family, and possibly was a student of Dr Hayden's. A few subsequent diary references, such as 'I will try to forget his unconceivable silliness',[97] indicate awkwardness or embarrassment about O'Carroll, who is believed to have proposed to Hayden.

What other suitors were there? Did the widowed Bischof in Bonn propose marriage to Hayden? In Athens in 1890 she received a letter from him (possibly a proposal) which vexed her. She had many times given him a plain answer to his question; the idea was absurd, she thought of him as an elderly man like her father.[98] Several very brief comments about Bischof seem to confirm that he had suggested marriage – 'I wish he would not write such letters ...'[99] To Bischof it could have been an attractive possibility to marry this intelligent, efficient woman who got on well with his children, spoke German and liked Bonn. However, the prospect had held no attraction for the then twenty-eight year old Irish woman.

On an emotional level, Hayden had experienced confusing feelings about Arthur Conan, the young student Markos and Frank Humphries. She was also quite prudish and experienced moral scruples in her reaction to any physical demonstration of affection from her male friends, even from Conan who had honourably declared his intentions. She was 'fairly frightened' when an acquaintance, Mr McLoone, bringing her home in a cab tried to put his arm around her; to add to the drama the cab driver was drunk and lost his way. Hayden described McLoone as an odious brute, a low cad of disgusting behaviour,[100] but he must have been forgiven as, some years later, she accepted his invitation to tea at Mitchell's, the Dublin restaurant.

Hayden had seen marriage as a loss of independence, imposing domestic and family constraints on a woman's life. Concerns of this nature did not deter feminists like Mary Colum and Hanna Sheehy Skeffingon from marrying. Feminists were beginning to reject the traditional middle-class concept of marriage which required strength in a husband and frailty in a wife.[101] Hayden enjoyed the companionship of men, whom she at times found to be more intellectually stimulating than some of her women acquaintances, and clearly by 1903 she had some desire for the company of a husband. Her ideal would have been marriage as a life companionship, as some feminists envisaged, between a self-respecting man and a self-respecting woman.[102] This was Hayden's image of the happy relationship of Hester and Donn Piatt. In the course of a letter (c. 1907) to Patrick Pearse in which she advised him to marry and have a family, she wrote 'there is a part of human nature that asks for human relationships and human sympathies'. She referred to a recent marriage (whose, we do not know) which she supposed went off well, and continued:

> It must be a queer sensation going to be married, something like what I used to call a 'confession feeling', a sort of sinking sensation, inter-mingled both with excitement and with fear, only much worse ... more important and final than anything else except death.[103]

However unconscious, there is a perception here that she has, for her part, neglected what might have been a significant life experience.

As a younger woman, Hayden's occasional references to men as coarse or brutish might suggest inhibition about the thought of sexual intercourse. She recorded a doctor's visit, when she had influenza in Athens, as a 'very bad two minutes for me' adding 'Men are horrid ... when they are coarse and most of them are'.[104] As for babies, it would be 'all well enough if one found them in cabbage plants'.[105] Similarly, Margaret Ward has written of Maud Gonne that her:

> distaste for the sexual act, a result no doubt of the puritan morality of the period, was a common feeling amongst women of her social class.[106]

The attraction Hayden had felt for Humphries, while intellectual was also partly sexual; it is not impossible that had he suggested marriage, and despite her disapproval of some of his exploits, her heart might have over-ruled her head. However as a rule, she was a dispassionate, self-contained person, conforming to the contemporary Victorian constraints on the sexual lives of women. Nor is there reason to think she might have been sexually attracted by women. She had many women friends, both married and single, at different periods throughout her life; no one of these is thought to have been as intimate as a lover.

While Hayden had not desired to have children of her own, she became personally involved with several small children towards the end of her thirties. Earlier, she had fulfilled with care, though perhaps without much affection, her duties as guardian of her cousin, Annie Ryan. Three other children appeared in her diaries towards whom she took on some responsibility, Tommie Rice, Percy Hurley and Violet Kelly. Rice, a grandson of Dr Thomas Hayden's brother John, was born in 1891 and, according to Hayden, had been somewhat neglected by his mother Maggie.[107] Hayden brought Tommie to and from school in Bath, shopped for his clothes, and had him staying with her at times in Dublin. On his return to school in September 1901 she wrote, 'I had seen the last of my boy for nearly a year. I shall miss him and his concerns a good deal'.[108] Once Hayden's diaries cease, we have no further information about Tommie Rice.

In 1903, Hayden mentioned Percy Hurley, 'such a wee mite for 3 years old'.[109] Percy was one, probably the youngest, of the children of Kathleen Hurley, a Crean relative, whose husband had absconded and who herself was addicted to alcohol and in ill health. Percy Hurley received passing mention in some correspondence of the 1930s, and seemed then to be living with the two Haydens, Mary and John. Described as 'my cousin Percy Hurley', he was the principal beneficiary of Hayden's will, upon the decease of her brother John; and he must be 'her adopted son' referred to by Agnes O'Farrelly.[110] Both Tommie Rice and Percy Hurley were her cousins, about whom Hayden felt a natural concern, but she also took on some personal responsibility for their well-being. She clearly had a genuine affection for Tommie Rice and, it would seem, also for Percy Hurley. Percy is believed to have been handicapped by polio, which could have added to her solicitude for him.[111]

Violet Kelly was the infant daughter of Hayden's friend Josephine McGauran and her husband Frank Kelly. The parents, whose marriage was somewhat unstable, first left the child with Josephine's family in Dublin, and then on their return from Australia in 1887, placed her in a convent at Chelsea, as noted with sadness by Hayden – 'dear little thing ... if she were my child, I would not part with her for anything'. Hayden also thought of taking the child, but quickly rejected the idea as imprudent. She felt sorry for Violet, 'worse than an orphan, whose parents do not care for her',[112] and visited her occasionally until 1893, but beyond that, we know no more.

Hayden's fondness for these various children made her willing to become personally involved, in very practical ways, with their lives and welfare, though there might have been other, more obvious but less willing, surrogate parents. Her involvement in social work had been increasing, but her experiences with these three children had some emotional content, revealing tender instincts which one might not suspect of this otherwise independent woman who had preferred studies and learning to marriage and motherhood.

Widening Horizons

In 1903 Hayden was over forty, accustomed to the independent life which she had deliberately chosen. It was to become a life of more public involvement, her concern for personal independence extending beyond herself to the feminine role in society. On her own Hayden had built a life for herself based on her interest in scholarship. Limitations on what she as a woman might do or might aim for were initially galling and as she grew older began to seem quite unjust. Hayden's attitude to her own life is an example of the feminist desire to exhibit singleness as a positive personal choice.[113] Liberating experiences for women to which Hayden took with enthusiasm included travel, smoking and cycling.

Contrary to nineteenth-century fashion, she wore her hair cut short from the age of twenty-one. At that age too, while on a brief visit to London to see John and while he was occupied at Grays Inn, she dined in 'a common, low, eating house, but I did it and rejoiced in the impropriety of the act'. Though these may now appear as relatively minor issues, they were at the time brave statements of unorthodoxy for a respectable woman to make. Hayden's willingness to challenge accepted conventions demonstrated her impatience with the accepted norms for women. In these and in other ways, such as her increasing desire to work on equal terms with men, Hayden conformed to a definition of 'the new woman' whose hallmark was personal freedom.[114]

Hayden's position on women's rights developed gradually, fuelled by the restrictions she encountered in her academic career. When accompanying her father at a medical conference on the Isle of Wight in 1881, she heard the President of the Medical Association make an 'ill-judged' address decrying the idea of women as doctors. (Women had gained access to the profession in the UK as a result of the Medical Qualification Act of 1876).[115] Though she considered the speech irrational and impertinent, she could not make up her own mind on the issue.[116] Much later in life she had no doubt about the suitability of women for professions like medicine and law. Equal opportunity for women to fulfil a role in the community was to become central to her thinking. This did not by any means imply a career outside the home for every woman. Hayden would stress the importance of a rounded education so that wives and mothers could intelligently and responsibly contribute to the welfare of the family and the upbringing of their children.

Such a role was not what she had ever desired for herself. The sense of exclusion was a recurrent experience for her, as it was for many women who developed a feminist consciousness. Even her father who encouraged her pursuit of education at secondary level had thought her schooling should then end. The comment about Hayden made by Frank Kelly, husband of her friend Josephine, that 'he hated women going out of their sphere',[117] is an example of a common reaction to women students. In his case, it could have been an expression of his envy of her academic endeavours. Women were still perceived as intellectually inferior beings who should be content to remain so. Kelly, however unconsciously, could well have seen Hayden and her like as a threat to his notion of his own superiority, the more so as his own prospects were somewhat uncertain. Hayden, though she liked him, had noted him as an 'an awful rolling stone ... within the last two years he has been in Europe, Asia, Africa, Australia and America, more or less'.[118] Education was central in the development of Hayden's feminist thinking. Since her youth she had been – perhaps patronisingly – critical of the poor education, indifference and frivolity of many girls growing up around her. Her own disappointment about the senior fellowship rankled, and one can see here the stirrings of her campaigning spirit, soon to be channelled into the plan, of which she was not the originator, to prepare and present to the (Robertson) Royal Commission the case for university education for women.

On the wider political scene, home rule remained an eventual prospect, if remote after the defeat of the 1893 bill in the House of Lords. The Local Government Act 1898 established a system of elected borough and county councils which provided an opportunity for the middle class, professional, commercial and farming, to demonstrate its ability for self government in local matters.[119] Women were included in the local government franchise on a similar basis to men, that is with certain property or university qualifications, as a result of the efforts of women like Anna Haslam. Haslam described the Act as 'the most significant political revolution in the history of Irish women'.[120] And women had begun to exercise effective roles as poor law guardians and rural district councillors. By the end of 1898, eighty-five women had been elected as poor law guardians, of whom thirty-one were also rural district councillors.[121] Growing demand from women, encouraged by their admission to the examinations of the Intermediate Board and of the Royal University, led to the organisation of a women's campaign for university facilities equal to those made available to men. This would be the first organised public campaign in which Hayden and many like her were involved. The women availing of the late nineteenth-century opportunities for secondary and university education were few in number and generally middle class, not typical of the wider female population in Ireland. Nor were they representative even of middle-class women as a whole. Those who campaigned for access to the university were pioneers, like their predecessors of earlier campaigns such as Isabella Tod, Anna Haslam, Anne Jellicoe and Margaret Byers, radicals in their contemporary context. Their achievement encapsulated in the Irish Universities Act 1908 was slowly but surely to encourage more women to proceed to higher education.

NOTES
1   Hayden Diary, 3 June, 1 July 1888.
2   Hayden Diary, 7 October 1896.

3   Hayden Diary, 8 January, 15 January, 26 February 1897. Robert Clive (1725–1774) and Warren Hastings (1732–1818) by military campaigns and administrative organisation created the British Empire in India, to the glory of their country and the financial profit of the East India Company; both men also acquired considerable personal wealth during their careers in India. *Oxford Dictionary of National Biography*, Vols 12, 25.

4   Hayden Diary, 3 June 1897.

5   Lilian Green, *Off the Beaten Track in South India: The Journal of Lilian Green, 1897* (Typed and published by Tealo Phillips, Cardiff, 1988), NLI. Ms. Accession no. 6314.

6   A.A. Kelly (ed.), *Wandering Women: Two Centuries of Travel Out of Ireland* (Dublin, 1995), pp 8–9.

7   *Ibid.*, p. 110.

8   Michelle Perrot, 'Stepping Out' in Genevieve Fraise and Michelle Perrot (eds), *A History of Women in the West, IV Emerging Feminism from Revolution to World War* (Harvard, 1993), pp 468–69.

9   Hayden Diary, 27 September 1883.

10   Hayden Diary, 22 August 1898.

11   Hayden Diary, August 1901.

12   Hayden Diary, 25 February 1896.

13   Hayden Diary, 12 May 1897.

14   Margaret Ward, *Hanna Sheehy Skeffington: A Life* (Cork, 1997), p. 27.

15   Elizabeth, Countess of Fingall, *Seventy Years Young* (Dublin, 2005), p. 230.

16   Hayden Diary, 17 May 1898.

17   Hayden Diary, 28 August 1897.

18   Hayden Diary, 6 and 8 August 1896.

19   See Maria Luddy, *Women and Philanthropy in Nineteenth Century Ireland* (Cambridge, 1995), pp 209–214.

20   Rosemary Cullen Owens, *A Social History of Women 1870–1970* (Dublin, 2005), p. 78.

21   Owens, *Ibid.*, pp 12–14.

22   Maria Luddy, 'Prostitution and Rescue Work in Nineteenth Century Ireland' in Maria Luddy and Cliona Murphy (eds), *Women Surviving: Studies in Irish Women's History in the 19th and 20th Centuries* (Dublin, 1989), pp 61–62; Luddy, *Women and Philanthropy*, pp 77–82.

23   Maria Luddy, *Women in Ireland, 1800–1918: A Documentary History* (Cork, 1995), p. 58.

24 Hayden Diary, 22 July 1882.

25 Carmel Quinlan, *Genteel Revolutionaries: Anna and Thomas Haslam and the Irish Women's Movement* (Cork, 2002), pp 75–77, 102–3.

26 Mary Cullen, 'Anna Maria Haslam' in Mary Cullen and Maria Luddy (eds), *Women, Power and Consciousness in 19th Century Ireland* (Dublin, 1995), pp 171–172.

27 Hayden Diary, November 1887.

28 Hayden Diary, 18 February, 1 and 3 March 1899.

29 Hayden Diary, 25 April 1884.

30 Hayden Diary, 4 June 1900.

31 Hayden Diary, 20 March 1892. Also Hayden Diary, 18 October 1885, 6 March 1892.

32 Mary E. Daly, *Dublin: The Deposed Capital: A Social and Economic History 1860–1914* (Cork, 1984), pp 295–301. *Alexandra College Magazine*, June 1914, p. 64; Maryann Gialanella Valiulis, 'Toward "The Moral and Material Improvement of the Working Classes": The Founding of the Alexandra College Guild Tenement Company, Dublin 1898', *Journal of Urban History*, Vol 23, No 3, March 1997, pp 295–315; Margaret Ó hÓgartaigh, *Kathleen Lynn: Irishwoman, Patriot, Doctor* (Dublin, 2006), pp 69–70.

33 Jacinta Prunty, 'Improving the Urban Environment: Public Health and Housing in Nineteenth Century Dublin' in Joseph Brady and Anngret Simms (eds), *Dublin Through Space and Time* (Dublin, 2001), pp 219–20.

34 Lady Aberdeen, *We Twa: Reminiscences of Lord and Lady Aberdeen* (London, 1925), Vol. II, p. 187.

35 Daly, *Dublin: The Deposed Capital*, p. 279.

36 Cullen Owens, *A Social History of Women in Ireland*, p. 61.

37 Luddy, *Women and Philanthropy*, pp 145–146.

38 *Alexandra College Magazine*, June 1912.

39 Hayden Diary, 18 March 1884.

40 Hayden Diary, 2 March 1888.

41 Hayden Diary, 16 March 1884.

42 Hayden Diary, 29 March 1892.

43 Hayden Diary, 22 October 1897, 2 July 1898.

44 Hayden Diary, 22 June 1902.

45 Hayden Diary, 22 May 1897.

46 See Leeann Lane, *Rosamond Jacob: Third Person Singular* (Dublin, 2010), p. 35.

47 Hayden Diary, 29? April 1888, (there are many torn pages at this point).
48 Hayden Diary, 10 February 1891.
49 Hayden Diary, 29 April 1891, 25 February 1901.
50 Carmel Quinlan, *op cit*, p. 35.
51 Quinlan, *ibid*, pp 15–16.
52 Ward, *op cit*, p. 125.
53 Subsequently published in *Journal of National Literary Society of Ireland*, Vol. 1, 1900.
54 Hayden Diary, 17? December 1898.
55 *The Sphere*, 29 September 1900.
56 Hayden Diary, 19 and 14 March 1899.
57 Hayden Diary, 21 April 1899.
58 Hayden Diary, 18 April and 25 April 1899. Hayden's letter to Donnelly is not in the Dublin Diocesan Archives, nor is there a letter to Walsh about the Fellowship; nor have any replies which Hayden received survived.
59 Hayden Diary, 21 April 1899.
60 Michael Tierney, 'A Weary Task' in Michael Tierney (ed.), *Struggle with Fortune* (Dublin, 1954), p. 11.
61 Hayden Diary, late January 1900.
62 William Delany SJ (1835–1924), a Jesuit priest and experienced educationalist, who became President of University College when the Catholic hierarchy entrusted its management to the Jesuits in 1883. He held the office until 1888 and again from 1897 to 1909 at the establishment of the new National University of Ireland with UCD as a constituent college. Delany re-invigorated the flagging college and would be one of many consulted during the negotiations leading to the university legislation of 1908, but he remained opposed to the co-education of women.
63 *Royal Commission on University Education in Ireland* [Robertson Commission] Third Report (Appendix) (1902), p. 360. See Chapter 4.
64 *Royal Commission* on *University Education in Ireland*, First Report, Appendix (1901), p. 213.
65 Hayden Diary, 2 October 1900.
66 Hayden Diary, 22 November 1899.
67 Hayden Diary, 26 January 1899.
68 Hayden Diary, 21 April 1900.
69 Hayden Diary, 26 and 28 November 1900.
70 Hayden Diary, 7 and 11 December 1900.

71 *Royal Commission on University Education in Ireland*, Third Report, Appendix (1902), p. 360.

72 *Royal Commission on University Education in* Ireland, First Report, Appendix (1901), pp 209–14.

73 Hayden Diary, 8 December 1900, 5 February 1901.

74 Hayden Diary, 18? January 1901.

75 Fathers of the Society of Jesus, *A Page of Irish History: Story of University College, Dublin 1883–1909* (Dublin and Cork, 1930), pp 214–5.

76 Hayden Diary, 22 November 1901.

77 Hayden Diary, 22 April 1902.

78 Hayden Diary, 18 June 1902.

79 Hayden Diary, 9 June 1901.

80 Mary Hayden, 'A Few Thoughts on Women in Universities and on University Women', *The National Student*, June 1935, p. 70.

81 Hayden Diary, 23 April 1897.

82 Hayden Diary, 12 November 1896.

83 Hayden Diary, 28 April, 15 and 29 November, 5 December 1897.

84 Hayden Diary, 12 and 21 January 1898.

85 For example, Hayden Diary, 21 April 1900.

86 Hayden Diary, 26 March 1898.

87 Hayden Diary, 4 April 1898.

88 Hayden Diary, 7 May 1898.

89 Hayden Diary, 17 May 1900.

90 Hayden Diary, 9, 10 September 1900.

91 Hayden Diary, 26 April 1903.

92 Hayden Diary, 4 July 1903.

93 Hayden Diary, June 1903.

94 Hayden Diary, 3 August 1903.

95 Hayden Diary, 30? April 1903.

96 Hayden Diary, 18 February 1901.

97 Hayden Diary, 25 December 1882, also 17 March 1884. Conan Kennedy (ed.), *The Diaries of Mary Hayden* (Killala, 2005), Volume V, p. 2149, footnote.

98 Hayden Diary, 17 May 1890.

99 For example, 22 May 1889, 11 January 1890.

100 Hayden Diary, 28, 29 May, 1 June 1889.

101 Carol Dyhouse, *Feminism and the Family in England 1880–1939* (Oxford, 1989), pp 147–49.

102 Dyhouse, *ibid*, p. 154.

103 Máire Ní Aodáin to Pearse (No date, probably 1907; see chapter 5), NLI P.H. Pearse papers, MS 21054 (4).

104 Hayden Diary, 24 January 1890.
105 Hayden Diary, 28 April 1887.
106 Margaret Ward, *Maud Gonne: Ireland's Joan of Arc* (London, 1990), p. 95.
107 Hayden Diary, 5 December 1901.
108 Hayden Diary, 7 September 1901.
109 Hayden Diary, 27 May 1903.
110 Agnes O'Farrelly, 'Mary Hayden', *Alexandra College Magazine*, December 1942.
111 I am grateful to Patricia Moorhead, a descendant of the Crean family, for this information about Percy Hurley. And see Conan Kennedy (ed.), *The Diaries of Mary Hayden* (Killala, 2005), Vol. V. pp 2267–68.
112 Hayden Diary, 1 September, 13 September 1887, 24 September 1888, 27 November, 24 December 1890.
113 Philippa Levine, *Feminist Lives in Victorian England: Private Roles and Public Commitment* (Oxford, 1990), p. 45.
114 Lucy Bland, *Banishing the Beast: English Feminism and Sexual Morality 1885–1914*, p. 144, cited in Quinlan, *Genteel Revolutionaries*, p. 154.
115 F.O.C. Meenan, *Cecilia Street: The Catholic University School of Medicine 1855–1931* (Dublin, 1987), p. 82
116 Hayden Diary, 13 August 1881.
117 Hayden Diary, 16 October 1883.
118 Hayden Diary, 25 June 1888.
119 Senia Pašeta, *Before the Revolution: Nationalism, Social Change and Ireland's Catholic Elite, 1879–1922* (Cork, 1995), p. 65.
120 Maria Luddy, 'Women and Politics in Nineteenth Century Ireland' in Maryann Valiulis and Mary O'Dowd (eds), *Women and Irish History* (Dublin, 1997), p. 107.
121 Quinlan, *Genteel Revolutionaries*, p. 136.

IV

MARY HAYDEN AND WOMEN'S ADMISSION TO THE UNIVERSITY
1902–1908

Better provision of university education for Irish Catholics had become a live issue by the beginning of the twentieth century, while women were also campaigning for equal university admission for women.[1] The establishment of a Royal Commission was an opportunity for women to make their case, and led to the formation of the first association of women graduates, of which Mary Hayden was a founding member.

Women and University Education
The desire for improved educational provision for women was being increasingly articulated in England and Ireland in the latter half of the nineteenth century. In England, higher education for women was slowly opening up, as some women attended lectures in scientific and cultural societies, and in colleges and institutes founded to train

them for a limited range of employment.[2] There were similar developments in Ireland, notably the work of Margaret Byers, Anne Jellicoe and Isabella Tod, from 1860 onwards, in establishing schools to educate and train women.[3] The degrees of the Royal University of Ireland were open to women from the establishment of the University by charter in 1880. The Royal College of Science from its foundation in 1866 had admitted women to its lectures. Women were permitted to take the examinations of the Royal College of Surgeons in Ireland from 1885, and they had access to the licentiate of the Royal College of Physicians in Ireland from 1876.[4]

Girton College, Cambridge was founded in 1869 by Emily Davies and Barbara Bodichon to provide for women a university education the same as that available to Cambridge men. From 1881 women were permitted to sit for degree examinations at Cambridge University but were not awarded degrees there until 1948. Other universities in England and Scotland had admitted women to degrees before the end of the nineteenth century, and Oxford did so at the end of the 1914–18 war. But women in the university were still not on equal terms with men or permitted to study all subjects.[5]

In Ireland though, the performance of women students at the Royal University examinations would testify to the high standard of teaching in the women's colleges.[6] Their exclusion from the Jesuit managed University College where half of the fellows of the Royal University, its examiners, were teaching[7] was for the women a concern and a grievance. In Hayden's words. 'The house on Stephen's Green was guarded as a male preserve'.[8] Hayden described how the first women graduates had to take the same examinations as the men without the benefit of lectures by the fellows.[9] A petition in 1888, signed by thirteen Catholic lady graduates headed by Mary T. Hayden MA,[10] for permission to attend the fellows' lectures was refused by the President, Fr William Delany, and subsequently rejected by the Royal University Senate on the ground of its inability to interfere with the institution where the fellows lectured.[11]

There had been gradual piecemeal admission of women to classes in the Queen's Colleges at Belfast, Cork and Galway in the mid 1880s, but the numbers were small and the attendance of Catholics was discouraged by their church.[12] The degrees of the Royal University were taken also by Protestant women who were not admitted to attendance at Trinity College or to the degrees of Dublin University. Trinity College had however agreed, on a request from Alexandra, to provide for women two examinations,[13] which, as noted, were taken by Hayden. Special examinations for women were also started by Queen's University, and in England girls had now been admitted to the Oxford and Cambridge Local Examinations.[14] Trinity professors were also employed by Alexandra College to lecture to its women students,[15] but efforts by CAISM to have women admitted to lectures and degrees in Trinity College were at the time unsuccessful.[16] However in 1895 Hayden recorded going to Trinity College to hear Professor Dowden who 'has opened his lectures to ladies this term'.[17] In University College, Delany, under pressure, conceded admission to some lectures by fellows to second and third year women honours students who continued to attend classes in the women's colleges. Women were listed as students for the first time in the University College register of 1901, the nineteen names including Agnes O'Farrelly and Johanna (Hanna) Sheehy,[18] and by the closing years of the Jesuit management there had been further concessions about women's attendance at classes.[19]

Conscious that the Royal University was regarded as no more than a temporary solution of the Irish university question[20] (even the Senate of the University was to call in

February 1901 for a commission to report on the greater extension and more efficient conduct of university education in Ireland)[21] women entered the debate to make the case for their inclusion on equal terms in whatever new provision the government might decide upon for university education in Ireland. It was pointed out that while the discussion of the Irish university question centred on Roman Catholic Irish men, there was 'another class with even greater disabilities', that of 'Irish women, Catholic and Protestant'. A petition to the government in 1896 from the women's colleges, Catholic and Protestant, and two associations of schoolmistresses, supported also by public figures, churchmen and fellows of the two Universities, requested endowment of university teaching for women and their admission to university prizes and degrees.[22] Hayden, with Katherine Murphy, the other woman junior fellow, went out, at the request of Mother Patrick Shiel of St Mary's Dominican College, to canvas signatures for the petition; she found it 'a hateful job though the people ... we went to [were] all nice and pleasant' except one who was deaf and another who was 'stuck-up'.[23] Shiel had sought support for the petition from the CAISM (of which convent schools were not members) while the CAISM was at the same time engaged in its own efforts to persuade the Board of Trinity College to admit women.[24] Hayden herself was a member of the CAISM, as might be expected from her association with Alexandra.

The Robertson and Fry Commissions

The appointment in 1901 of a Royal Commission on University Education in Ireland (Robertson) was the impetus which led to the formation of the Irish Association of Women Graduates and Candidate Graduates for the purpose of presenting a coherent case to the Commission. Hayden's diary notes 'great talk of University Commission' and meetings at Alice Oldham's house to decide upon evidence to be presented to the Commission and to prepare a survey to be sent to women graduates of the Royal University.[25] Oldham, Hayden, Agnes O'Farrelly and Hanna Sheehy worked on the circular sent to 400 women graduates, to which about 300 replies were received.[26] The new Association was then established at a meeting in the Gresham Hotel on 14 March 1902.[27] Oldham, the teacher in Alexandra who had been one of the first nine women RUI graduates in 1884, and who was the energetic secretary of the CAISM, became President of the new Association and Mary Hayden, a graduate of the following year, its Vice-President.

The results of the survey of women graduates, presented to the Robertson Commission, showed that of 300 replies received, large majorities favoured common colleges, common teaching, and equal advantages in university education for men and women. Also requested was a fixed test for the award of fellowships.[28] A majority also opted for retention of the Royal University, reconstituted as a teaching university with affiliated colleges, at least one for Catholics and another for Protestants. Endowment of the existing women's colleges as residential halls was also suggested.

Oral evidence to the Robertson Commission on behalf of the IAWGCG, given by Annie M'Elderry MA, Principal of Rutland School Dublin, and Agnes O'Farrelly MA, Lecturer in Irish in Alexandra and Loreto Colleges, stressed that attendance at recognised lectures should be compulsory, that women should not be 'shut up in women's colleges' and that convocation, senate, fellowships and appointments should be open to women.[29] As an able advocate and the most senior of the Catholic women graduates who could represent the College, Hayden appeared on behalf of St Mary's where she had taught since its establishment. The other college for Catholic women, Loreto, was represented before the

Commission by James Macken, a professor at St Patrick's teacher training college for men. Hayden presented a list of the distinctions gained by students of St Mary's, and on 11 June 1902 attended to give her persuasive oral evidence. She is described in the Report as 'MA Ex-Junior Fellow of the Royal University of Ireland', and in response to questions she commenced by recounting her own qualifications and her unsuccessful attempts to gain a senior fellowship, including her disagreement with Delany's statements that women were ineligible for these appointments. In her diary she noted that 'I let myself go rather regarding Dr Delany, which was both wrong and foolish. In the other part I got on better. It lasted only about 35 minutes'.[30] During her evidence Hayden recounted that she and another woman junior fellow had petitioned the Standing Committee of the University Senate about the senior fellowships and had been referred to the authorities of University College where the President (Delany) told them he could not recommend the appointment of a woman. He had also asked if renewal, by a special arrangement, of the salaries of women junior fellows would satisfy them, which she had rejected.[31] The issue of women's university education had become a matter of principle for Hayden, in which compromise was not the solution; equality with men in university opportunity was her requirement.

Hayden went on to speak to the Commission of the importance of higher education for women whether as wives and mothers, or supporting themselves by employment, an opinion she was to voice frequently throughout the rest of her career. She argued for equal access for women to the university facilities provided for men, and opposed any idea of separate colleges for women. Describing the difficult financial circumstances for St Mary's, Hayden argued for the endowment of the women's colleges as halls of residence and tutorial work.

In the early years of the women's colleges at Cambridge and Oxford, women were not permitted to attend the lectures for men students, and 'sympathetic dons had to give the same lecture' again to the women.[32] But included in the documentation submitted by the IAWGCG was a letter obtained from W.B. Harris, Commissioner of Education in the United States, as evidence of the favourable experience of co-education in schools and higher institutions in that country.[33] In America there were well established colleges for women, such as Vassar, Wellesley, and Bryn Mawr, but by 1900 the majority of women students were in co-educational institutions, though still excluded from Ivy League institutions like Yale and Harvard.[34]

Separate or common teaching was the only issue on which there were divided opinions among the advocates of the women's case. The women's colleges, established to satisfy a need for university level teaching for women, had never been formally recognised within the RUI or represented on its Senate, nor had a fellow of the RU ever been appointed to teach in a women's college.[35] Not surprisingly many of the colleges, including Alexandra, Loreto and Victoria Belfast, hoped for formal recognition and endowment within the university, but the IAWGCG was against this suggestion, and it is notable that Hayden, although appearing for St Mary's College, nevertheless unequivocally presented the Association's stance, with the support of Mother Patrick Shiel.[36] When preparing for her appearance before the Commission, Hayden had consulted Shiel.[37] Also notable is that Alice Oldham, president of the women graduates, appearing however on behalf of CAISM, while unequivocally asking for the admission of women to university lectures, favoured also the endowment of 'residential women's colleges, something like the colleges in Oxford and Cambridge',[38] but she did not favour the recognition as a university college of

Alexandra, where she herself was a teacher.[39] Hayden, it will be recalled, had been unenthusiastic about the women's colleges at Cambridge when visiting the university with her father in 1880.

The dilemma was that if there were to be common university colleges open to women, the women's colleges would not survive. Furthermore there were some, clergy and laity, who preferred separate education for women, whether for moral or educational reasons. The proponents of mixed colleges sought common teaching as a guarantee of equality for women in university education, and particularly feared that degrees awarded to students of women's colleges could be regarded as inferior.[40]

The arguments presented for equal university facilities for men and women proved convincing to the Commission, particularly the eight recommendations received from the IAWGCG which were in effect adopted by the Commission. Its Report noted that its recommendations 'are in general accord with the views of those who are best acquainted with the requirements of Ireland in regard to the higher education of women' and went on to recommend that lectures, examinations, colleges, degrees and other privileges of the university 'should be open without distinction of sex'.[41]

Delany informed the Commission of the concessions admitting honours women students to certain lectures in University College by re-arranging accommodation and timetables.[42] Later explanation by the Jesuits of the reluctance to admit women as equal members of the College concentrated on inadequacies of accommodation and finance, and opined 'that a good case could be made out for the authorities of the College'.[43] But Delany was fundamentally opposed to co-education. An anonymous correspondent in *The Leader* in 1908 accused him of wanting 'to secure to the regular [i.e. male] students at University College a monopoly of [the fellows'] lectures'.[44]

In his evidence to the Commission Delany stated that he was 'a strong advocate for the higher education of women', but in answer to further questions he gave his view that University College should be open to women as it was 'at the present moment', and that there should be provision for the women's colleges. Delany appeared again on 11 June, the date of Hayden's evidence, to give supplementary evidence on the finances and organisation of University College. He took the opportunity to refer to the appointments 'specially criticised' to senior fellowships when Hayden had been the unsuccessful applicant. Defending the appointments and qualifications of Fr George O'Neill and Mr John Bacon, Delany added that the Standing Committee (of the University Senate) 'also knew that I as President did not feel myself authorised to introduce so strange a novelty in a Catholic University College' as a lady lecturing to men, 'whereas Trinity College has persistently excluded ladies altogether'.[45] Reluctance to appoint women to university posts was common. A professor in London in 1888 considered it 'undesirable that any teaching in University College should be conducted by a woman'. At the University of Edinburgh in 1894 a woman enquiring about lectureships was informed that 'the appointment of women to these posts' was not contemplated.[46] And even in 1914, Dr Alice Barry was rejected for the fellowship of the Royal College of Physicians in Ireland on grounds of sex.[47]

During the evidence to the Commission from the IAWGCG, Most Reverend Dr John Healy (Catholic bishop of Clonfert) stated his opposition to the suggestion that ladies might lecture 'where most of the students are young gentlemen', to which Annie M'Elderry responded 'if they have proved themselves fully qualified, why not'. Another Commissioner, Ambrose Birmingham, Professor of Anatomy and Registrar of the Catholic University School of Medicine in Cecilia Street, to which women students had been admitted since 1896, said there were no more satisfactory pupils than the lady students and 'we have found that their admission to the School was productive of nothing but good to the institution'.[48] The Medical School facilitated the admission of women students, of whom there were fifteen in 1900–01.[49]

Having marshalled its case for the Royal Commission, the IAWGCG kept up its pressure, presenting a memorial to Trinity College in December 1902 urging the claims of women, the favourable result of which is noted both in the minute book and in Hayden's diary.[50] After some years of resistance and debate, Trinity finally admitted women to its degree courses, though not to fellowships or foundation scholarships, in January 1904.[51] There was increasing sympathy in Trinity for the women's demand; and in the context of the deliberations of the Robertson Commission this limited concession might avoid any more drastic possibility such as a Catholic college within the University of Dublin, or recognition within the University of a women's college such as Alexandra.[52] There was also the realisation that Protestant women would otherwise attend whatever new national university might be established to replace the Royal University.[53] The admission of women to Trinity was a significant advance, particularly for Protestant women like Alice Oldham. Hayden, if it had been an option in her youth, might well have attended Trinity in spite of clerical disapproval; her father had allowed her brother to register there.

Also in 1904 a memorial presented by the IAWGCG to University College received a reply which was considered 'anything but satisfactory'[54] which the committee decided to forward to the Chief Secretary. The advisability of publishing this correspondence was later considered by the IAWGCG committee and decided against as 'injudicious',[55] an example of caution in the pursuit of the campaign. Though at the time radical in their claim for equality in university education, the women of the Association tended towards prudence in what was for most of them a quite new experience, organised agitation on behalf of women.

Women engaged also in the demand for better provision of university education for middle-class Catholic men, a demand advocated by the Irish Parliamentary Party as a preliminary to its hoped for achievement of Home Rule. Legislation did not follow immediately upon the Robertson Commission Report, its recommendations as a whole for the conversion of the Royal University into a federal teaching university meeting a mixed reception.[56] Impatience with the delay led to the foundation in 1904 of the Catholic Graduates and Undergraduates Association which called for immediate settlement of the university question, and urged all Catholic graduates to join. Included among its graduate members were the names of Arthur Clery, Felix Hackett, Patrick Pearse, John Marcus O'Sullivan, Tom Kettle, Mary Hayden, Agnes O'Farrelly, Mary Bowler (later Macken) and several other women graduates. Clery, Hackett, O'Sullivan and Kettle had all been students at the Jesuit University College, St Stephen's Green, and all were later, like Hayden and Macken, appointed to professorships in the new UCD. (Kettle who married Mary Sheehy, sister of Hanna, was elected MP in 1906; he was killed at the Somme in September 1916. O'Sullivan became a member of Dáil Éireann in 1923 and was Minister for Education in the Cumann na nGaedheal government 1926–32. Pearse, like the others a graduate of the Royal University, was teaching a weekly class in Irish at University College and studying for admission to the Bar at the King's Inns).

The inclusion of women in an eventual settlement seems to have been taken for granted, since they had been included in the earlier Royal University legislation. The issue of common or separate teaching received no special mention in the Catholic Graduates and Undergraduates Association. Mary Hayden was listed as Vice-Chairman in the report of the first committee meeting, held on 28 January 1904, and she, with Clery, Kettle and the two honorary secretaries comprised the sub-committee appointed to draw up a statement on the university question for general distribution.[57] The Association expressed its support for the Irish parliamentary representatives, lobbying many of them on the university question.[58] Addressing a meeting of this Association in December 1904, the Irish Party MP John Dillon, calling for a national university for Ireland 'which will represent the ideals of our people', urged that it be extremely democratic.[59] While participating in the demand for a university acceptable to nationalists and to Catholics, women also pursued their own particular concern for equality within the new university. The strength of the women's case lay in the IAWGCG whose members, irrespective of their religious affiliations, sought to achieve for women access to whatever university provision might be accorded to men. Dillon, along with most members of the Irish Party, would later be opposed to women's suffrage, partly though not solely for fear of endangering the passage of a home rule measure. On the university issue it was important for the Irish Party to secure a solution acceptable to nationalists, educationalists and the Catholic hierarchy. If the momentum of the claim in both Ireland and England for higher education for women, combined with the willingness of the Liberal government in England, was to ensure the inclusion of women in the legislation, the Irish MPs would not object. By 1900, women constituted about 15 per cent of students in British universities and, for instance, the charter of the University of Wales (1893), on which the charter of the NUI would eventually be based, stated that women should be treated as full members of the University.[60]

The establishment by the Catholic bishops in 1905 of scholarships for men and women students at University College, Loreto and St Mary's Colleges was welcomed by the IAWGCG committee, on the proposal of Oldham seconded by Hayden. Not to be deflected from their ultimate goal, the resolution added the hope that the teaching of the fellows of the RUI at University College would be 'open alike to the women scholars and to the men, thus ensuring them the full benefits of a University education'. This request was also forwarded to University College and acknowledged by Delany who agreed to bring it to his scholarship committee.[61]

Another Royal Commission was established in 1906, this time on Trinity College Dublin and the University of Dublin, to advise how its 'usefulness to the country' might be increased. One possibility was the establishment of a new Catholic college within the University.[62] The IAWGCG promptly decided to send to this, the Fry Commission (its chairman being Sir Edward Fry), a statement of the success of women since their admission to Dublin University, with a request that 'no reactionary measures' be taken to affect women's position there.[63] The Association was represented at the Fry Commission by Agnes O'Farrelly and Ethel Hanan BA, one of TCD's earliest women graduates. Some of the material submitted by the Association relating to its dealings with University College was considered by the Commission to be 'outside the scope of' its inquiry,[64] and much of O'Farrelly's oral evidence expounding on university education for all women students in Ireland was similarly regarded as not relevant. Hanan was more to the point, saying that the arrangements for women in Trinity since 1904 were satisfactory and should not be altered. The addition of a residential hostel and playing fields would be welcome. She was opposed to extern teaching or separate education for women students on grounds of quality, standing and the social 'cleavage' which it would involve. Here she and the IAWGCG differed from the position of Henrietta White, Alexandra Principal, who in a written submission and oral evidence strongly urged the case of Alexandra for recognition by Dublin University. Margaret Byers made a similar case for Victoria College, Belfast. But the concern of O'Farrelly and Hanan was that if a new college were to be established within the University of Dublin it should be open on equal terms to women and men.[65]

The Fry Commission, unlike its Robertson predecessor, recommended in favour of separate colleges for women[66] but the IAWGCG adhered to its position as presented to both Robertson and Fry. A proposal to ascertain the support for women's colleges was rejected, as 'entirely opposed to the principles upon which this Association is founded'.[67] But the fact of the proposal suggests that there were some in the Association who thought otherwise.

In early 1908 a paper on 'Women in Universities' by Norah Meade, a young Royal University Scholar, favoured separate colleges for women. A reply written by Hayden and Hanna Sheehy Skeffington to which there was a rejoinder by Meade and a further reply by Hayden and Sheehy Skeffington, amounted to a controversy extending over four issues of the *Irish Educational Review*.[68] Meade advocated women's colleges where women fellows would teach, combined with general lectures in the university for all students, women and men. Only a separate women's college would produce a highly cultured, refined and self-reliant woman, she believed, and she disliked competition between the sexes.

In their reply, Hayden and Sheehy Skeffington argued strongly against any suggestion of separate colleges or separate teaching for women. They referred to the survey carried out in 1902 in which a majority of the respondents favoured mixed colleges. It was feared that separate colleges would provide an inferior level of teaching as the fellows would be unlikely to repeat their lectures. Evidence given by the IAWGCG to the Robertson Commission had opposed women's colleges. The authors wished to see women appointed to fellowships gained in open competition, who would then lecture to mixed classes. Also they favoured the social intercourse of men and women working and chatting together. Noting that St Mary's, the college where Meade was a student, was disinterested enough to support what it considered 'most beneficial to the education of women in general', the authors implicitly acknowledged the courageous impartiality of Mother Patrick Shiel, with whose approval Hayden, when representing St Mary's before the Robertson Commission, had rejected separate colleges for women.[69] The subject Domestic Economy, suggested by Meade, was dismissed as quite out of place in a university. (The inclusion of domestic science was a subject of some debate, which had been suggested by others, such as Lady Aberdeen, wife of the Viceroy and campaigner on women's health, Lillian M. Faithful, the Principal of Cheltenham Ladies College, and Margaret Byers of Victoria College).[70] But for Hayden and Sheehy Skeffington, the model was the curriculum provided for men, and common, shared facilities.

Irish Universities Act
With university legislation clearly in the offing, the Association decided at the end of the year to put the case directly to the Chief Secretary, Augustine Birrell,[71] having previously written to the Permanent Under-Secretary of State for Ireland, Sir Antony MacDonnell, to seek support for their requests for equal treatment.[72]

The pressure was irresistible, particularly in view of the gradual concessions to women students over the previous thirty years, and it was not surprising that when it came the Irish Universities Act (1908) and accompanying university and college charters provided equality for women in the university, its offices and authorities.[73] The publication of the university bill was welcomed by the IAWGCG in a resolution passed unanimously by the committee on 11 May 1908 in which they expressed satisfaction that the claims of women to full membership of the university had been recognised, and noted the representation accorded to women on the governing bodies for Dublin and Belfast, which they asked should be extended also to Cork and Galway.

Critics of the bill for its non-denominational character included Fr Peter Finlay who saw it dealing a heavy blow to the higher education of women in its failure to accord university status to the women's colleges. He objected to co-education, on behalf both of 'many Catholic parents' and of nuns who 'could not, under any circumstances' participate. He made no reference to the women who held a different view, or to their successful campaign.[74] Delany, writing to Walsh, gave his view that co-education tended 'to diminish refinement amongst women students and to lessen markedly in the men students the love of courtesy and consideration for women'.[75] The issue of the co-education of women and men aroused more concern than did the admission of women to university education, which by this date had become an acceptable middle-class expectation. An article entitled 'Co-education in the National University' which expressed opposition to the co-education of girls whose parents did not wish it, was typical of this reaction.[76] And indeed as far back as 1897, Alice Oldham had written of the 'widespread objection in this country ... to men and women studying together at college lectures'.[77] The question would continue to be raised until finally disposed of in 1912.

The final solution to the university education issue was the work of the new Chief Secretary, Augustine Birrell appointed in 1907, who in consultation with Archbishop

William Walsh, William Delany, and the leaders of the Irish Parliamentary Party produced an arrangement which was broadly acceptable.[78] The Irish Universities Act of 1908 dissolved the Royal University of Ireland and established two new universities, the National University of Ireland with three constituent colleges (to provide teaching) at Dublin, Cork and Galway, and Queen's University Belfast, all open on equal terms to women as well as men. The federal structure of the NUI with constituent colleges in different cities was modelled on the University of Wales with its colleges at Cardiff, Bangor and Aberystwyth. That women were included on equal terms in the legislation, the primary purpose of which was to satisfy the nationalist expectation of acceptable university provision for men, particularly Catholic men, was an achievement by women due almost entirely to their own sustained efforts. The ethos of 'self-help' in contemporary initiatives such as the Gaelic League and the Irish Agricultural Organisation Society may be seen also in the origin and achievement of the IAWGCG,[79] which has been described as fulfilling 'the most radical demand made by the Irish movement for women's higher education',[80] but this did not become clear for some years as the issue of women's colleges lingered on, and the IAWGCG remained apprehensive about the possibility of recognition for separate women's colleges within the university. Mary Hayden and Agnes O'Farrelly were nominated in the UCD charter as members of its Governing Body. Hayden was similarly appointed to the NUI Senate. These appointments may have been token gestures, but they would have been acceptable to the Irish Parliamentary Party and to the Gaelic element within nationalism, as well as being a reflection of the attitude towards women of contemporary English liberalism. Trinity College was not included in the 1908 Act, and the Fry Commission on that university did not lead to legislative change in its structure.

University teaching and degrees were now available to women in Ireland, who by 1925 would constitute 30% of all Irish university students, comparing well with other western European countries.[81] In UCD's first session 1909–10, of the total 530 students, 42 were women; and two years later, women had increased to 137 in a total student number of 765.[82] Custom can prove more difficult to change than regulations; the Literary and Historical Society UCD delayed acceptance of women as members until December 1910, and the matter remained a contentious issue until settled in a revision of the rules of the Society in 1915, which however was long before their admission to the premier debating societies in Oxford, Cambridge and TCD.[83]

Hayden and Hanna Sheehy Skeffington were active participants in the growing demands for women's suffrage – a campaign in which surprisingly the IAWGCG appears to have taken no part. The suffrage agitation was more aggressive, more publicly visible than had been the more modest campaign for university access which consisted mainly of resolutions, petitions, published articles, repeated applications to University College, the Royal University, and Trinity College, submissions to two Royal Commissions, and letters to government figures. Noisy public meetings were not part of the effort. Moreover, the IAWGCG preferred to avoid directly political involvement on the issue,[84] in contrast to the Catholic Graduates and Undergraduates Association which had expressed support for the Irish Parliamentary Party and lobbied individual Irish MPs.[85] At least some in the IAWGCG were satisfied that the university issue was resolved and even considered dissolving the association. Hayden who became its President in 1913 saw an important future for the organisation in the furtherance of educational and employment opportunities for women; she led it and its immediate successor the National University Women Graduates' Association for almost three decades.

More immediately, on the suffrage issue Hayden, as well as writing, would speak and preside at public meetings to advocate the parliamentary franchise for women as a matter of equity on the route to full citizenship. Hanna Sheehy Skeffington's willingness to engage in militant action, her experiences of imprisonment, the murder of her husband Frank in 1916 on the orders of a deranged British officer, and her unwavering republican convictions, all contributed to a public image of an easily recognised, independent-minded woman. She was very different in political terms from Hayden who was non-militant and non-republican, but the two were to remain friends throughout their lives and, as convinced feminists, would work in association on successive issues of women's rights. So far, Hayden, like many of her contemporaries, had expressed her feminism in efforts to catch up with men. The concept of 'gender difference and the complementary talents which women would essentially bring to public life',[86] was a perspective she would develop during the suffrage campaign and maintain to the end of her life. Hayden was also now about to become a senior member of the new university, an achievement which would enhance both her academic reputation and her status in the community at large, and on a personal level would strengthen her self-confidence.

NOTES

1   See Judith Harford, *The Opening of University Education to Women in Ireland* (Dublin, 2008); Also Joyce Padbury, 'Mary Hayden and Women's Admission to the University: The Establishment of the National University of Ireland in 1908', *Dublin Historical Record*, Vol LXI, No 1, Spring 2008, pp 78–86.

2   Deirdre Raftery, *Women and Learning in English Writing 1600– 1900* (Dublin, 1997), p. 216.

3   Mary Cullen, 'Women, Emancipation and Politics 1860–1984' in J.R. Hill (ed.), *A New History of Ireland,* Vol. VII (Oxford, 2003), p. 836.

4   Susan M. Parkes and Judith Harford, 'Women and Higher Education in Ireland' in Deirdre Raftery and Susan M. Parkes (eds), *Female Education in Ireland 1760–1900: Minerva or Madonna* (Dublin, 2007), pp 116–17.

5   June Purvis, *A History of Women's Education in England* (Milton Keynes, 1991), pp 113–116.

6   Eibhlin Breathnach, 'Charting New Waters, Women's Experience in Higher Education, 1879–1908' in Mary Cullen (ed.), *Girls Don't Do Honours: Irish Women in Education in the 19th and 20th Centuries* (Dublin, 1987), p. 69.

7   Donal McCartney, *UCD. A National Idea: The History of University College Dublin* (Dublin, 1999), p. 30.

8   Mary Hayden, 'A Few Thoughts on Women in Universities and on University Women', *The National Student,* June 1935, p. 70.

9   (Mary Hayden), 'Three Notable Irishwomen', NLI, Hayden papers, Ms 24,007 Box 14.

10   Mary Macken, 'Women in the University and the College' in Michael Tierney (ed.), *Struggle with Fortune* (Dublin, 1954), p. 143.

11   Fathers of the Society of Jesus, *A Page of Irish History: The Story of University College Dublin 1883–1909* (Dublin and Cork, 1930), p. 455.

12   John A. Murphy, *The College: A History of Queen's/University College Cork 1845–1995* (Cork 1995), pp 128–130; See also Margaret Ó hÓgartaigh, *Quiet Revolutionaries: Irish Women in Education, Medicine and Sport, 1861–1964* (Dublin, 2011), Ch. 4.

13   Luce, *Trinity College Dublin,* pp 117–118.

14   Susan M. Parkes, 'Intermediate Education for Girls' in Raftery and Parkes (eds), *Female Education in Ireland,* pp 74–75.

15   Anne V. O'Connor, 'The Revolution in Girls' Secondary Education in Ireland, 1860–1910' in Cullen, *op cit,* p. 33.

16   Breathnach, 'Charting New Waters', pp 62–63.

17   Hayden Diary, 8 November 1895.

18   McCartney, *op cit,* p. 73.

19   *Ibid.,* p. 77.

20   Breathnach, 'Charting New Waters', p. 69.

21   McCartney, *op cit,* p. 25.

22   Alice Oldham, 'Women and the Irish University Question', *New Ireland Review,* VI (January, 1897), pp 257–63.

23 Hayden Diary, 20 February 1896.
24 Lucinda Thompson, 'The Campaign for Admission 1870–1904' in Susan M. Parkes (ed.), *A Danger to the Men: A History of Women in Trinity College Dublin 1904–2004* (Dublin, 2004), p. 43.
25 Hayden Diary, 20 November, 30 November, 5 December 1901.
26 Deirdre Raftery, 'The Higher Education of Women in Ireland 1860–1904' in Parkes (ed.), *A Danger to the Men*, p. 17.
27 Minute Book, March 1902, NUWGA 2/1, UCD Archives.
28 *Royal Commission on University Education in Ireland. Third Report* (Appendix) (1902), pp 566–68.
29 *Ibid.*, Third Report (Appendix) (1902), pp 318–22.
30 Hayden Diary, 11 June 1902.
31 *Royal Commission,* Third Report, *op cit*, pp 357–59.
32 Martha Vicinus, *Independent Women: Work and Community for Single Women 1850–1920* (Chicago, 1988), pp 126–27.
33 *Royal Commission,* Third Report, *op cit*, p. 565.
34 Barbara Miller Solomon, *In the Company of Educated Women: A History of Women and Higher Education in America* (Yale, 1985), pp 47–58.
35 Breathnach, 'Charting New Waters', p. 69.
36 Margaret Mac Curtain, 'St Mary's University College', *University Review,* III, no. 4 (1963), pp 41–47.
37 Hayden Diary, 8 June 1902.
38 *Royal Commission on University Education in Ireland,* First Report (Appendix) (1901), p. 218.
39 Lucinda Thompson, 'The Campaign for Admission, 1870–1904' in Parkes (ed.), *A Danger to the Men*, p. 45.
40 Breathnach, 'Charting New Waters', p. 71.
41 *Royal Commission on University Education in Ireland,* Final Report (1903), pp 49–50.
42 Fathers of the Society of Jesus, *A Page of Irish History: Story of University College Dublin 1883–1909* (Dublin and Cork, 1930), pp 457–458.
43 *Ibid*, pp 451–472.
44 *The Leader,* 16 July 1905, cited in Thomas J. Morrissey SJ, *Towards a National University: William Delany SJ 1835–1924* (Dublin, 1983), p. 281.
45 *Royal Commission,* Third Report, *op cit*, p. 360.
46 Cited in Carol Dyhouse, *No Distinction of Sex? Women in British Universities 1870–1939* (London, 1995), pp 134–140.
47 F.O.C. Meenan, *Cecilia Street: The Catholic University School of Medicine 1855–1931* (Dublin, 1987), p. 82.

48   *Royal Commission,* Third Report, *op cit,* p. 333.
49   Meenan, *Cecilia Street,* p. 82.
50   Minute Book, 16 January 1903, NUWGA 2/1, UCD Archives. Hayden Diary, 10 June 1903.
51   Luce, *Trinity College Dublin,* pp 117–118.
52   Susan M. Parkes (ed.), *A Danger to the Men,* Introduction, p. 3.
53   Lucinda Thompson, 'The Campaign for Admission 1870–1904' in Parkes (ed.), *A Danger to the Men,* p. 53.
54   Minute Book, 7 June 1904, NUWGA 2/1, UCD Archives.
55   *Ibid.,* 13 December 1904.
56   McCartney, *op cit,* p. 25.
57   J.B. Lyons, *The Enigma of Tom Kettle: Irish Patriot, Essayist, Poet, British Soldier 1880–1916* (Dublin, 1983), p. 116.
58   Catholic Graduates and Undergraduates Association, Minutes of Committee Meetings. UCD Library, Special Collections, Curran papers, CUR Ms 25.
59   McCartney, *op cit,* p. 36.
60   Dyhouse, *op cit,* pp 7, 12.
61   Minute Book, NUWGA, 16 June 1905, 29 September 1905. 2/1 UCD Archives.
62   McCartney, *op cit,* pp 25–26.
63   Minute Book, 2 July 1906, NUWGA 2/1 UCD Archives.
64   *Royal Commission on Trinity College, Dublin, and the University of Dublin,* Final Report (Appendix) (1907), p. 406.
65   *Ibid.,* Final Report (Appendix) (1907), p. 267.
66   McCartney, *op cit,* p. 76.
67   Minute Book, 9 March 1907, NUWGA, 2/1 UCD Archives.
68   See *Irish Educational Review,* January, February, March, April 1908.
69   See Mac Curtain, *op cit,* pp 33–47.
70   Margaret Ó hÓgartaigh, *Kathleen Lynn: Irishwoman, Patriot, Doctor* (Dublin, 2006), p. 66; L.M. Faithful, 'Home Science' in Dale Spender (ed.), *The Education Papers: Women's Quest for Equality in Britain 1850–1912* (London, 1987), p. 327; Harford, *op cit,* p. 138; Dyhouse, *op cit,* p. 139.
71   Minute Book, 31 December 1907, NUWGA, 2/1 UCD Archives.
72   *Ibid.,* 26 February 1907.
73   McCartney, *op cit,* pp 78–79.
74   Sacerdos [i.e. Peter Finlay] 'Mr Birrell's University Bill', *New Ireland Review,* 29 (June 1908), pp 210–220.
75   Delany to Walsh, 8 April 1908, cited in Morrissey, *op cit,* p. 283.

76 M. Sullivan, 'Co-education in the National University of Ireland', *Irish Educational Review*, vol. 3 (1909–10), p. 577.

77 Alice Oldham, 'Women and the Irish University Question', *New Ireland Review* VI (January 1897), p. 258.

78 McCartney, *op cit*, p. 26.

79 P.J. Mathews, *Revival* (Cork, 2003), p. 8; Breathnach, 'Charting New Waters', p. 77.

80 Breathnach, *ibid*, p. 76.

81 Margaret Ó hÓgartaigh, 'Women in University Education in Ireland: The Historical Background' in Anne Macdona (ed.), *From Newman to New Woman: UCD Women Remember* (Dublin, 2001), p. x.

82 *Report of the President, UCD 1975–76*, p. 110.

83 Eugene McCague, *Arthur Cox 1891–1965* (Dublin, 1994), p. 29; Cahir Davitt, 'The New College 1908–1916' in James Meenan (ed.), *Centenary History of the Literary and Historical Society of University College Dublin 1855–1955* (Dublin, 2005, 2nd ed.), p. 115.

84 Minute book, 31 December 1907, NUWGA 2/1, UCD Archives.

85 Catholic Graduates and Undergraduates Association, Minutes, 18 January, 26 May 1904. UCD Library, Special Collections, Curran papers, CUR Ms 25.

86 Maria Luddy, 'Women and Politics in Nineteenth Century Ireland' in Maryann Valiulis and Mary O'Dowd (eds), *Women and Irish History* (Dublin, 1997), p. 102.

V

MARY HAYDEN AND THE GAELIC LEAGUE
1900–1913

Mary Hayden became an enthusiastic member of the Gaelic League and a student of the Irish language. She met Patrick Pearse with whom a friendship developed which lasted for many years. She grew to believe in constitutional nationalism, and the need for a home rule arrangement in the best interests of the country. The prospect of university legislation aroused another demand, quite distinct from the issue of the admission of women, but one in which Hayden again was involved, namely the academic status to be accorded to the Irish language in any new university.

Douglas Hyde's famous lecture in 1892 to the National Literary Society, 'The Necessity for de-Anglicising the Irish Nation', proved to be an influential statement in the cultural climate of the Celtic renaissance.[1] The literary revival derived much encouragement from the Celtic scholarship of the preceding decades, which gave rise also to language societies such as the Society for the Preservation of the Irish Language. George Sigerson, a founder of the National Literary Society, had as early as 1860 published his first collection and translation of Irish poetry.[2] Hayden was en route to Greece in November 1892 when Hyde gave his lecture, but it must have become known to her and is likely to have aroused her interest in learning Irish. For instance, her feeling of shame in 1896 about 'our lost language, our poor little set always copying England' and 'our national dress despised even by the peasants' reflects the influence of Hyde's lecture.[3] Hyde's theme of the folly of neglecting what is Irish and his extolling of earlier Gaelic literature was the direction along which Hayden's thinking was developing. The distinguishing characteristics of Irish nationality, language and custom should be recognised and treasured, Hyde urged, and could be so embraced within a bilingual society which continued to use English in contexts where it was necessary. In 1894 Hayden heard Hyde's lecture on Irish literature, given to the National Literary Society; she 'liked his account of the bardic schools particularly'.[4]

Possibly the most significant event of the literary revival was the foundation of the Gaelic League in 1893 with the aim of reviving and encouraging the knowledge and use of the Irish language, spoken and written. Its founder, Eoin MacNeill, was a family friend of Mary and John Hayden. Both MacNeill and the League's President, Hyde, would later be university colleagues of Hayden's. The League was the first association to admit men and women on equal terms.[5] Hayden started to learn Irish towards the end of 1897.[6] She found it 'rather interesting' and persevered, a year later attending lessons at the Gaelic League with her friend Hester Sigerson.[7] For Hayden after her intensive studies of German, French, Latin and Greek, the prospect of tackling another language was apparently not too daunting. In Connemara in 1900 she began to understand 'the general drift of a conversation in Irish' though she could not participate,[8] and some months later at a meeting of the Gaelic League she was agreeably surprised by how much she understood of the speeches.[9] The National Literary Society granted some use of its premises to the new League, and itself initiated Irish language classes with, from 1901, Hayden and Agnes O'Farrelly included among the teachers.[10] Hayden was the seconder of a resolution, proposed by Sigerson and adopted by the Council of the National Literary Society in July 1900, calling for the teaching and examining of Irish as an ordinary school subject in Irish speaking districts.

Friendship with Patrick Pearse

Hayden first met Patrick Pearse when he was not yet twenty, preparing for the BA degree of the Royal University and for legal qualification at the King's Inns. They both moved in the stimulating environment of the literary revival. But it was through her Irish language studies that Hayden became friendly with Pearse, and it is in this context that he appears in her diaries.[11] In March 1902 they were both among a party of five men and nine women who went to Cashel, Connemara, to study the language. Hayden recorded that she 'got on with the others all right and induced Mr Pearse to talk – he turns out to be only 22, so I suppose he's just shy'.[12] Back in Dublin their friendship developed, Pearse often accompanying her home after Gaelic League meetings, and in May, at the Oireachtas competitions, Hayden 'had lunch in the refreshment room with Mr Pierse [sic] and got him to talk quite a lot'.[13]

In January 1903, they were both again in Connemara to practise Irish speaking. Over the preceding Christmas Hayden had been in continued touch with Pearse about arrangements for their accommodation. It was she who was making the booking, which was finally concluded with the hotel in Letterfrack. There were to be at least two other members of the party, who dropped out. The lack of other companions on this occasion caused comment, for instance from Hester Sigerson who did not think it proper, but Hayden observed that she was old enough to be Pearse's mother had she married very young. They talked 'a lot on all sorts of subjects' and she found 'him most companionable, a really nice fellow'.[14] Hayden remained in the west some days longer than Pearse, but on her return to Dublin he met her 'at the train. It was really very good of him; he wheeled [her] laden bicycle right across town'. Other brief diary mentions show that she had got quite used to Pearse's company; and she noted 'such a boy he seemed, with his young fresh face! I might easily have been his mother'.[15] However her regard for him was not maternal, and in fact, as the friendship developed it had something of the character of a favourite nephew with a companionable and compatible aunt.

Hayden, Pearse, O'Farrelly and others often met to speak Irish, and for their Gaelic League activities sometimes met for tea at O'Farrelly's home. Hayden was co-opted to the Coiste Gnótha (executive committee) of the Gaelic League on 28 February 1902; thereafter elected and re-elected annually, her membership continued until 1913. Other members of the Coiste Gnótha were Pearse, O'Farrelly, and George A Moonan, who many years later would collaborate with Hayden on *A Short History of the Irish People*. In a contest in 1903 for the editorship of the League's newspaper *An Claidheamh Soluis*, Hayden supported Pearse's candidature which was successful.[16] Congratulating him, she looked 'forward to the *Claidheamh* flashing out in fine style within the next few weeks'.[17] Almost immediately controversy erupted about an anonymous article in the newspaper which criticised the bishops' Lenten Pastorals for lack of reference to the Irish language. Opinions differ as to editorial responsibility for the article in the issue which appeared just five days after Pearse's appointment, and which in any event he might have written.[18] Hayden was among the moderates in the League who were alarmed by the tone of the article. She considered it 'grossly imprudent', writing that many bishops and priests would be glad to ruin the Gaelic League, an organisation of which they were jealous, and she blamed Pearse.[19]

On another occasion, Hayden was, as she wrote to Pearse, 'rather sorrowful' about the *Claidheamh*. 'Your last article was a little bit over defiant in my humble opinion ... though I agree with every word of it'. And to soften her criticism in this instance, she wrote 'I here assume the character of the *candid friend* – and hope you won't be vexed'. She was probably referring to his article on the rejection of the Irish Council Bill, in which Pearse trenchantly defended his role as editor and his legitimate, if unpopular, attitude in support of the Bill.[20] Hayden's comment that 'we should be the better for trying ourselves a bit in shallow waters; we've had time to forget how to swim'[21] suggests that she, like Pearse, favoured acceptance of the Bill, which was a proposal for minor administrative devolution of eight departments of the Irish administration, and which Pearse considered acceptable for its inclusion of education among the departments to be transferred to Irish control. However the Bill was widely condemned in Ireland as an inadequate substitute for Home Rule, and was withdrawn. Hayden tells us, many years later, that she had a long argument with Pearse about the Irish Council Bill of 1907, which, she noted, he thought 'ought to have been accepted',[22] and so, it seems, did she.[23] It would confirm her moderate attitude to piecemeal concession of self-government measures.

A genuine friendship developed between Hayden and Pearse. Pearse's sister, Mary Brigid, later wrote that Hayden 'was a great friend of my brother'[24] and Ruth Dudley Edwards has described her as 'Pearse's closest woman friend'.[25] He was a sensitive friend, whose kindness when they first met was appreciated, as evidenced by the diary entries. There are some letters from Hayden to Pearse,[26] written from Manchester where she had gone to study Old Irish with Dr John Strachan, one of the founders of the School of Irish Learning,[27] and which cover a variety of subjects. The letters are in part quite personal and are in reply to his letters in which he possibly expressed concern for her wellbeing. He had apologised for delay in writing, and sent her birthday wishes, to which she replied 'Thanks very much for your wishes of *returns*, but I don't feel as if I wanted many of them'. A short letter written by Hayden from France, also undated and in reply to one from Pearse, includes the words 'I can't say that I feel in any better spirits', again suggesting that Pearse had been solicitous on her account. And for him, it was encouraging to have the endorsement of this respected member of the Dublin cultural scene.

Pearse's side of this correspondence has not survived, and we can only judge its content by the replies. Pearse wrote to her both about practical matters, and more personally on his ideas for his own future. It was the latter which provoked her advice to him to marry and have a family. She wrote:

> No, I don't want you to have such a future as you plan for yourself ... There is a part of human nature that asks for human relationships and human sympathies ... [She hoped to see him] settled as a paterfamilias with children'.

And she added '*Tá tú óg fós*[28] [you are still young]. In another letter, she advised him to be 'often in the company of young people'. And she felt it necessary to modify his idealised view of women and to defend the character of men. 'I've got to stand up for men to you; you are so hard on them – If there were none, where would you be?' Hayden's observations on male and female characteristics, including her thought:

that the finest type of men have much of the woman about them as the finest type of women much of the man – which only means I suppose that they unite the best qualities of both sexes

are a telling rejection of gender stereotyping.[29]

Hayden's letters to Pearse became quite chatty. The initial 'Dear Mr Pearse' became '*A chara*' which clearly was more friendly; and she signed off as '*Mise do fíor chara*, [your true friend] Máire Ní Aodáin' (but never just Máire or Mary).[30] Hayden has told us that until about 1914 she saw a great deal of Pearse, 'especially in summer when we often went cycling together'.[31] And their participation in expeditions of Irish language enthusiasts continued. She wrote of 'the Drogheda trip' in June 1903,[32] and there are photographs of a group, including Hayden and Pearse, in Omeath in 1905.

This friendship commenced at an opportune time for Hayden who, though a strong, busy character, was experiencing a sense of loneliness, compounded by the death of Arthur Conan and the failure of her applications for a senior fellowship. As she wrote in one letter, 'I've had a lot of partings from places and still more and worse from people, and every new one recalls the others, more or less'.[33] The companionship of Pearse, the chats and cycle rides with him, and the shared Gaelic League activities were satisfying, enjoyable, supportive, and without emotional complication. In another letter to him, she wrote, 'I do want some thought-interchange and some gossip too'.[34] Hayden liked the shy young man, his intelligence, his idealism, and his propriety – as she recalled, 'from a doubtful story or jest he shrank as from a blow'.[35] The comment that Hayden and O'Farrelly had 'more pretensions to intellect than personal charm'[36] may well be true. Pearse's seriousness of purpose attracted her. Furthermore, the sense of exclusion, of which she and other women were conscious in many aspects of public life, was not part of her experience in the Gaelic League. Pearse treated her as an intellectual equal; she similarly regarded him as one with whom she could engage in debate. She found him 'not much interested in actual politics, though his love for Ireland was then, as always, intense and passionate'. In tune with her own lack of interest in party politics, she noted that Pearse paid little attention 'to questions of party intrigue' and preferred to 'think on broad lines ... an inevitable result of his idealism'.[37]

Pearse, like Hayden, became a member of the Catholic Graduates and Undergraduates Association which was exerting pressure on the Irish MPs on the university issue. Each participated, according to their particular concerns, in the general clamour for acceptable provision of university education for Irish Catholics – his that the university be truly national, and hers that women be admitted on equal terms with men.

The Language Revival

Unlike previous Irish language organisations, the Gaelic League was a popular, rather than an exclusively scholarly movement.[38] By 1903, there were 400 branches.[39] Mary Colum described how in the Dublin of her young days men and women of all classes and occupations took to the activities of the Gaelic League, the language lessons, the native games and dances, and in her words 'a good time was had by all'.[40] Another student, Mary Macken, recalled how she, with a few other university girls and boys, attended Gaelic League classes in 1899 where the teacher was 'an undergraduate named Pearse, enthusiastic, nervous and shy'.[41] There was fertile ground for the generation of national consciousness on a political level also. As early as 1908, Eoin MacNeill felt that the language movement was 'steadily building up the foundations of political freedom'.[42]

Hayden's feminist instincts, which were not party political, propelled her into public life at the time when pride in the national heritage was also exercising a strong attraction. Two of Hayden's lasting friendships, originating in the circles of women in higher education, were with Agnes O'Farrelly and Hanna Sheehy Skeffington, both feminists with a nationalist outlook.

O'Farrelly was the most forceful of the women in the League at the time,[43] but the prominence in the League of Hayden and O'Farrelly is acknowledged by Sean O'Casey's inclusion of them, as Mary Ní Hayadawn and Oona Ní Merrily, in his ironic account of the League's participation in a Dublin procession in 1903.[44] Hayden found it a novel experience to go in the League's procession, when she rode in the second carriage, behind the President (Hyde).[45] O'Farrelly was to be Hayden's lifelong associate and one of her closest friends. O'Farrelly was the younger by about twelve years. She gained the MA degree in 1900 and, like Hayden, was a founder member of the IAWGCG.

Not as constantly active in the Gaelic League as her academic colleague O'Farrelly to judge from the *Annual Reports*, Hayden's participation was usually on educational issues, and she continued to feel optimism about the progress of the language movement and the increasing numbers of teachers and pupils.[46] Hayden and O'Farrelly were members of an education sub-committee in 1903, of which MacNeill was chairman. Having had notable success with the encouragement of Irish language teaching in primary and secondary schools, with the subject included in 1900 in the curriculum for the Intermediate Board examinations,[47] the League was turning its attention to the study of the language at university level. At the Ard Fheis in 1905 an ambitious proposal was discussed for the establishment of an Irish Academy to which admission would be by examination, and by means of which higher-level qualifications might be awarded. Hayden advised against a proposal from MacNeill and O'Farrelly for the establishment of an Ollscoil Ghaedhealach, urging that efforts and available finance should more wisely concentrate on primary education to save the spoken language, endangered as the literary language was not.[48] She suggested the translation of common phrases into Irish to MacNeill as a method of teaching the language.[49]

There are two publications by Hayden on the Gaelic League which illustrate the significance which she attached to the language revival and her intellectual appreciation of the language, its history and tradition. Her article 'The Irish Language Movement and the Gaelic League' published in the *Alexandra College Magazine*[50] recounted the foundation of the League, its aims, and its achievements, concluding with her opinion that the arousal of national pride was important, but not the elimination of English, a bi-lingual Ireland being the desired goal of all but the extremists in the movement. Here Hayden can be read as reflecting the influence of Hyde. Alexandra College had introduced its first class in Irish in December 1900, taught by Agnes O'Farrelly,[51] who was succeeded by Pearse in 1904. The other publication by Hayden was a Gaelic League pamphlet *Facts About the Irish Language and the Irish Language Movement* (1910). This was intended for visitors to Ireland, particularly Irish-Americans. It gave simple accounts of the history and structure of the language, its decay in the nineteenth century, arguments for its revival, and described the foundation and work of the League. The pamphlet ended with suggestions how visitors might help the League 'in its battle against powerful forces of anglicisation which seek to crush the national spirit of Ireland'.[52] Hayden requested financial contributions for the League, and that visitors should not encourage emigration, each emigrant being blood 'drawn from the veins of our poor Mother Erin', emotive language of a style not previously noted from Hayden. She did not favour emigration, to judge from her comment to Pearse in 1904 that emigration could prove economically unrewarding.[53] Her observations, published elsewhere, about 'young people flying by shiploads from our shores, bringing the riches of their strength to the stranger, and leaving poverty and weakness at home'[54] illustrate what has been described as the intelligentsia's disappointment with 'the Connacht people's propensity to emigrate'.[55] These two publications on the League express quite consciously their author's pride in her newfound national heritage, and it seems to have been her work with the Gaelic League which led to the formulation of her nationalist thinking; at the same time in both articles she stressed the non-political and non-sectarian origins of the League.

Typically Hayden's application to the study of the Irish language was wholehearted, and having come to grips with modern Irish she proceeded to learn Old Irish, studying under Kuno Meyer, John Strachan and Osborn Bergin in Liverpool, Manchester and at the School of Irish Learning in Dublin.[56] Meyer and Strachan were Celtic scholars, professors in Liverpool and Manchester respectively; Bergin lectured in Celtic at Queen's College Cork, and became a foundation professor in UCD (1909–1940).[57] When attending classes in Manchester, Hayden wrote that she liked Strachan 'immensely, he takes such interest in each student'.[58] The School of Irish Learning had been established in 1903 at the instigation of Kuno Meyer then lecturing at the University of Liverpool. Meyer, Strachan and Bergin all lectured at the School of Irish Learning which attracted to its summer courses students of Old and Middle Irish from Europe and America, as well as candidates for the Royal University degrees.

What was recorded as Hayden's 'scholarly paper on Some Early Irish Translations' read to the National

Literary Society in 1909[59] may have been an early product of these studies. Also that year, she had a long review in the *Freeman's Journal* of a work which contained articles by 'three Keltologists of worldwide fame' – as she described Heinrich Zimmer, Kuno Meyer and Ludwig Stern. Her detailed account of the matters treated by these three authors, 'the results of the latest research', displayed her familiarity at least with Old Irish law and the literature of the various Celtic languages. Published some months before the submission of her application for the university lectureship to which she was appointed in October 1909, the review left no doubt about her scholarly background.[60] In time she was to have at least one significant Early Irish publication, her edition and translation of 'The Songs of Buchet's House' (a twelfth century Irish manuscript poem) in *Zeitschrift fur Celtische Philologie,* 8 (1912).[61]

Hayden's Awakening Nationalism

Hayden's enthusiasm for the literary heritage in both English and Irish expanded to embrace the entire gamut of the country's history and governance. Eoin MacNeill's comment that he 'would accept any settlement that would enable Irishmen to freely control their own affairs' expressed the attitude of many.[62] Hayden was now proceeding from her youthful lack of interest in national politics, and would become a convinced Home Ruler seeing a native parliament as a pre-requisite for any political, economic and cultural advancement for the country. More particularly, the 1908 university legislation which included the admission of women was a political measure, and other rights for women might be claimed in the arena of parliamentary politics.

Previously Hayden had been comfortable with United Kingdom status and did not object to rule from Westminster. But as far back as 1889, when attending a Liberal-Unionist meeting presided over by Millicent

Fawcett, the English suffragist, Hayden had been displeased by 'the anti-Irishness of the sentiments expressed', while she repeated her usual lack of interest in politics.[63] The political structure of government was of little consequence to her. She moved easily between Dublin and London, frequently crossing to London to visit friends and relations, to read in the British Museum, or en route to the continent. The circles in which she moved in Ireland included people who might join the British military and colonial services. When living in Bonn or Athens she had regarded herself as part of the English set, and she enjoyed the entrée to embassy society in Athens, as mentioned by Agnes O'Farrelly,[64] while not unmindful however of her own distinct origins – the Olympic Games success of John Pius Boland she had welcomed as the 'triumph of my country'.[65] Hayden in earlier years had not been averse to the West British lifestyles and aspirations which the professions, the civil and imperial services, and other respectable occupations encouraged.[66] However in 1903, with her awakening sense of a national identity, she criticised the female members of the Crean family for their lack 'of national feeling; they run after English respectability and her society in a way that is quite funny'.[67] Writing in *An Claidheamh Soluis*, Hayden deplored those who looked to England for their standards.[68]

Hayden's awakening national consciousness was not yet inspired by deep political conviction. At the time of the Boer War her strong criticism of British military action in the Transvaal was pragmatically based as much on its cost and its damage to England's prestige as on an objection to imperial rule. These views, expressed during a debate at Alexandra College, placed her in a small minority against the motion approving of the war which was passed overwhelmingly.[69] On the same theme, Douglas Hyde, writing of the influence of the Boer War on national feeling in Ireland, included 'the heavy blows [the Boers] inflicted on England's prestige' among the factors contributing to the national mood.[70] There were many Irishmen in the British Army, but an anti-recruitment campaign was launched by the Transvaal Committee, which had been established in 1899 to arouse public sympathy for the Boers. Arthur Griffith, who had spent some time in South Africa,[71] was a principal figure on this committee. Irish nationalist opinion in general was supportive of the Boers in their resistance to British imperialism. The great increase in membership of the Gaelic League by 1902 is attributed in large measure 'to the galvanic effect of the Boer War'.[72] The war 'focused much moderate Irish opinion into an anti-imperial mould',[73] and in Hayden's case the mixed feelings she had felt about a 'terrible British defeat' in January 1900 had changed by 1902 to satisfaction that the British had suffered a fine defeat from the Boers, 'more power to them'.[74] On a personal level she worried for the safety of Tom Crean, who was a medical doctor with the British Army in South Africa.[75] (He came home in 1902, wounded and with a Victoria Cross). While not questioning the sovereignty of Britain and its Queen, Hayden criticised the exercise of power by government and parliament, and would begin to do so on home ground as she became converted to the idea of Home Rule. Her attitude was that of many in the Irish Catholic middle class, influenced as it was by British liberal ideas. Her growing appreciation of a national identity was still within the context of union with Britain, a view sometimes expressed by Parnell.[76]

Another leading participant in the Transvaal Committee was Maud Gonne. Hayden had encountered her at the Contemporary Club and thought her 'a lovely woman, most fascinating'.[77] Hayden was not a member of the association of women, Inghinidhe na hÉireann (Daughters of Ireland), founded by Gonne in 1900, which pledged 'the principle of independent nationality for Ireland', though its aims to encourage the study of the Irish language, literature and history were another expression of the contemporary cultural revival.[78] It enabled women to develop self-confidence in contributing to political activity and 'opened up a whole world of new possibilities for women'. But, described by Gonne as 'one of the first societies for open Revolutionary work',[79] it posed a challenge to more conservative nationalists like Hayden who were at home in the more sedate Gaelic League. The Inghinidhe offered women an opportunity to participate on their own terms, by organising their own events, entertainments, and protests on nationalist issues such as the visit of King Edward VII in 1903.[80] Hayden was not in Dublin at the time of the royal visit, and her diary makes no mention of the protests.

Through the feminist organisations, the Ladies' Land League, Inghinidhe na hÉireann, and later Cumann na mBan – none of which Hayden joined – women were proclaiming their right to take part in national politics. The language, cultural and educational activities of the Gaelic League were satisfying for Hayden; and the first women's associations which she joined, the Irish Women's Suffrage and Local Government Association (IWSLGA) and the IAWGCG, had the advancement of women as their primary purpose.

Irish in the National University

In 1907 the Gaelic League Ard Fheis noted the increase in the numbers of students studying the national language for the examinations of the Royal University. When in 1908 details of the proposed university legislation were known, the League held a special Ard Fheis in June to demand a favourable place for Irish studies in the new university, with the language as an essential subject for matriculation. Hyde and MacNeill had been criticised in the newspaper

Sinn Féin for accepting appointment to the University Senate before the language issue was resolved, and the Coiste Gnótha was similarly at fault for not achieving an assurance on the status of Irish in the legislation.[81] An organised nationwide campaign produced resolutions of support from county councils and other public bodies. The League's views had been forwarded to the Chief Secretary, Augustine Birrell, who responded that the matter, being essentially academic and within the discretion of the university, would not be dealt with in the forthcoming Act and Charters and might be taken up with the Commission which would have the responsibility of preparing the first statutes of the new university.[82]

A deputation from the Coiste Gnótha, which included MacNeill, Hayden, O'Farrelly and Pearse, presented the case for essential Irish to the Commission on 27 April 1909, to be told by the chairman, Chief Baron Palles, that the matter was not the business of the Commission.[83] According to one of the Commissioners, John Pius Boland, the matter had been keenly debated, he being strongly in favour and Stephen Gwynn opposed to compulsory Irish for matriculation. The Commission agreed the issue was one for decision by the University; but Boland also brought it to the National Convention of the Irish Parliamentary Party where his motion was adopted by a sizeable majority, though opposed by John Dillon and Stephen Gwynn.[84] The language was becoming a badge of nationalism even for those who had not learned it, though not all nationalist sympathisers approved of its compulsory imposition in the new university. The Coiste Gnótha then turned its attention to the Senate of the University, calling on it to deal with the matter.

Hayden's attitude to compulsory Irish was unambiguous but moderate. To the large public meeting on 'Irish in the National University' held in the Rotunda on 7 December 1908 she sent a telegram 'Sorry cannot attend. Completely sympathise with demand'.[85] She had two letters on the subject published in the *Freeman's Journal*[86] in which she disputed arguments by opponents of compulsion – that matriculation candidates had no facilities for learning Irish, that compulsory requirements for university entry were not usual (citing the example of Germany), or that students would be driven to attend Trinity and other universities. She pointed to the numbers presenting Irish as a subject in the examinations of the Intermediate Board. With her experience as both learner and teacher of languages she expected that the matriculation standard would not be too high for the average student to reach in twelve months. A reasonable number of students studying Irish was in her view a necessary foundation for a first-rate school of Celtic Studies. There had been much correspondence to the newspapers on the subject. Hayden deplored the tone of the more controversial, writing that the 'flinging of epithets is not argument', and that fair expressions of opinion should be tolerated.

The bishops' standing committee had stated that the curriculum was a matter for the University Senate, and was not convinced of the advisability for the Irish language of compulsion.[87] However, the League's position was favoured by many younger clergy. But the bishops' pronouncements were received unfavourably in the League's manifesto, 'Irish in the National University', published over the names of Hyde, MacNeill and other officers.[88] This pamphlet, written by MacNeill, was probably decisive in the eventual success of the campaign.[89] In university circles also opinion was divided. Delany, though demonstrably sympathetic to the encouragement of the Irish language, history and archaeology, was opposed to compulsion at entry, fearing, as Dillon did, divisive implications nationally and also anticipating a restrictive effect on entrants from Ireland

and abroad to the new university,[90] one of the objections disputed by Hayden. The Women Graduates' Association (IAWGCG) too, though well disposed to the encouragement of Irish studies in the new university, was divided on the advisability of compulsory Irish for matriculation.[91]

At the Coiste Gnótha, Hayden cautioned against a demand for the immediate enforcement of essential Irish for matriculation, proposing that the University Senate be called on to deal with the matter as soon as its board of studies had been appointed.[92] The League was fortunate to have Hayden, MacNeill and Hyde on the Senate. However, Hayden was not confident of success,[93] and she criticised the use of the adjective 'compulsory' (as suggestive of tyranny) instead of 'essential' in the Senate minutes and agenda, for which she blamed the University Registrar.[94] From its first meeting on 17 December 1908 the Senate had been in receipt of resolutions from Gaelic League branches, county councils and public bodies. The subject was raised by Hyde, referred to the board of studies and to the three constituent colleges, and finally came back to the Senate on 23 June 1910 when the decision was taken that Irish be an essential subject for matriculation from 1913. The twenty-one votes for the decision included those of Hayden, Hyde, MacNeill, Coffey and Conway (UCD President and Registrar respectively), and Sigerson. Against the decision there were twelve voters, including Delany, Christopher Nixon (the Vice-Chancellor), Chief Baron Palles, Monsignor Mannix and Archbishop Healy of Tuam.[95] In the Senate, the nationalist UCD representatives had outweighed the opposition of some members from UCC and UCG where a British and unionist outlook existed among some staff appointed during the Queen's Colleges era.[96] The Gaelic League considered the outcome very satisfactory and promised full support to the university.[97] It was the

League's 'greatest victory'.[98] Hyde saw the victory as the achievement of a truly Irish National University which would revolutionise 'the entire intellectual outlook of Ireland'.[99] Thanks to the non-political stance of the League, the Parliamentary Party had supported the campaign for Irish in the National University,[100] the University being a significant achievement on the Party's way towards winning Home Rule.

The Teaching of Irish

Hayden seems to have felt satisfied that once university entrants had a modest knowledge of the language, the university could be expected to pursue the more advanced study of the language and its literature, and of Celtic Studies in the widest sense. In the basic work of restoring the language, she attached importance to national schools. Though the language was now an acceptable subject for the curriculum, there were insufficient competent teachers, provoking the League constantly to press for improved funding for national schools and payment for teachers of Irish. Hayden was the seconder of a motion passed unanimously at the Ard Fheis in 1905 proposing joint action on trade union lines with the teachers' organisation to seek an increase in the 'miserable salaries' offered to teachers. Specifically on the teaching of Irish she was one of the proposers of a motion at the Ard Fheis in 1913 requesting payment for teachers of Irish in every school in the Gaeltacht areas.

Hayden's university stature, her role in the Gaelic League and her friendship with Pearse made her an obvious choice for membership of the board of governors of St Enda's, the bilingual private school he had established in 1908, when in 1910 he was moving it to new premises at Rathfarnham, The Hermitage, and appealing for funds for its support.[101] St Enda's was a school for Catholic boys, where the teaching, based on Pearse's educational theories, included commitment to an Irish Ireland and to the Irish language, respect for the pupils and their character formation, and learning for its own sake rather than for examination purposes. A 1913–14 prospectus lists Hayden as one of the ten-member Council.[102] Extern Lecturers listed in the Prospectus 1910–11 included Hayden, O'Farrelly, MacNeill, Hyde, Yeats and Padraic Colum. In 1909 Hayden gave a lecture on 'Anglo-Saxon Literature', described in the school magazine as 'a very animated and animating talk'. The subject, a return to her early literary studies, provided an opportunity for her to make favourable references to figures in early Irish epic history, a reflection of her more recent studies of early Irish texts.[103]

No longer on the Coiste Gnótha after 1913, she seems to have dropped out of active participation in the business of the Gaelic League and it may well be that, like Hyde who resigned from its Presidency in 1915, she disliked the increasingly political tone of the League's activities, which 'obscured the importance of the purely language movement' as recorded in a later work of which she was co-author.[104] O'Farrelly was a strong supporter of Hyde in his wish to keep the League apart from nationalist politics.[105] Hayden's contacts with Pearse were also ceasing, though not her personal regard for him.[106] By now Hayden was keenly involved in the movement for women's suffrage and convinced of the desirability of a home rule parliament expected once the Great War was over. However, her membership of the League had been a significant influence in the awakening of her national pride and sympathy. While remaining on the whole detached from party politics, she had become a convinced nationalist. But for Hayden herself, women's suffrage was the more immediate issue, and the one in which she was already personally involved.

At the same time, aside from the issue of women's suffrage, Hayden had new pre-occupations in her teaching and governing role in the new UCD, the successor to the college managed by the Jesuits to which women had not been admitted.

NOTES

1   R.F. Foster, *Modern Ireland 1600–1972* (London, 1989), pp 448–451.
2   F.S.L. Lyons, *Ireland Since the Famine* (Glasgow, 1973, 2nd ed.), p. 228.
3   Hayden Diary, 27 May 1896.
4   Hayden Diary, 16 January 1894.
5   Carol Coulter, *The Hidden Tradition: Feminism, Women and Nationalism in Ireland* (Cork, 1993), p. 20.
6   Hayden Diary, 8 December 1897.
7   Hayden Diary, 24 October 1898.
8   Hayden Diary, 11 August 1900.
9   Hayden Diary, 3 October 1900.
10 National Literary Society, Minute Book, Annual Report 1901–1902, NLI Ms 646.
11 Joyce Padbury, 'A Young Schoolmaster of Great Literary Talent': Mary Hayden's Friend, Patrick Pearse' in Roisín Higgins and Regina Uí Chollatáin (eds), *The Life and After-Life of P.H. Pearse* (Dublin, 2009), pp 33–44.
12 Hayden Diary, 31 March 1902.
13 Hayden Diary, 21 May 1902.
14 Hayden Diary, 1 January 1903.
15 Hayden Diary, 28 January 1903.
16 Hayden Diary, 2 March 1903.
17 Hayden to Pearse, 7 March [1903], NLI, Patrick Pearse papers, Ms 21054 (4).
18 Padbury, 'A Young Schoolmaster', p. 37; Ruth Dudley Edwards, *Patrick Pearse: The Triumph of Failure* (London, 1979, 2nd ed.), p. 64; Regina Uí Chollatáin, *An Claidheamh Soluis agus Fáinne an Lae* (Dublin, 2004), p. 90.
19 Hayden Diary, 10 March, 15 May 1903.
20 'The Dead Bill and Ourselves', *An Claidheamh Soluis,* 25 May 1907.

21 Hayden to Pearse, 1 June [1907?], NLI, Patrick Pearse papers, Ms 21054 (4). Two undated letters from Manchester are written on black-bordered notepaper, which originally suggested they were written in 1904 when Hayden was in mourning for the death of Arthur Conan. But there is evidence that she was in Dublin at this time. A more likely date for her stay in Manchester is 1907, when the mourning notepaper could relate to the death, on 25 April 1907, of her uncle, John Hayden. Her teacher in Manchester, John Strachan, died in autumn 1907.

22 Mary Hayden, 'My Recollections of Pádraig Pearse', p. 148.

23 Hayden to Pearse, 1 June [1907?], NLI, Patrick Pearse papers, Ms. 21054 (4).

24 Mary Brigid Pearse (ed.), *The Home-Life of Pádraig Pearse* (Dublin, 1935), p. 147.

25 Edwards, *Patrick Pearse*, p. 120.

26 Hayden to Pearse, [no date, but see note 21], NLI, Patrick Pearse papers, Ms.21054(4).

27 John Strachan (1862–1907), philologist and celticist, professor at Owens College, Manchester. *Dictionary of Irish Biography* (2009) Vol. 9.

28 Hayden to Pearse [1907?], NLI, Patrick Pearse papers, Ms 21054(4).

29 Hayden to Pearse, 1 June [1907?], NLI, Patrick Pearse papers, Ms 21054(4).

30 Hayden to Pearse, 14 March 1905, NLI, Pearse papers, Ms. 21050.

31 Mary Hayden 'My Recollections of Pádraig Pearse' in Mary Brigid Pearse, (ed.), *op cit*, pp 147–150.

32 Hayden to Pearse, 4 June 1903, TCD, Ms. 8265/154.

33 Hayden to Pearse [1907?] NLI, Patrick Pearse papers, Ms. 21054(4).

34 Hayden to Pearse, 1 June [1907?], NLI, Patrick Pearse papers, Ms. 21054(4).

35 Mary Hayden, 'My Recollections of Pádraig Pearse', *op cit*, p. 149.

36 Edwards, *Patrick Pearse*, p. 55.

37 Mary Hayden, 'My Recollections of Pádraig Pearse', pp 147–48.

38 P.J. Mathews, *Revival* (Cork, 2003), p. 23.

39 Michael Tierney, *Eoin MacNeill: Scholar and Man of Action, 1867–1945* (Oxford, 1980), p. 28.

40 Mary Colum, *Life and the Dream* (Dublin, 1966, rev. ed.), p. 96.

41 Mary M. Macken, 'Musings and Memories: Helena Concannon M.A., D.Litt.', *Studies*, vol. XLII, March 1953, p. 92.

42 Cited in Michael Laffan, *The Resurrection of Ireland: The Sinn Féin Party 1916–1923* (Cambridge, 1999), p. 10.

43 Mairead Ní Chinnéide, *Máire de Buitléir: Bean Athbheochana* (Dublin, 1993), p. 49; On Agnes O'Farrelly see Ríona Nic Congáil, *Úna Ní Fhaircheallaigh agus an Fhís Útóipeach Ghaelach* (Dublin, 2010).

44 Sean O'Casey, *Drums Under the Windows* (London, 1945), p. 127.

45 Hayden Diary, 15 March 1903.

46 M.H, 'The Celtic Languages. Articles by Professors Zimmer, Meyer and Stern', *Freeman's Journal*, 10 April 1909; Joost Augusteijn, *Patrick Pearse: The Making of a Revolutionary* (Basingstoke and New York, 2010), p. 131.

47 Thomas J. Morrissey, *William J. Walsh: Archbishop of Dublin 1841–1921* (Dublin, 2000), p. 232.

48 Gaelic League Annual Report, Ard Fheis 1905 (Dublin, 1905), p. 136. Nic Congáil, *Úna Ní Fhaircheallaigh*, p. 173.

49 Hayden to MacNeill, 17 September 1906. NLI MacNeill papers, MS 10,881.

50 *Alexandra College Magazine*, December 1903, pp 3–9.

51 Anne V. O'Connor and Susan M. Parkes, *Gladly Learn and Gladly Teach: Alexandra College and School 1866–1966* (Dublin, 1984), p. 58.

52 Mary Hayden, *Facts About the Irish Language and the Irish Language Movement* (Gaelic League, Dublin 1910), p. 29.

53 Hayden to Pearse, 2 June 1904, Trinity College Dublin, Ms 8265/182.

54 M. Ní A., 'Living for Ireland', *An Claidheamh Soluis*, 25 January 1908.

55 Foster, *op cit*, p. 449.

56 Mary Hayden, Application for Lectureship in Modern Irish History, 6 August 1909, National University of Ireland Archives.

57 Kuno Meyer (1858–1919), born Hamburg. With Strachan, founded the School of Irish Learning. *Dictionary of Irish Biography* (2009), Vol. 6; Osborn Bergin (1873–1950), born Cork. First professor of medieval and early Irish at UCD (1909–1940), *Dictionary of Irish Biography*, Vol. 1.

58 Hayden to Pearse, 1 June [1907?], NLI, Patrick Pearse papers, Ms 21054(4).

59   National Literary Society, Minute Book, Annual Report 1909, NLI Ms 646.
60   M.H, 'The Celtic Languages. Articles by Professors Zimmer, Meyer and Stern', *The Freeman's Journal*, 10 April 1909.
61   Noted in *Irish Historical Studies*, vol. iii, September 1943, p. 39, where the publication date is recorded as 1911.
62   Cited in Foster, *op cit*, p. 456.
63   Hayden Diary, 22 May 1889.
64   Agnes O'Farrelly, 'Mary Hayden', *Alexandra College Magazine*, December 1942.
65   Hayden Diary, 11 April 1896.
66   Senia Pašeta, *Before the Revolution: Nationalism, Social Change and Ireland's Catholic Elite, 1879–1922* (Cork, 1999), p. 98.
67   Hayden Diary, 15 March 1903.
68   Máire Ní Aodáin, 'The Golden Mean', *An Claidheamh Soluis*, 7 and 14 January 1905; M. Ní A. 'Living for Ireland', *An Claidheamh Soluis*, 25 January 1908.
69   Report of Students' Union Debate, *Alexandra College Magazine*, December 1900, pp 101–2.
70   Douglas Hyde, 'My Memories of the Irish Revival' in William G. FitzGerald (ed.), *The Voice of Ireland* (Dublin, 1924), p. 456.
71   Donal P. McCracken, *The Irish Pro-Boers 1877–1902* (Johannesburg, 1989), pp 58–61.
72   Foster, *op cit*, p. 448.
73   *Ibid.*, p. 433.
74   Hayden Diary, 11 March 1902.
75   Hayden Diary, 27 January 1900.
76   Pauric Travers, 'Reading Between the Lines: The Political Speeches of Charles Stewart Parnell' in Donal McCartney and Pauric Travers (eds), *The Ivy Leaf: The Parnells Remembered* (Dublin, 2006), pp 62–3.
77   Hayden Diary, 2 December 1898.
78   Maria Luddy, *Women in Ireland 1800–1918: A Documentary History* (Cork, 1995), pp 300–1.
79   Maud Gonne MacBride, *A Servant of the Queen* (Gerrard's Cross, 1994/1st ed., 1938), p. 268.
80   Margaret Ward, *Unmanageable Revolutionaries: Women and Irish Nationalism* (London, 1995 ed.), pp 58–64, 86.
81   Mairead Ní Chinnéide, *Máire de Buitléir*. p. 101.
82   Gaelic League Annual Report, Special Ard Fheis 1908 (Dublin, 1908).
83   Gaelic League, Annual Report 1909 (Dublin, 1909).

84   John Boland, *Irishman's Day: A Day in the Life of an Irish M.P.* (London, c. 1944), pp 62, 131–33.

85   *Freeman's Journal,* 8 December 1908.

86   *Freeman's Journal,* 28 December 1908, 5 February 1909.

87   Thomas J. Morrissey, *Towards a National University: William Delany SJ (1835–1924)* (Dublin, 1983), p. 334.

88   Gaelic League, Report Ard Fheis 1909. Annual Report 1909.

89   Michael Tierney, 'Eoin MacNeill: A Biographical Study' in John Ryan (ed.), *Saint Patrick by Eoin MacNeill* (Dublin, 1964), p. 25.

90   Morrissey, *William Delany,* pp 323–24, 336.

91   IAWGCG Annual General Meeting, 5 December 1908, NUWGA 2/1, UCD Archives.

92   Gaelic League Annual Report 1909.

93   Hayden to MacNeill, 28 October 1908. NLI MacNeill papers, MS 10881.

94   Hayden to MacNeill, 21 January 1909. NLI MacNeill papers, MS 10,881.

95   National University of Ireland, Senate Minutes 23 June 1910.

96   Donal McCartney, *UCD: A National Idea* (Dublin, 1999), p. 40.

97   Gaelic League Annual Report, Ard Fheis 1910.

98   Hayden and Moonan, *A Short History of the Irish People* (Dublin, no date), p. 571.

99   Janet and Gareth Dunleavy, *Douglas Hyde: A Maker of Modern Ireland* (California, 1991), p. 316.

100   *Ibid.,* p. 326.

101   Ruth Dudley Edwards, *Patrick Pearse,* p. 146.

102   UCD Library, Special Collections, 4.5.14/23.

103   *An Macaomh,* Vol. 1, No. 1, 1909, p. 85.

104   Hayden and Moonan, *op cit,* p. 572. While the literary sections of this book were the work of Moonan, parts at least of this chapter, 'Literature and Language' could have been written by Hayden. Also see Nic Congáil, *Úna Ní Fhaircheallaigh,* pp 257–8.

105   Mairead Ní Chinnéide, *Máire de Buitléir,* p. 115.

106   Mary Hayden, 'My Recollections of Pádraig Pearse', *op cit,* p. 147.

Mary Hayden
university professor

VI

THE UNIVERSITY PROFESSOR (1)
1909–1924

Hayden was appointed to the foundation staff of the new UCD, and in 1911 she became the first Professor of Modern Irish History, one of three women professors. She was also appointed to the Governing Body of the College and to the Senate of the National University of Ireland. Thus began a long and distinguished career in the University, as teacher, writer and notable presence. The question of separate colleges for women was finally disposed of. University College survived the political disturbances of the years 1916–23, in which Hayden took no part.

The New University College

With the university legislation of 1908, the college on St Stephen's Green, managed by the Jesuits since 1883 and originally the Catholic University of Ireland, became UCD, the largest of the three constituent colleges of the new NUI. The Irish Universities Act included provision for the appointment of a body, the Dublin Commissioners, to be responsible for making the initial statutes for the new university and its colleges, and for the first appointment to all offices. The Governing Body of UCD (of which Hayden and O'Farrelly were both members) which first met on 29 December 1908 was required to draft statutes and propose names for appointment for submission to the Commissioners. Though English literature had been Hayden's principal subject of study, she did not apply for either of the two professorships established in that subject, presumably exercising a wisdom acquired from her earlier unhappy experiences with the senior fellowship. George O'Neill SJ, who had been awarded the fellowship when she first applied, was appointed to the Professorship of English Language and Philology, but the other senior fellow whose appointment had so annoyed her, John W. Bacon, did not succeed in securing the more senior chair, the Professorship of English Literature. Bacon was appointed instead to the Office of Secretary (and Bursar), which he held until his retirement in 1938.

In History there were two chairs established, that of Early (including Medieval) Irish History to which Eoin MacNeill was appointed, and History, reluctantly accepted by John Marcus O'Sullivan.[1] O'Sullivan, whose Heidelberg doctorate was in philosophy, had hoped for a chair in that subject. Considered too young or not sufficiently orthodox according to different accounts, he was persuaded to apply for the chair of History for which the first list of applicants had been considered unsatisfactory. O'Sullivan had studied History at first year level only but, according to one account, he was advised that Philosophy and History made a good combination; what the young men were interested in was ideas.[2] He became a highly regarded, if unproductive, professor;[3] a colleague, Mary Macken, later believed that O'Sullivan's 'philosophical training made his teaching of history especially valuable for our students'.[4] In the early decades of the twentieth century, history was not ranked among the most prestigious of academic subjects, either in the school curriculum or the professional world. Primary school inspectors frequently noted that teachers were ignorant of or uninterested in history, their teaching of the subject suffering accordingly.[5] O'Sullivan would, early in his tenure, lament the poor regard for history as a subject for study or for employment in the civil service.[6] And in the 1930s Hayden, in a letter to her former student Dudley Edwards about his employment prospects, would comment that secondary schools 'think too little of History to get a specialist to teach it'.[7]

Of the fifty-one senior posts (professors and lecturers) four went to women; the proportion of women to men in academic appointments would subsequently diminish until the late decades of the century.[8] Three of the women appointed were experienced, well-known teachers, and advocates of higher education for women.

The subject Modern Irish History was provided for by a Lectureship to which Mary Hayden was appointed. Also in the Lecturer category were the three other women foundation appointments, Mary Macken in German, Maria Degani in Italian and Spanish, and Agnes O'Farrelly in Irish Language, a post for which Pearse had been a candidate. The annual salaries for these posts varied, Hayden's lectureship being worth £250 per annum. She was quite satisfied, and was described sitting in the National Library 'her mind at peace with the world' as she received the congratulations of R.I. Best who also noted that she had triumphed over the historian Rev E.A. D'Alton, another applicant for the post.[9] Edmund Curtis, later appointed to a professorship in TCD, had been another candidate.[10] Hayden was by far the most experienced teacher, an important consideration for the Commissioners, as also was the connection with the Royal University. The perception that she had been unfortunate in her dealings with Delany might also have entered the minds of Walsh and Boland, two of the Commissioners. Within two years, nine of the lecturers first appointed were raised to the status of professor. Mary Hayden and Mary Macken thus became professors, though with no immediate change in salary. Although the first appointments made under the Irish Universities Act were temporary, once confirmed by the University Senate as they were in 1916, Hayden and Macken thenceforth held appointments tenable until retirement.

Macken and O'Farrelly shared Hayden's views on university education for women, and both were active members of the Women Graduates' Association. Somewhat younger than Hayden they were, like her, graduates of the Royal University. Macken had briefly been a private student of Hayden's for a course of English literature. As a student she had experienced the stimulus of the literary revival, the Gaelic League, the National Literary Society and the Contemporary Club, where she met W.B. Yeats and John O'Leary. She had studied in Berlin and Paris, and then was awarded a studentship which brought her to Cambridge, an experience which would have delighted Hayden in her earlier days. Macken later was to write many articles on German literary figures, particularly German Catholic writers, and on the Catholic Action movement among German women.[11] Macken had been a member of Inghinidhe na hÉireann, which suggests her early political thinking to have been more akin to O'Farrelly than Hayden. Macken, like her two colleagues, was strongly feminist, and insisted on the compatibility of feminism and Catholicism, as she would do in 1937 on the subject of the new Irish Constitution. In 1916 Macken was to join the other two on the Governing Body, and together they constituted an effective voice on matters affecting women as occasion arose.

The confirmation of another appointment, that of Eoin MacNeill, posed a problem for the College in the resolution of which Hayden played a part. MacNeill was in prison following the Easter Rising when the Governing Body on 23 May met to consider the posts then about to become legally vacant and to recommend to the University Senate the re-appointment of the holders. Consideration of this particular professorship was postponed then, and again in July when notice of MacNeill's trial and sentence to life imprisonment had been officially received (thereby making him ineligible to hold the post or for re-appointment by the Senate). In January 1917 the Governing Body further postponed consideration of the future of the chair. MacNeill was released in June 1917, the vacant professorship was advertised early the following year and MacNeill was re-appointed, the whole delaying episode being an example of the discretion with which the President, Denis Coffey, steered the College through those politically tempestuous years.[12] He had arranged that the lectures in Early Irish History would be given by R.A. Macalister, the Professor of Archaeology, and Mary Hayden – the period 1000–1485 to be her responsibility.[13] Hayden and Macalister both offered half their salaries to MacNeill's wife Agnes, an offer which though appreciated was not accepted.[14]

The Years of Political Tumult

The first fifteen years of Hayden's professorship bridged momentous events in Irish political history. The long desired home rule measure was eventually passed with its implementation postponed to the end of the First World War. The Easter Rising was initially unpopular, but there was a subsequent wave of public sympathy following the executions of the leaders, including a UCD lecturer, Thomas MacDonagh. Then came the defeat of the Home Rule Party and the victory of Sinn Féin at the 1918 election, the first Dáil Éireann, the War of Independence, the Treaty with the British Government and the establishment of the

Irish Free State, followed by the Civil War between opponents and adherents of the Treaty. As a later President of the College, J.J. Hogan, was to write, the:

> Rising, though destined to be a turning point of our history, was a minority action, which initially surprised and shocked the majority of Irish nationalists, in the College as well as outside.[15]

Of the years 1915–16 a student, James Hogan, later Professor of History in UCC, recalled that though he and some others were members of the Volunteers, the atmosphere in UCD was non-political with no 'expectation of anything unusual to come', and that debates in student societies were more literary than politically inclined.[16] Hogan and other students became actively involved in the War of Independence 1920–21, while the work of the College went on. C.S. Andrews, another student, found the Literary and Historical (the premier debating society) to be run by 'sons of Castle Catholics and the detritus of the Irish Party'.[17] He met more congenial company in the Soccer Club, and soon combined his attendance at lectures with increasing IRA activity.

During the years 1919–23 UCD, no less than the country, experienced constant interruption of its work, with raids, arrests, imprisonment of staff, and the execution of two students. But it remained open; the prime concern of the President, Denis Coffey, was to establish the College on a secure basis, avoiding political involvement or publicity for provocative actions by students or staff.[18] On the occasion of a military raid in 1921, the 'wanted' students could not be identified as the President had left the roll-book at his home.[19] In 1916 Hayden had noted that Coffey 'is anxious not to further identify the College with the rising', when she sent to Pearse's mother 'a kind personal article on your son'. In deference to Coffey's concern, Hayden 'signed only initials', but she was willing to see the article published for Margaret Pearse's sake. Her initials might easily have identified the author. An article 'Patrick Pearse' published over the initials M.H. in the *London Herald*, is very probably the piece in question.[20] In her accompanying letter to his mother, Hayden wrote that Pearse:

> is constantly in my mind ... I see him in all sorts of places in which we were together. I regret very very much that I saw so little of him lately, but I suppose it could not be well helped; he was heart and soul in a cause which, deeply as I sympathise with everything done for Ireland, I could not in conscience help. I do wish though that I had seen him even once in the last few months.[21]

The Governing Body

The Governing Body endeavouring to establish the newly-chartered University College on a firm foundation had a delicate task. Until 1922, it was dependent on the British Government for its endowment. With the completion of the new building on Earlsfort Terrace, which was the last major building project of the British administration in Dublin,[22] teaching moved there from St Stephen's Green in 1918–19. The President acceded to the request of Dáil Éireann for the use of the Earlsfort Terrace building for the Treaty debates in early 1922. C.S. Andrews described how he wangled his way in to hear the debates.[23] He was one who would interrupt his university course to participate in resistance to the Treaty, and there were others. There were supporters and opponents of the Treaty among the students and the staff, but the majority favoured the Treaty. The Governing Body tried to avoid being caught up in political controversy while proceeding with the management and academic work of the College. The College not only survived without a break, but experienced continuous growth. The student numbers increased from 530 in its first session 1909–10 to 1,684 in 1930,[24] and sound academic foundations were laid.[25]

Hayden was a publicly active figure during these years but was not a participant in these major events. She differed from her longtime friend, Agnes O'Farrelly, in not giving precedence to the national issue and in being opposed to militant action. Hayden's activism was most cogently expressed by her participation in the suffrage campaign where she made a significant contribution both by the arguments she advanced for women's franchise and by her status as a professor of the new National University. Feminism was more important than nationalism for Hayden, and was to remain so to the end of her life. Within UCD, while her academic and teaching credentials were indisputable, her role as one of the first women professors was novel. Fulfilling this role in the predominantly male environment of the university did not inhibit her from her suffrage campaigning outside. Nor did the suffrage issue distract her from a committed involvement both to her own teaching and to the general development of the fledgling institution.

Though both Hayden and O'Farrelly were appointed to the foundation staff, Hayden's academic career advanced more rapidly, achieving the rank of professor in 1911, whereas O'Farrelly's professorial appointment (modern Irish poetry) was not obtained until 1932.[26] In 1909 Hayden had expressed concern that there might be 'no opening for Miss O'Farrelly' in the new College.[27] The warmth of O'Farrelly's obituary on Hayden[28] attests to a genuine friendship between the two women, for which their activities together in the Gaelic League, in the Governing Body and with the Women Graduates' Association is also evidence. But during the decade prior to the Treaty, they also had their separate concerns, Hayden with the suffrage movement and her social work in Dublin, and O'Farrelly with the foundation of Cumann na mBan. Hanna Sheehy Skeffington criticised this organisation for its subordinate role of helping the Volunteers, an organisation from which women were excluded. O'Farrelly, Louise Gavan Duffy and Mary Colum among others, accepted their role as auxiliaries in the nationalist cause. Though Hayden is not recorded on this issue, her view would have been that of Sheehy Skeffington; women's role was not that of helper. Nor on the whole was Hayden in favour of militant action, nor indeed did O'Farrelly take an active part in the 1916 Rising. Both women were to support the Treaty.

The first Governing Body, which had the task of recommending on the first statutes and foundation appointments, had its members named in the Charter, Hayden and O'Farrelly among them, an acknowledgement of their prominence. Hayden was a member of the provisional committee appointed by the Governing Body to make suggestions on the initial statutes, as directed by the Dublin Commissioners. She corresponded with one of the Commissioners, Archbishop Walsh, on the status within the new University and the new College of those RUI graduates who had not been registered students of the former Jesuit conducted University College at St Stephen's Green.[29] This category, while it included many men who had studied elsewhere for their RUI degrees, applied to all the women graduates of the RUI. Hayden was reported years later as having referred to the early statutes of the University as *Equus instar montis inferni Palladis arte.* Her knowledge of the Latin classics allowed her to adapt Virgil's line about the Trojan horse to describe the statutes as a hollow gift and to include a reference to their principal author, the Right Honourable Christopher Palles, the chairman of the Commissioners and a member of the Governing Body.[30]

It was the first year of the Governing Body's existence, before the College opened to students in November 1909. Meetings were held in the Senate Room of the Royal University building on Earlsfort Terrace where there was a large hall for ceremonial occasions, but teaching in the initial years was mainly at 85 and 86 St Stephen's Green. The period of office of the first Governing Body ended in January 1913. Hayden was then elected by the Academic Council as one of its representatives on the second Governing Body and re-elected on the next two occasions. In 1923 she was a co-opted member, and in the three subsequent Governing Bodies she was nominated by the Government. Her twenty-seven years' uninterrupted membership ended on 31 January 1935. Re-appointment by a Fianna Fáil government would have been unlikely, given her support for the Treaty and her earlier contacts with Unionist sympathisers. Agnes O'Farrelly returned to the second and subsequent Governing Bodies as a representative of the graduates or as a co-opted member, largely through the efforts of the Women Graduates' Association, which in 1916 supported the election also of Mary Macken.

Women's Colleges

While the Irish Universities Act 1908 had included women equally with men in its provisions, an important issue hanging over since the debates on the university question was the status of the two colleges for women, the Dominican St Mary's and the Loreto Institute. This was now a matter for the Governing Body. The charter of the National University contained provision for the Senate, on receipt of a recommendation from one of the constituent colleges, to grant the status of recognised college (i.e. in association with one of the constituent colleges) to an institution which satisfied certain conditions as to standards, staff and the level of education provided. The opportunity was taken by St Patrick's College, Maynooth, to apply early in 1909. Birrell, the Chief Secretary, though convinced that Maynooth should be recognised had realised that the university legislation would not get through the House of Commons were it to include what would be seen as a denominational provision, but he intended the University Senate to deal favourably with the matter.[31] Having obtained the necessary approval of the Governing Body of UCD,[32] St Patrick's was granted the status of a recognised college by the NUI Senate as from November 1909.[33]

The IAWGCG was conscious of the risk that recognition might similarly be accorded to the women's colleges, a possibility which had been opposed by the Association (though not all its members) in evidence to the Robertson and Fry Commissions. Women's colleges within the university meant segregation, which Hayden and others saw as a denial of equal facilities and equal opportunity, and as a continuation of the exclusion which the IAWGCG had been founded to combat. Of course, women were now included on equal terms in the 1908 Act and Charters, and had access to the constituent University Colleges from which they could not be excluded even if recognised status were to be accorded to certain women's colleges. The outcome could have meant a choice for women between attendance at a University College or at a recognised college for women, which some women or their parents might have preferred. As was pointed out in the student magazine, *National Student*, women opting for UCD might be frowned on as 'brazen-faced', whereas they might consider inadequate the resources and possibilities of a women's college.[34] Hayden, O'Farrelly and many others in the IAWGCG, remained adamantly opposed to separate teaching for women.

Even with the new legislation, the IAWGCG, still insistent on common teaching and common facilities, found it advisable in December 1909 to urge the Senate of the University not to allow separate lectures for women. Hayden, O'Farrelly and Sheehy Skeffington were members of a deputation to present the views of the Association to the Chancellor and Senate.[35] Although women's colleges were the model in Oxford and Cambridge, there were by now many co-educational universities in England and Scotland. The University of Wales, the model for the NUI, was co-educational, as were other universities in Europe, for instance Berlin, Geneva and Brussels, and in America, such as Boston, Michigan and Cornell.[36]

The university provisions for the granting of recognised college status stipulated that an application must secure the approval of the governing body of the relevant constituent college before it could be considered by the Senate. The UCD Governing Body in 1910 received an application from St Mary's, followed by one from Loreto.[37] Note was taken of a petition to the Senate with 3,000 signatures in favour of the application, and of letters protesting against the recognition of women's colleges from the IAWGCG and the Teachers Guild of Great Britain and Ireland. Proposals to grant recognition to the two colleges for women students in Arts, and subsequently for first university courses for women, were both defeated, Hayden and O'Farrelly in the majority voting against. The Governing Body then reported to the Senate that it did not consent to the recognition of either college.[38]

The issue was crucial for the nuns as, without recognition of some sort within the university, these independent colleges for women would not survive. Furthermore, their own nuns who wished to obtain degrees would be required to attend the mixed UCD, an unacceptable idea for virtually enclosed orders. Some members of the Catholic hierarchy thought that a single agreed, limited application might succeed.[39] However, the two colleges again separately sought recognition for first year courses. The Loreto application obtained initial approval for three years, Hayden and O'Farrelly opposing.[40] Hayden had anticipated this result, having written to MacNeill that 'the good nuns seem to have talked over several of the Governing Body'.[41] She hoped

176

nevertheless to put up a good fight when the matter came before the Senate and wrote that she was 'intriguing hard'.[42] When the St Mary's application came to the Governing Body, it too was approved, O'Farrelly and three others opposing, and Hayden this time abstaining.[43] These two applications for recognition were in fact turned down by the University Senate. The IAWGCG noted that the Senate, in consequence of legal opinion had decided to let the matter drop.[44] The legal advice was that no institution belonging to a body also engaged in secondary education could be recognised as a college of the university.[45]

The aim of the IAWGCG and of Hayden herself had been achieved. Her abstention in the final Governing Body vote on St Mary's may be attributed to loyalty to the college where she had taught for many years, more particularly as the partial recognition requested had, in spite of her opposition, been recommended for Loreto. She had informed Mother Patrick of her strong opposition to recognition of any outside college, but she had also undertaken to oppose the exclusion of St Mary's if recognition were to be granted to another college.[46]

However inadequate the facilities for university education in Ireland in the earlier years of the twentieth century, there were at least no organisational or legal impediments to the participation of women equally with men in lectures, examinations, degrees and prizes of the NUI, unlike the contemporary situation at Oxford and Cambridge. In Trinity College women had been admitted to lectures, examinations and degrees, but the distinctions of Fellow and Foundation Scholar were not open to them until 1968. The IAWGCG had shown itself more radical than some of its members and allies in the campaign for women's admission to the university. Those whose ambition would have been satisfied by women's colleges were no less determined in their desire for equality in university education, but in hindsight their more modest goal suggests their fundamental conservatism.

On the other hand, it has been suggested that the absence of separate women's colleges inspired with a strong sense of competition might, in part at least, account for the failure of women to increase their numbers in the senior academic ranks during the middle decades of the twentieth century. Hayden and other women academics of the new University College had all come from lecturing in the pre-1908 women's colleges.[47] Research in America in the later twentieth century has found that, while the overwhelming majority of women students were in co-educational institutions, 'they have not flourished there ... in numbers commensurate with their presence'.[48] For the years 1910–1960 graduates of women's colleges were twice as likely as women graduates of coeducational institutions to be cited for career achievements in *Who's Who of American Women*.[49] However, it is more than likely that in twentieth-century Ireland university colleges exclusively for women would have suffered even more than did the co-educational colleges from under endowment and inadequate facilities – inequalities from which the early women graduates were determined to escape. The two colleges, Dominican and Loreto, were granted recognition as places of residence for women students attending UCD, as had been suggested by Hayden and others in evidence to the Robertson Commission in 1902. The nuns themselves began to attend as regular students at UCD where, through the good offices of Agnes O'Farrelly, they were assigned their own reading room. England and the United States continued to have women's colleges at university level throughout most of the century.

Later debate has noted that while education remained within the control of men it continued to be about men, concentrating on male experience and structuring 'inequality by enhancing the image of men, at the expense of women'.[50] Such further issues began to be examined in the contexts of women's studies, gender studies and equality studies. But the path had been laid by the women who first surmounted the hurdle of admission to the university; they ensured that women ceased to be seen as extraneous to the provision of university education. Hayden was satisfied, writing in later years that 'Now-a-days women are looked on as an ordinary part of the student body'.[51] And for the University it was her view that co-education, far from encouraging 'distraction, flirtation, inefficiency and slackness ... had brought increased efficiency and promoted good discipline'.[52]

Opportunities for Educated Women

Access to university education and to the franchise were two strands of emancipation for women, both middle-class concerns. Hayden had always wished for some public purpose in her life; becoming a teacher, and now a university professor, had been satisfying. She also saw women as medical doctors, whom she knew in both the Women Graduates' Association and the suffrage movement. The desirability of women in the legal profession was also aired in relation to court cases affecting women and children, and would become possible under the Sex Disqualification (Removal) Act 1919.

Hayden's perception of the possibilities for women had become defined well beyond the limits she had noted in her younger days. She had arrived at the conviction that women should have equal opportunities in professions like medicine, law, accountancy, and had spoken on 'Women in Business' to an educational meeting of the IWSLGA in 1910.[53] Concerns about employment of women were often aired in the Women Graduates' Association. Hayden herself in 1910 had raised the question of women's eligibility for membership of Intermediate and National Boards of Education;[54] she was a member of a deputation from the Association in 1914 received by Sir Matthew Nathan, the Under Secretary, on this issue.[55] The liberating experience of her education at Alexandra, the role models she encountered there, the opportunities she had seized to earn her living, her acceptance as an independent woman in Dublin's cultural circles and in the Gaelic League, all contributed to a conviction of self-worth, confirmed by her status as a university professor. She now saw as open to challenge the patriarchal structure of society, which as a young girl she had instinctively queried. Hayden dated her own feminism from the mid-1890s,[56] which were the years of her junior fellowship and her awakening interest in women's suffrage. The development of her thinking can be traced through the rest of her life in pronouncements on education, suffrage, jury service, employment, and the Irish Constitution.

Hayden became the third President of the IAWGCG in 1913. The following year the Association, having achieved its initial purpose, divided into separate organisations for the three universities, Queen's University, Belfast, Dublin University (TCD), and the NUI with Hayden as its first President. The NUWGA though most active in Dublin had members in the other two constituent colleges at Cork and Galway. Conscious of the value of having three of its members on the UCD Governing Body, the Women Graduates' Association was mindful of employment opportunities for women which it might bring to the attention of the Governing Body. It was important for the Governing Body to promote the employability of its graduates, male and female, which it attempted to address by establishing an Appointments Committee (1914) of which the three women governors, Hayden, O'Farrelly and Macken were all members.

The Professor

To her professorship Mary Hayden brought long experience as a teacher and a particular concern for the educational development of women. History had been an examination subject for her; its secondary place in her interests no doubt a reflection of its then less prestigious rank among the established disciplines.[57] The historian was seen then as:

> a man of letters who combined scholarship with commentary on contemporary affairs, a role personified in Ireland by the two most well-known historians of nineteenth century Ireland, J.A. Froude and W.E.H. Lecky.[58]

Lecky, whose hero was Henry Grattan, underrated the social, the economic, the emotional and the irrational forces in history, in the words of his biographer Donal McCartney.[59] History was usually presented as narrative and often as a division of literature, as art rather than science. The professionalisation of the subject as an academic discipline was only beginning towards the end of the century. Hayden's relief to learn that history was but a minor portion of the examination for the junior fellowship will be recalled. For Hayden in her earlier years, history was the context in which literary works were written; in her application for her lectureship in 1909 she had mentioned that history had been included with the subject English when she took the examinations of the Intermediate Board. Her scholarly background was in literature. The path from literature to history was not unusual. That was the route followed, for example, by Helena Concannon who took her degrees in modern languages and was an applicant for a lectureship in Italian in 1909. Turning to the lives of saints, heroes and heroines, she wrote a prize-winning *Life of St Columban*, and several works on the historical roles of women which were widely read[60] and which have been suggested as useful starting points for research on women in Ireland.[61] Within the university with her appointment in History, Hayden had two women contemporaries, Mary Donovan O'Sullivan appointed Professor in UCG in 1914, and Constantia Maxwell, the first woman academic staff member in TCD from 1909. O'Sullivan and Maxwell worked mainly in the developing disciplines of economic and social history, more consistently and in more detail than did Hayden who would move from aspects of social history to the political history of Ireland, which she presented from a nationalist standpoint, as she herself would acknowledge.

Hayden's earliest efforts at scholarly writing in the early 1890s had been on medieval literary texts, a progression from her study of literature for the MA degree. Articles on the *chanson de geste* and 'The Song of Dermot and the Earl' were undertaken for their literary value, but the historical content of the material could not fail to arouse the interest of a committed scholar and moreover a woman becoming increasingly conscious of the civil and cultural limitations of her environment. The descriptions of society, customs, behaviour, of the lives of men, women, wives, husbands, sons, daughters, suggested themes which might deserve serious study in a broadened interpretation of the limits of historical scholarship. The earliest of her publications which might perhaps be regarded as in some sense historical was the article 'Medieval Etiquette' in *New Ireland Review* (1896), based on her reading of medieval texts and on secondary sources listed. In similar style based on literary references was her article 'Children in the Middle Ages' in the *Alexandra College Magazine* (December 1906), and she returned to the same material for her article 'Women in the Middle Ages' published in two parts in *The Irish Review* (August and September 1913). She found in these literary texts a revelation of a world which both resembled and differed from the society of her day. She was drawn particularly to the many references to the experiences of women and children as individuals, both honoured and downtrodden. These subjects provided much material for articles from 1890 to 1913, and again later in her life. These attempts at historical interpretation of the lives of women and children suggest Hayden's awareness of the developing research into the history of women, pioneered in England by some women scholars associated with the London School of Economics.[62] Like Hayden, the medievalist Eileen Power gave much attention to the social and economic position of women; and she too was a feminist and supporter of suffrage.[63] Hayden's 'Women in the Middle Ages' looked to an earlier golden age for women as an encouragement to feminists during the height of the suffrage campaign. Hayden was to write again in this vein during the feminist opposition to the 1937 Constitution.

The *Alexandra College Magazine* congratulating Hayden on her university lectureship added that she 'had of recent years devoted herself almost entirely to Irish History and Archaeology, her enthusiasm for which is well known'.[64] Speaking in Alexandra in 1908 on the training of children for citizenship, Hayden had suggested that old Irish history should be taught to inculcate a spirit of patriotism, but lamented that there were few suitable textbooks.[65] What textbooks she had used as a teacher we do not know, but one possibility could have been *An Illustrated History of Ireland 400–1800* (1868) by Mary Frances Cusack, a work intended for popular consumption; its author believed as Hayden did in the patriotic value of teaching history in schools and like Hayden was an admirer of Daniel O'Connell.[66] At the time of her appointment to the university lectureship, Hayden was an advising examiner in History to the Board of Intermediate Education where her accurate and extensive knowledge of History in general and of Modern Irish History was attested to by a former colleague who hoped that she would write a 'much wanted' book on modern Irish history.[67] She was also commended for her review articles on Irish history in the English magazine *The Sphere* in which she criticised erroneous representations of Irish history for English readers.

In these three articles[68] Hayden was concerned to demolish the treatment of Irish history as exemplified in an *Introduction to the History of England* by C.R. Fletcher, Fellow of Magdalen College, Oxford. Hayden deplored the author's misleading accounts of events in Irish history, for example his prejudiced treatment of Shane O'Neill, of the shipwrecked Armada sailors in Connaught, or 'shillelaghs in sixteenth century warfare – fancy!' Hayden disputed Fletcher's statements about trade, agriculture and roads in Ireland, quoting Alice Stopford Green as her authority and citing earlier sources used by Green such as Spenser, Fynes Moryson, and the *Annals of the Four Masters*. On Irish learning, Hayden referred to the work of Zimmer, Kuno Meyer and other scholars which represented Ireland in early medieval times as the university of western Europe. Fletcher's erroneous representation of Ireland and its people was not calculated to promote good feeling between the two countries, concluded Hayden, notably as the book appeared to be intended for school children, the future men and women of England. As a corrective to the depiction of a barbarous race of Hibernian savages, Hayden recommended the recent work by Alice Stopford Green, *The Making of Ireland and its Undoing*. Green argued that English historians misrepresented Irish history to serve the political purpose of a colonial government.[69] Hayden shared Green's admiration for the civilisation of Gaelic Ireland, and was informed by her interpretation. But Hayden's own book published in 1921 would be seen as a more balanced presentation.[70] Some months later Green herself had occasion to criticise derogatory and ill-informed views on Ireland and its history, in response to a harsh review of her own book by Robert Dunlop.[71] The two women must have known each other in Dublin through the School of Irish Learning. Alice Stopford Green was a historian and nationalist whose encouragement and finance had helped to start the School of Irish Learning of which she was a governor. Stopford Green and Hayden were both impressed by the importance which the literary revival attached to the distinctly native content of Irish history and culture, in contrast to earlier historians such as Lecky for whom history was an account of the political development of settlers and their descendants.

How the two history professors, O'Sullivan and Hayden, regarded each other, we do not know. O'Sullivan's approach to his subject was more concerned with ideas than was Hayden's factual narrative. They both attended the Third International Congress of Historical Studies in London in 1913, and wrote short notes about the meeting for *Studies*.[72] O'Sullivan took a broad view of changes in the approach to historical scholarship and he bemoaned the scant regard for history as a subject for study and the absence of specialised work on source material essential for scientific study. He concluded his report by praising Germany as 'the motherland of modern historical study'. O'Sullivan was an admirer of Germany's progress during the nineteenth century. His own philosophical training had introduced him to intellectual developments in that country, where advances in the scientific study of the past were particularly influential in the evolution of the subject as a scholarly discipline with exacting standards.[73]

Hayden did not find the meeting particularly useful. She criticised the practical arrangements, the small attention to Irish history, the formality of the discussions and the lack of human interest in papers based on obscure legal documents. She also noted that only two women read papers. O'Sullivan wrote that new approaches to historical studies required attention to the spiritual, social and economic conditions in which people lived, his recognition of the expanding possibilities of the subject. Hayden in her previously published articles was of the same mind, though the bulk of her historical writing was still to come. She considered the discussion following a paper by G. Orpen on Norman rule 'the most barren of any'. History as she preferred to present it was not a dry subject. Others of her articles were to deal with individual people – Lambert Simnel, Giraldus Cambrensis, and she had previously written on Maria Edgeworth. In her writing about the past there is appreciation that it is real, the human touch to which she referred more than once is there. It was still a narrative of particulars, derived from secondary sources, and did not lead her towards thematic analysis.

The University Senate

Hayden's distinction in women's education had been acknowledged in 1908 by her nomination in their charters both to the UCD Governing Body and to the NUI Senate. Her membership of the Senate continued, with re-appointment by His Majesty, until 1924. When the appointment of the second Senate was due in 1914 she seemed reasonably confident of her re-appointment by the Crown (i.e. the government) and was unwilling to seek election by Convocation where she thought the clerical vote would 'prevent the election of any woman',[74] and where she might be perceived as an establishment, non-nationalist candidate. In fact Agnes O'Farrelly was elected, her nationalist credentials being possibly an election asset. Hayden was again appointed by the Crown in 1919. She was frequently referred to as Senator Mary Hayden in newspapers, her presence bringing prestige to public events, notably suffrage meetings.

In the first Senate, as in the Governing Body, Hayden was appointed to various committees, to make representations on the statutes, to consider a design for the university seal and the possibility of providing a university mace, and to draft regulations in accordance with the proposed statutes. She was also a member of the first Standing Committee of the Senate, but this appointment was not renewed after 1914. Nor was Hayden's membership of the Senate itself renewed once the Crown had been replaced by the government of the Irish Free State, though that government did appoint her on three occasions to the Governing Body of UCD. The membership of the Senate is completed by co-option, and when the fourth Senate of the University met in November 1924 Hayden's name was proposed for co-option, but was eliminated after the first count, thus ending her sixteen years' membership.

One of the earliest issues before the Senate was the question of Irish as an essential subject for matriculation, wholeheartedly favoured by Hayden. Hayden had heard the name of Douglas Hyde rumoured for the office of Chancellor of the University. Her own preference was for George Sigerson who she considered deserved 'this tardy recognition', nor did she think it wise for the Gaelic League to have its President so directly attached to the new University before its success had been assured.[75] In the event, the Senate unanimously elected William Walsh, Archbishop of Dublin, as Chancellor, an understandable recognition of his significant role, culminating in detailed negotiations with Chief Secretary Birrell, leading to the establishment of the University. Walsh died in April 1921 and was succeeded as Chancellor by Éamon de Valera. In summer 1921 de Valera, President of Sinn Féin, was invited by a cross section of members of the University to accept nomination for the office to which election was henceforth by Convocation (i.e. the graduates). A graduate of the Royal University, he was an obvious and acceptable choice as a political embodiment of the struggle for national independence, and was welcomed as Chancellor at a reception on 19 November 1921. He attended his first formal Senate meeting on 19 December and did not attend again until December 1924, the intervening period being occupied with the Treaty debates, his departure from the Dáil, the Civil War and his imprisonment.[76]

Much of the business of the Senate was concerned with making appointments in the three constituent colleges. Another woman gained a chair of History when in October 1914 the Senate appointed Mary J. Donovan MA to a Professorship of History in UCG. Hayden was the initiator of the proposal to confer an honorary degree on George Sigerson, her longtime friend and associate in the National Literary Society, which was duly approved. In 1919 she was included in a Senate committee to consider a proposal to the government from UCC for the establishment of a separate University of Munster.[77] A separate university in Cork had been a long held ambition of the UCC President, Bertram Windle, which gained momentum in 1918–19 but came to nothing in the face of opposition from a variety of sources of which the NUI Senate was but one. The Senate procedure was a delaying tactic, while Sinn Féin in Cork opposed the idea of an independent university pending the settlement of the national question, seeing Windle's negotiations with the Government as a unionist, pro-British manoeuvre.[78] Hayden was one of the University's delegates to a Conference of the Universities of the Empire in July 1921 in London and Oxford.[79] Participation in this imperial gathering was unlikely to present a problem for her, or for her constitutional nationalism; she was at this time, as we shall see, a member of the short-lived Irish Dominion League. In 1922 she was one of the University's two representatives appointed to meet the Dáil Éireann Commission on Secondary Education on the question of introducing an honours leaving certificate examination.[80]

Hayden's nationalism was inspired by the literary and language movements of the late nineteenth century. The success of the Irish Parliamentary Party in achieving the establishment of the NUI was now an encouragement to people like Hayden to adopt the cause of Home Rule, foreseeing further beneficial developments for the country. While occupied with and committed to her academic life, she was convinced that the parliamentary franchise must be achieved for women, and she was recognised both within the university and beyond it as a leading proponent of women's rights.

NOTES

1   John Marcus O'Sullivan (1881–1948), *Dictionary of Irish Biography* (Cambridge, 2009), Vol. 7.

2   Thomas J. Morrissey, *Towards a National University: William Delany SJ (1835–1924)* (Dublin, 1983), p. 350.

3   Mary O'Dowd, 'From Morgan to Mac Curtain: Women Historians in Ireland from the 1790s to the 1990s' in Maryann Valiulis and Mary O'Dowd (eds), *Women and Irish History* (Dublin, 1997), p. 50; See also Donal McCartney, *UCD A National Idea: The History of University College, Dublin* (Dublin, 1999), pp 64–5.

4   Mary Macken, 'John Marcus O'Sullivan', *Studies*, March 1948 Vol. xxxviii, No. 145, p. 5.

5   David Fitzpatrick, 'The Futility of History: A Failed Experiment in Irish Education' in C. Brady (ed.), *Ideology and the Historian* (Historical Studies XVII, Conference of Irish Historians 1989), pp 182–183. I am grateful to Maria Luddy for this reference.

6   J.M. O'Sullivan, 'The Congress of Historical Studies', *Studies*, ii, June 1913, p. 99.

7   Hayden to Edwards, 4 August (1936?) UCD Archives, LA 22/129 (4).

8   McCartney, *op cit,* pp 83–84.

9   R.I. Best to Kuno Meyer, 30 October 1909, NLI MS No 11002, quoted in Sean Ó Luing, *Kuno Meyer 1858–1919: A Biography* (Dublin, 1991), p. 78.

10 Irish Universities Act 1908. Dublin Commission. University College Dublin. Applications for Professorships, Lectureships and Other Offices. Vol. II Printed for the use of the Commissioners (Dublin, 1909). NUI Archives.

11   Mary M. Macken, 'The German Catholic Women's League', *Studies*, December 1931, Vol. XX, pp 555–569.

12   See J.J. Hogan, 'The Work of Dr Coffey and Dr Conway' in Michael Tierney (ed.), *Struggle with Fortune* (Dublin, 1954), pp 81–102; T.D. Williams, 'The College and the Nation' in Tierney, *Struggle with Fortune*, pp 166–192.

13   F.X. Martin, 'The Vacant Chair at University College Dublin' in F.X. Martin and F.J. Byrne (eds), *The Scholar Revolutionary: Eoin MacNeill 1867–1945* (Shannon, 1973), pp 387–390.

14   Michael Tierney, *Eoin MacNeill: Scholar and Man of Action, 1867–1945* (Oxford, 1980), p. 245.

15   J.J. Hogan, 'Introduction' in F.X. Martin (ed.), *1916 and University College Dublin* (Dublin, 1966), p. vii.

16   James Hogan, 'Memoir 1913–1937' in Donnchadh Ó Corráin (ed.), *James Hogan: Revolutionary, Historian and Political Scientist* (Dublin, 2001), p. 187.

17   C.S. Andrews, *Dublin Made Me* (Dublin, 1979), p. 125.

18   McCartney, *op cit* (Dublin, 1999), pp 106–111.

19   Mary Macken, 'Dr Denis J.Coffey', *Studies*, xxix (June 1940), p. 185.

20   M.H., 'Patrick Pearse', *London Herald* (no date), cutting included in scrapbook of Frank Martin, NLI, Ms 32,695/1, cited in Joost Augusteijn, *Patrick Pearse: The Making of a Revolutionary* (Basingstoke and New York, 2010), pp 355. N. 194, 356, N. 214. Much of this article was used again by Hayden in 'My Recollections of Pádraig Pearse' in Mary Brigid Pearse (ed.), *The Home-Life of Pádraig Pearse* (1934).

21   Mary Hayden to Mrs Pearse, 11 June 1916, Pearse Papers, NLI, Ms 21059.

22   Donal McCartney, 'History of UCD at Earlsfort Terrace' in Niamh Puirséil and Ruth Ferguson (eds), *Farewell to the Terrace* (Dublin, 2007), p. 5.

23   Andrews, *op cit*, p. 206.

24   *Report of the President University College Dublin 1975–76* (Dublin, 1976), p. 110.

25   McCartney, *op cit*, pp 109–111.

26   On Agnes O'Farrelly see Ríona Nic Congáil, *Una Ni Fhaircheallaigh agus an Fhís Utóipeach Ghaelach* (Dublin, 2010).

27   Hayden to MacNeill, 12 January 1909, MacNeill Papers, NLI Ms.10,881.

28   *Alexandra College Magazine*, December 1942, pp 32–35.

29 Hayden to Walsh, 23 December 1908, Dublin Diocesan Archives, Walsh papers, File no 12. Hayden to Walsh, 8 June 1909, DDA Walsh papers File no.6.

30 Thomas Dillon, 'The Origin and History of the National University, Part II', *University Review,* Autumn 1955, p. 20. I am grateful to Victor Connerty for the identification and elucidation of the Latin phrase reportedly used by Hayden – Virgil, *The Aeneid* Book II line 15.

31 Grainne O'Flynn, 'Augustine Birrell and Archbishop William Walsh's Influence on the Founding of the National University of Ireland', *Capuchin Annual* (1976), pp 145–162.

32 UCD Governing Body Minutes, 8 December 1909.

33 NUI Senate Minutes, 23 February 1910.

34 *National Student,* July 1911.

35 Minute Book, 8 December 1909, 11 March 1910, UCD Archives, NUWGA, 2/1.

36 Susan M. Parkes, 'Introduction' in Parkes (ed.), *A Danger to the Men: A History of Women in Trinity College Dublin 1904–2004* (Dublin, 2004), p. 2.

37 Governing Body Minutes, 21 February and 22 March 1910.

38 Governing Body Minutes, 19 April 1910.

39 Eibhlín Breathnach, 'Charting New Waters: Women's Experience in Higher Education 1879–1908' in Mary Cullen (ed.), *Girls Don't Do Honours: Irish Women in Education in the 19th and 20th Centuries* (Dublin, 1987), p. 75.

40 Governing Body Minutes, 1 June 1911.

41 Hayden to MacNeill, 29 May 1911. NLI MacNeill papers, Ms 10,881.

42 Hayden to MacNeill 16 June 1911, NLI MacNeill papers, Ms 10,881.

43 Governing Body Minutes, 15 July 1911.

44 Minute Book, 23 January 1912, UCD Archives, NUWGA 2/1.

45 NUI Senate Minutes, 30 October 1912. See also McCartney, *op cit,* pp 80–81.

46 Judith Harford, *The Opening of University Education to Women in Ireland* (Dublin, 2008), p. 153.

47 McCartney, *op cit,* p. 84. See also Carol Dyhouse, *No Distinction of Sex? Women in British Universities 1870–1939* (London, 1995), pp 138–40.

48 M. Elizabeth Tidball, 'Women's Colleges and Women Achievers Revisited' in Elizabeth Minnick, Jean O'Barr and Rachel

Rosenfeld (eds), *Reconstructing the Academy: Women's Education and Women's Studies* (Chicago, 1988), p. 219.

49 Joy K. Rice and Annette Hemmings, 'Women's Colleges and Women Achievers: an Update' in *Reconstructing the Academy*, p. 220.

50 Dale Spender, 'Introduction' in Dale S. Spender (ed.), *The Education Papers: Women's Quest for Equality in Britain, 1850–1912* (London, 1987), pp 6–7.

51 Mary Hayden, 'A Few Thoughts on Women in Universities and on University Women', *The National Student,* June 1935, p. 70.

52 *Irish Citizen,* 11 December 1915.

53 Irish Women's Suffrage and Local Government Association. Report 1910. NLI, Ir 3996 i 3.

54 Minute Book, 17 May 1910, UCD Archives, NUWGA 2/1.

55 Minute Book, 25 January 1915, UCD Archives, NUWGA 2/2.

56 Mary Hayden, 'The New Woman: A Reply', NLI. Hayden papers, Typescript (1935), Ms 24011.

57 Mary O'Dowd, 'From Morgan to Mac Curtain', p. 50.

58 *Ibid.,* p. 44.

59 Donal McCartney, *W.E.H. Lecky: Historian and Politician (1838–1903)* (Dublin, 1994), pp 187, 188.

60 Mary M. Macken, 'Musings and Memories, Helena Concannon M.A., D.Litt.', *Studies,* March 1953, Vol XLII, pp 95–6.

61 O'Dowd, 'From Morgan to Mac Curtain', p. 42.

62 O'Dowd, 'From Morgan to Mac Curtain', p. 45.

63 Maxine Berg, 'A Woman in History: Eileen Power and the Early Years of Social History' in Mary O'Dowd and Sabine Wichert (eds), *Chattel, Servant or Citizen* (Belfast, 1995).

64 *Alexandra College Magazine,* December1909, pp 41–2.

65 *Alexandra College Magazine,* June 1908, p. 49.

66 O'Dowd, 'From Morgan to Mac Curtain', p. 43.

67 Professor William Graham, Queen's University Belfast. Testimonial included with Hayden's application to the Dublin Commissioners. NUI Archives.

68 Mary Hayden, 'Irish History as She is Written', *The Sphere,* 22, 29 August, 19 September 1908.

69 Nadia Smith, *A Manly Study? Irish Women Historians, 1868–1949* (Basingstoke, 2006), pp 43–46.

70 *Ibid,* pp 70–75.

71 Alice Stopford Green, 'Tradition in Irish History', *The Nineteenth Century and After* (March 1909), reprinted in Green, *The Old Irish World* (Dublin, 1912), pp 168–97.

72 J.M. O'Sullivan, M.T. Hayden, 'The Congress of Historical Studies', *Studies,* Vol. II (June 1913), pp 99–102.

73 Herbert Butterfield, *History and Human Relations* (London, 1951), pp 158–59.

74 Hayden to Hanna Sheehy Skeffington, 26 and 28 September 1914. NLI, Hanna Sheehy Skeffington Papers, MS 22,667 (i).

75 Hayden to MacNeill, 5 February 1908. NLI MacNeill Papers, Ms 10,881.

76 Donal McCartney, *The National University of Ireland and Eamon de Valera* (Dublin, 1983).

77 NUI Senate Minutes, 28 February 1919.

78 See John A. Murphy, *The College: A History of Queen's/University College Cork, 1845–1995* (Cork, 1995), pp 175–81, 201–207.

79 NUI Senate Minutes, 17 December 1920.

80 NUI Senate Minutes, 12 July 1922.

VII

THE SUFFRAGIST
1908–1922

Hayden had become interested in the suffrage movement by the end of the nineteenth century and she joined various organisations seeking rights for women. Working with Hanna Sheehy Skeffington, she often figured in the *Irish Citizen*, the newspaper established by Francis Sheehy Skeffington and James Cousins, who was, with his wife Margaret Cousins, another university graduate, engaged in the campaign for women's suffrage until 1913 when they left Ireland; from 1915 their lives were spent in India where they continued to be politically active.

Contemporaneously with her work in UCD, Hayden spoke and presided at suffrage meetings. In writing she argued the case for enfranchisement and engaged with various issues of deprivation affecting women in Dublin. While she was now a supporter of the claim for Home Rule, the priority for her was women's suffrage.

Background to Suffrage Claim

Not until the nineteenth century did the male population in general in England and Ireland, apart from wealthy landowners and members of the aristocracy, have the right to vote for members of parliament. From 1832 onwards gradual extension of the franchise included the growing prosperous male middle class. Wider male franchise remained an issue throughout the century until granted towards the end of the 1914–18 war.

The first petition to parliament at Westminster for women's suffrage (1866) had included the signatures of twenty-five Irish women, including Anna Haslam. From the first debates on female suffrage (1867),[1] the subject of votes for women was subsequently discussed many times in Westminster. By the end of the century there were many women's suffrage societies in England, holding meetings and organising petitions. Eventually, the vote for women would be granted in the Representation of the People Act (1918), though only for women aged thirty and over.

The women's suffrage movement in Ireland is traced from the 1870s. The first suffrage society was founded in Belfast in 1871 by Isabella Tod,[2] and in 1876 Anna Haslam started the society which became the Irish Women's Suffrage and Local Government Association (IWSLGA).[3] Haslam and Tod had been prominent in the movement to have women included in the provisions of the Intermediate Education Act 1878 and admitted to the examinations of the Royal University. Anna Haslam and her husband Thomas were committed to the emancipation of women. Thomas had published pamphlets in 1874 advocating suffrage and 'a more positive legal status' for women.[4]

The new educational opportunities available helped develop an articulate body of women who came increasingly to believe that women's suffrage was not only a natural right but also the only means by which legislation could be made more relevant to conditions affecting the lives of women and children. The principle was conceded by the Local Government (Ireland) Act 1898 which included women as local government electors on the same basis as men, that is with certain property or university qualifications. The acknowledged success of local government by elected councils was subsequently cited as an argument in favour of Home Rule, and by some as an argument also for conceding the parliamentary franchise to women. However, the parliamentary vote proved more difficult to achieve. In Westminster both the Liberal and Conservative parties, and the Irish party, all feared the possible effect on their representation of the addition of women voters to the electorate. And many still preferred to believe that parliamentary business was no concern of women. For instance, a writer in the *Roscommon Herald* in 1916 would describe votes for women as a crank notion.[5]

The reviving interest in romantic nationalism also influenced women, such as those who joined Inghinidhe na hÉireann in which the significant objective was political independence. Calls for women's franchise were considered a diversion from the national issue and a reflection of the suffrage movement in England.

Education for Citizenship

During the years leading to the resolution of the university issue in 1908 Hayden had joined in the then fairly genteel suffrage movement as a member of the IWSLGA, which had contacts with Alexandra College. She remained a lifelong admirer of its founder, Anna Haslam. As far back as 1893 Hayden had participated in debates on women's suffrage, though her views on the subject had not yet taken shape. Nor did she make reference in her diary to the achievement in 1898 of the local government franchise for women, though as a university graduate she should have been eligible to vote.

Hayden was becoming convinced that women should have a role in public life towards which they should be educated. She expounded on this subject in 1908 in an article 'Training of Irish Girls for Citizenship'.[6] Though avoiding the 'vexed question' of women's suffrage, the article, in writing of women as citizens, implied that women should exercise the responsibilities and duties of citizenship, one of which is the vote. Hayden was provoked by a reverend gentleman's speech on the ideals of education which allocated the duties of citizenship to boys, whereas, as she put it, the capacity to cook a chop or iron a shirt seemed to be the feminine equivalents for patriotism, municipal virtue and public spirit. The exclusion of women from public roles was a regular feminist concern about which Hayden had become increasingly conscious.

The paramount influence of mothers on their children was constantly stressed by Hayden, and as a consequence the importance of women's education. This theme, which was expressed briefly in Hayden's evidence to the Robertson Commission, would continue to inform her attitude to issues of women's role, citizenship and education. The education of girls should therefore equip them to use their influence in the home and in the community with enlightenment and judgement. Her often repeated criticism of the education of girls was concentrated now on their ignorance of public affairs, for which both school and home were blamed, and to which women's indifference to public duties was attributed.

Hayden saw a great need for Catholic lay women to undertake charitable work in hospitals, workhouses and clubs, though women engaging in philanthropic work tended to be excluded from an authority role. Her criticism of many middle- and upper-class women who have nothing to do but amuse themselves expressed an opinion which she often repeated. The implication that these unengaged women are the drones, not fully occupied domestically as the poorer classes are, nor earning their living as Hayden and her like do, underlies Hayden's view of middle-class married women. On the other hand, as Hayden acknowledged, women in public life 'have tended by their influence to raise the standard of political morality'.[7] These are the kind of women admired by Hayden, achievers perhaps as she herself wished to be and was now becoming. She was confident that the honourable and intelligent mother will train her children, girls and boys, to be good citizens. Hayden presumably saw herself as a good citizen, though she had once, when aged about twenty, suggested that her own independent spirit might have been encouraged by the absence of a mother.

Hayden's suggestions for the cultivation of a healthy sense of public duty in Irish girls included organised games, philanthropic work, reading newspapers, some knowledge of the machinery of government, of public bodies and the franchise, subjects like history and geography within a broad objective attitude to encompass a spirit of patriotism, a study of native industries and a critique of emigration.

Educated women shared Hayden's views in general on the significance of schooling. S.M.R. wrote, in another issue of the *Irish Educational Review*.[8] 'If woman be educated up to the level of man, she will be found to be a powerful factor in helping to regenerate her race'. But the same author's suggestion that woman's purpose was not to be the 'rival of man in intellectual attainments, but rather … his helpmate and support …' did not coincide with Hayden's attitude who did wish to rival men intellectually and who disliked the role of helper. S.M.R. was apparently a nun, and it has been suggested that women religious, while intent on equality, were not consciously feminist in outlook.[9] S.M.R.'s approval of woman 'as the inspirer of noble deeds [rather] than as the actual performer' is not how Hayden envisaged her own role. She wanted to be the performer.

Irish Women's Franchise League

The desire, in the lively cultural and political life of the new century in Dublin, for a more active association than the small IWSLGA led to the formation in 1908 of the Irish Women's Franchise League (IWFL). Initially a very small group started by Hanna Sheehy Skeffington and Margaret Cousins, its aim, like that of the older group, was to persuade every Irish member of parliament to vote for every women's suffrage bill that might be introduced into the House of Commons.[10] The founders of this new organisation admired the Women's Social and Political Union (WSPU) founded in Manchester in 1903 by Emmeline Pankhurst, which had brought more militant and publicly active methods to the suffrage claim in England. The women who joined the IWFL were pioneers in a conservative society, who taught themselves to address meetings, to preach the cause of women's suffrage, and to engage in controversy and propaganda.[11] Many were university graduates and some, such as Hanna Sheehy Skeffington and Mary Hayden, were veterans of the campaign for university education for women. The members and supporters of the League were part of the Irish renaissance of writers, actors and the language revival in the early years of the twentieth century;[12] they were representative of the increasingly confident and nationalist middle class. In the suffrage campaign Hanna was very much to the fore; she has been described as the political brain and pre-eminent strategist of the suffrage movement.[13]

Hayden wrote and spoke frequently on the issue of the franchise, where discrimination against women was, in her thinking, as unacceptable as it had been in university education. As early as 1906 she had proposed and spoken on resolutions calling for the parliamentary franchise for women,[14] and in February 1909 she was one of the speakers at a meeting in the Abbey Theatre when the suffragists were accused of neglecting nationalist aspirations.[15] Her distinguished position in Dublin life was appreciated, as she was regularly described in newspaper reports as Professor Mary Hayden, Miss Hayden M.A., or Senator Mary Hayden, recognising her membership of the Senate of the new National University. Though courageous and vocal in the demand for votes for women, she was opposed to any resort to militant or violent methods to achieve the goal. And, while a committed member of the IWFL, she remained loyal also to the IWSLGA, involved in its drawing room and education meetings.[16]

Political Background

The political background (1910) was that Asquith's Liberal government had become dependent in the House of Commons on Irish votes.[17] The abolition of the Lords' veto by the Parliament Act of 1911 made the passage of a Home Rule Bill a possibility for the Irish MPs, and at the same time was seen by suffragists in both England and Ireland as the removal of an obstacle to their enfranchisement.[18] The two issues, of suffrage and Home Rule, thus became closely associated. The Irish Party members in the Commons were on the whole opposed to women's suffrage, some fearing the issue would impede the achievement of a home rule measure, or believing that the matter should be postponed for consideration by a Dublin parliament, others as in England apprehensive of an electorate to include women voters, and some including the party leader, John Redmond, implacably against the enfranchisement of women. Another Irish MP, John Dillon, believed that woman's suffrage would 'be the ruin of western civilisation. It will destroy the home, challenging the headship of man ...'[19] Nor did the Irish Party wish to antagonise the Prime Minister, Asquith, who was not then in favour of women's suffrage, or to precipitate a general election which might result in a diminution of influence for the party.[20] Individual Irish MPs such as Willie Redmond, Tom Kettle and Stephen Gwynn favoured women's suffrage, but had to accept the party line in the interests of the home rule issue. Efforts by suffragists in Ireland to win over the Irish MPs intensified, with deputations to politicians, heckling of their speeches at public meetings and the organisation of public meetings to publicise the cause.

Irish Suffrage Campaign: Hayden's Participation

Irish suffragists kept in touch with progress abroad, such as the enfranchisement of women in some of the American states. Anna Haslam and others were in regular contact with the movement in England. Speakers from England, America and Australia came to address meetings in Ireland, and many English feminist journals were read by Irish women. Particularly in the early years, there were many contacts between suffrage groups in Ireland and England, towards their common purpose of inducing the Westminster parliament to enfranchise women in both countries. Emmeline Pankhurst and her daughters Christabel and Sylvia visited Ireland several times, and Irish suffragists spoke at meetings in England.[21] But the IWFL did not welcome the arrival of WSPU branches in Dublin and Belfast in 1912[22] nor the three English women who threw a hatchet at Asquith and engaged in other violence during his visit to Dublin the same year. (The name 'suffragette' was coined to distinguish militant from constitutional suffragists who preferred to campaign strictly within the law).[23] The IWFL did not prefer any particular political party, but concentrated on obtaining votes for women either by the enfranchisement of women in both Britain and Ireland or as a provision of any measure for Irish Home Rule.[24] Smaller branches of the IWFL and other societies with similar aims were established.[25] Five principal societies were listed in a review of the situation published in the first issue of the *Irish Citizen* in 1912.[26]

In that same first issue, it was reported that Hayden, addressing a meeting of the IWFL, described the denial of votes for women as 'a flagrant and crying injustice, which should not be tolerated another instant'. She said the women of Ireland should have a share in a home rule government. If men were entitled to a vote as of right, they could not then regard the vote as a cruel burden for a woman who should decide for herself whether to accept these responsibilities; she should be allowed to work with men. Irish women's loyalty to their political parties, both unionist and nationalist, should have its reward in the unique opportunity of the suffrage amendment to the Home Rule Bill to settle the question and avoid a possibly bitter contest under a new Irish Parliament. While a strong Home Ruler, she did not see how pressing for this amendment could possibly endanger the Home Rule Bill. In pointing to the beneficial effects for public life in general to come from women's influence, Hayden was in tune with some Catholic writers mildly supportive of women's emancipation.[27] For example, Arthur Clery wrote several articles on women's suffrage which he favoured on the grounds that women were naturally moral and religious.[28] But Hayden's feminism implied a more fundamentally altered role for women, rejecting the notion of subservience. Women's participation in society should be as equal members bringing their own intelligent contribution and not as helpmates. Displaying her support for the home rule campaign, Hayden was reported in attendance among a large group from UCD at a major rally on Sunday 31 March 1912, on O'Connell Street, where the student section was addressed by Dr Coffey, the College President.[29]

Nevertheless, suffrage was paramount. At a mass meeting of the different suffrage groups on 1 June 1912 to demand the inclusion of women's suffrage in the Home Rule Bill, Hayden, presiding, asked in 'a perfectly constitutional manner' for redress of a great wrong. The Home Rule Bill contemplated the continued exclusion of women from the constitutional right of a voice in making the laws of the country. Women were not untried electors, having voted in municipal elections. Nationalist and unionist suffragists 'have joined on this one issue without sacrificing our individual political opinions', and she asked all political parties in the British Parliament to help obtain this measure of justice to women.[30] Other speakers at this meeting included Hanna Sheehy Skeffington and Jennie Wyse Power, and messages of support included those from James Connolly and Maud Gonne.[31] The resolution, enthusiastically adopted, called on the government to amend the Home Rule Bill then under consideration by adopting the Local Government Register which included women as the basis for the election of the new parliament.

The resolution from the mass meeting having produced no response, the first militant protest in Dublin took place on 13 June when eight members of the IWFL broke windows on government buildings. The women, who included Hanna Sheehy Skeffington, were tried and, refusing to pay fines, were sentenced to imprisonment for terms from two to six months. Hayden was one of many signatories to the IWFL request for privileged status for the women who saw themselves as political prisoners. Added to the pressure of public opinion, and the desire of the prison authorities to avoid trouble, this resulted in first class status for the prisoners.[32]

The following month Hayden had a two part article in the *Irish Citizen* entitled 'Women Citizens, their Duties and Training' in which she lamented the indifference to public affairs in the education of the average Irish girl, and the comic depiction of the 'advanced woman' as one who neglects husband and children.[33] This is almost the same article which Hayden had published in the *Irish Educational Review* in October 1908. Hayden's criticism of the indifference of better-off women, oft repeated, was shared by Louie Bennett who wrote of 'hundreds of well-to-do women who never do anything of public value ...'[34] Hayden and Bennett were themselves privileged women who had time and opportunity to engage in public activity, and had developed the confidence to do so. Now forthcoming with her views on public issues which impinged on women's emancipation, Hayden was no longer indifferent to politics, and was herself in the widest sense a political figure.

Asquith's visit to Dublin in 1912 was marked by violence which led Hayden to complain in the *Freeman's Journal* about 'the atrocious treatment of inoffensive women, real or supposed Suffragettes ... [which] has disgraced our city'.[35] She continued that the 'huge majority ... act within the limits of the law'. The association of militant protest with the campaign was damaging the suffrage cause and generating mob violence, and, as Hayden noted, individual women might be assaulted in the street. Constance Markievicz and Jennie Wyse Power were both threatened by hostile crowds.[36] While women's suffrage was supported by prominent intellectuals like James Stephens and George Russell, the socialist James Connolly and the nationalist Patrick Pearse, many Catholic clergy disapproved of the suffrage women; the *Church of Ireland Gazette* advocated deportation for militant suffragettes, and the student magazine of UCD expressed opposition to the suffrage movement.[37]

Hayden had occasion to write to the *Freeman's Journal* again in September, this time on the dismissal of Hanna Sheehy Skeffington from her part-time teaching job in Rathmines School of Commerce following her release from Mountjoy Prison.[38] Hayden had seen no comment in the Dublin press on this 'flagrant injustice'. The ostensible reasons for the dismissal, such as declining student numbers, she described as a flimsy pretext, the undoubted reason being the political offence. Hayden continued that she herself was 'wholly opposed to militant Suffragette tactics, at least in Ireland at present', but where men receive sympathy when suffering for political principles and when such suffering not infrequently leads to their 'advancement to offices of public trust and emolument', a woman who had shown equal courage should not be deprived of her means of livelihood without a voice raised in her defence. The double standards by which the conduct of men and women was judged had been noted by Hayden as a young woman visiting a Magdalen Asylum (a home for the rescue of 'fallen women').[39] A circular prepared by Hayden, Jennie Wyse Power and others repeated the protest against the 'summary dismissal without sufficient reason of Mrs Hanna Sheehy Skeffington'.[40]

By 1913 suffrage societies in Ireland were numerous, with much common membership. For instance Hayden, a member of both the IWFL and the IWSLGA, is not infrequently noted as taking the chair or speaking at meetings of the Irish Women's Reform League (IWRL, founded in 1911 by Louie Bennett).[41] Hayden, like many middle-class women, had engaged in philanthropic work, but the IWRL was an example of how the movement for women's rights brought women from relatively sheltered homes to an appreciation of the realities of life for working-class women. The IWRL was concerned with conditions for working-class women and their children, health and safety, trade union and educational activities; other concerns were court cases involving women, and the need for women police and women lawyers.[42] Bennett had also founded in 1911 the Irish Women's Suffrage Federation (IWSF) to co-ordinate the work of the many small suffrage societies and possibly to lead to an organisation concerned with other issues of women's rights.[43] The Federation, which involved groups throughout the country including Belfast, had twenty-four affiliated societies by 1917 when Hayden became its President.[44] Hayden had been a member also of the committee of the IWSLGA continuously from 1906.

Legislation to allow for the release and re-imprisonment of prisoners weakened by hunger strike, which became known as the Cat and Mouse Act, was passed in 1913, with the support of the Irish Party,[45] but its provisions were not applied in Ireland as a result of the widely supported campaign of opposition in Dublin in summer 1913.[46] A protest meeting in the Mansion House on 28 June heard speakers who included Louie Bennett, T.M. Kettle, Kathleen Lynn, Hanna Sheehy Skeffington, Charles Oldham of TCD, and Constance Markievicz. Hayden's speech, reported under a sub-heading, 'Cowardly and Spiteful', described the Act as a spiteful, weak piece of legislation by people who felt they were not in the right. 'If they were satisfied that they were right, why not let the women die?' She trusted that the Irish Party 'without compromising their opinions on women's suffrage, would at least join in a protest on this question and so prevent an added legacy of bitterness'.[47] The Act was condemned as a dangerous weapon of political oppression. The *Irish Citizen* published protests against the Act from P.H. Pearse, Jennie Wyse Power and Maud Gonne, and an IWFL petition included Hayden among its signatories.[48]

Humour was often used as an effective medium to get points across during the suffrage campaign, involving verbal skill and acute observation.[49] Hayden's feminist confidence is evident in her ironic article, published in four parts in the *Irish Citizen* in August 1913,[50] where she derided as nonsense contemporary perceptions of inferior ability, capacity or potential in women. Headed 'Report of Debate in the Parliament of Amazonia on the Representation of the People (Men) Bill', the article purportedly recounts a debate on a proposal to confer the parliamentary franchise on male property owners and on husbands of females entitled to vote. The arguments against the proposal are that men already have enough work to do, that the mere payment of taxes does not constitute a right to vote, that a vote given to men will lead to quarrels over the dinner table, that cobblers will discuss foreign politics instead of mending shoes, that seats in the House, the Cabinet and the judiciary will then be demanded by men who, however ignorant, will have a voice in making decisions. Questioning what contribution to the State by the average man could equal that of the mother who had borne and reared a large family, Hayden included her constant emphasis on the significance of the role of mothers.

The speakers in favour argue that men have the brains and capacity to exercise the vote, that many intelligent men have no female relative to voice their views, and more in this vein. Sure of her subject, Hayden poked fun at men and cited several references to the parliamentary debates to demonstrate how ridiculous were the arguments against women's suffrage. She made use again of this article some years later as a paper to the Irish Catholic Women's Suffrage Association (ICWSA).[51]

On a more serious note her article on 'Women in the Middle Ages' was published in 1913;[52] this social history theme and her conclusions were very relevant to the contemporary suffrage cause. The criticism of English law in Ireland implicit in her comment on women's loss of succession rights was one she would repeat in other contexts. Examining descriptions of women's position in society at various times, Hayden believed there was nothing extraordinary about the demands of twentieth century feminists,[53] an argument she would advance again in another article, 'Women in Ancient Ireland' (*The Catholic Citizen*, 15 November 1920). The Gaelic revival image of a golden age for women in medieval Ireland, influenced by the work of women scholars such as Alice Stopford Green, Eleanor Hull and Sophie Bryant, was clearly acceptable to Hayden who must have known their work.[54]

Industrial strife in Dublin in 1913 and a lockout of workers drew support for strikers' families from members of the IWFL and the IWRL, notably in the soup kitchen in Liberty Hall presided over by Constance Markievicz. Hayden was one of several academics at a Mansion House meeting in October which established an industrial peace committee to appeal to disinterested public opinion and achieve a truce between Jim Larkin's transport union and the employers, so that a settlement might be reached. This initiative was led by Tom Kettle with a series of articles in the *Freeman's Journal*.[55] Speakers and attendance at the meeting included Catholic and Protestant clergy, university lecturers, writers, the painter William Orpen and the surgeon Oliver St John Gogarty.[56] The peace committee was later described by one of its members as 'theoretically neutral, but ... our sympathies were with the workers'.[57] The committee ended in November when its final report blamed the employers primarily for the continuation of the dispute.[58] Hayden's participation in this effort is an instance of her belief in dialogue for the resolution of conflict. She was willing to commit herself to a public issue not specifically feminist, here and again in 1919 with the Irish Dominion League, exemplifying her advice to women to participate in civic activity. However, the average woman might have found circles such as those mentioned less accessible than did the well-known professor.

Hayden was announced as 'the advocate of the suffrage cause' for a debate planned for a Suffrage Week in Dublin organised by the IWSF in December 1913. A varied programme was designed to appeal to suffragists of differing approaches.[59] The great debate was a somewhat one-sided event, as described in the *Irish Citizen*. Hayden, representing the IWRL, made an opening and a second speech. Starting with 'an admirably condensed and logical summary of the case for Woman's Suffrage', she said that even if few women demanded this right, its denial was unjust. Women had to obey laws on which they had not been consulted, though consultation was not enough. She detailed inequalities between men and women, especially teachers' pay. On militancy, Hayden said all women could not be responsible for the sins of the militants unless all men were to shoulder all the crimes of men.[60] The opposing view on suffrage was represented by Mabel Smith, a speaker imported from London whose ignorance of the Irish situation got her into difficulties. The motion that women should be enfranchised in the interests of justice was carried by an overwhelming majority. The Connaught Women's Franchise League was represented at this Suffrage Week by Mary J. Donovan (later Mary Donovan O'Sullivan), then lecturing at UCG before being appointed Professor of History in 1914.[61]

There had always been tension between suffragist and nationalist women as far back as Inghinidhe na hÉireann, and from 1914 with its successor Cumann na mBan, though there were suffragists in both. For ardent nationalists, political independence took priority and in this regard republican and home rule women were of the same mind in fearing damage to their own cause from the distraction of the suffrage demand. Some republicans in particular rejected the suggestion of a franchise bestowed by Westminster, preferring to achieve it from a native authority – an argument also propounded by some supporters of Home Rule. For Hayden, the franchise was detached from contemporary national issues and need not interfere with current aims. In fact she had more confidence in Westminster, fearing further delays if the question of votes for women was left for the attention of the anticipated parliament in Dublin. Here she differed from Agnes O'Farrelly who had 'confidence that one of the first acts of an Irish Parliament will be to enfranchise the women of the country'.[62] Critical of the lack of support for women's suffrage from the Irish MPs, Hayden nevertheless advised against outright opposition to the Irish Party, or to its home rule policy which she herself supported. As the decision on women's suffrage lay with nationalist men, they should, she wrote, be given 'no pretext to oppose our cause'.[63]

Home Rule Act and War in Europe

By early summer 1914 the passage of the Home Rule Bill seemed assured and efforts were renewed to have an amendment included enfranchising women.[64] In June all the Irish suffrage groups joined in an unsuccessful effort to secure the desired amendment.[65] The Home Rule Act became law in September with an exclusively male franchise, its implementation postponed till the end of the world war which had just commenced. The *Irish Citizen* asked 'Will Ireland Lead?' and conferred responsibility on Irish suffragists to ensure that the Irish parliament when established should enfranchise Irish women.[66] Replies to its question were published by the newspaper in succeeding issues.

Hayden's response considered that as the Home Rule Parliament would deal with internal administration only, women might be allowed to vote for male candidates for this less important assembly. However, her opinion was that the Irish were 'naturally conservative and dread novelty' and that Redmond's concept of 'democratic franchise' did not include women. Her belief was that women's suffrage for the Imperial Parliament would come first, making it then inevitable for the local Irish legislature. Hayden saw little use in active propaganda on suffrage during the war, but there was an enormous amount of social work which women suffragists should do. When co-operating with men, they should do so 'only on equal terms' and should avoid working as 'associates' or 'auxiliaries' or under exclusively male committees. For men to see women in positions of authority and responsibility, working not under them but beside them as their loyal comrades for the good of the human race, would she believed promote the cause of suffrage.[67] By now, of course, Hayden had her own experience of authority and responsibility as a professor working beside men in UCD, the sort of opportunity not shared by many of her companions among the suffragists. But, like Hayden, many suffragists saw war work as an opportunity for women to prove their entitlement to the vote.[68]

In Ireland, the majority of women were occupied in home, including farming, duties. Women in employment were mostly in domestic work or in factories and shops, and, among the better educated, in offices or teaching and nursing. In 1912 the *Irish Citizen* had noted the new departure in the Bank of Ireland of admitting women to clerkships.[69] In an address to the IWFL, Hayden took a positive view on openings for women during the war, describing the situation in England where, with men going to the front, there could be opportunities for women to enter occupations previously closed to them – medical, legal, banking, clerkships, waiters, barbers and manual occupations like tram-driving and conducting, and agricultural labour. Women could show their ability to work as well as men, and might retain these positions after the war; it could never again be said they were unfit for them.[70]

But in 1917 when more manpower was needed for the war front and the employment in vacant civilian jobs of men aged 16 to 62 was forbidden, the move was widely viewed as 'economic conscription' and a prelude to military conscription for Ireland. A writer in the *Irish Citizen* in 1918 noted the increased numbers of women doing the work of 'the men who are absent' and deplored the lower pay of the women.[71] But the successful resistance to conscription in Ireland in 1918 did not include concern for the unequal pay of women, although the anti-conscription protest had sought and received the support of women. This has been seen as an instance of women's acceptance of their inferior economic status, to be encountered again during the 1920s and 1930s.[72] Though Hayden frequently raised the question of equal pay, she did not specify it on this occasion.

The Irish feminist movement had a broad agenda, and while suffrage was primarily of interest to middle-class women, many of them were also actively concerned about the welfare of working-class women, which was often discussed in the *Irish Citizen*.[73] The IWRL was engaged with social conditions, the provision of meals for children, trade union and educational work. In Hayden's thinking these were compelling social issues to which she and like-minded women should devote their energies during the years 1914–1918 when purely political agitation for the franchise was less likely to be productive. Drunkenness and prostitution in Dublin were serious problems. The IWSLGA, the IWRL and other women's groups had campaigned for years about prostitution. Their calls for the appointment of women police were intensified during the war years with the absence of men who had joined the army. Hayden was 'continually bombarding the Irish members of the British Parliament about the addition of women police to the old Dublin Metropolitan Police', as remembered by Professor Michael Hayes in 1958 when recruitment of women to the Garda Síochána was decided. Adding that 'she was absolutely right', his tribute, during the Senate debate, to the work of Hayden and her women associates was endorsed by Owen Sheehy Skeffington and W.B. Stanford.[74] Hayden and others were involved in the establishment of a recreation room for soldiers' wives to provide sympathy and comfort as an antidote to drink while their men were at the front. A Joint Committee of Women's Organisations came together to organise Women Patrols in an effort to combat prostitution, following the example in England, leading to an Irish Women's Patrol Committee with Hayden and Anna Haslam as joint Presidents. Hayden herself did active police work in night-time Dublin according to a UCD colleague.[75] This committee was one of a long list of societies supporting a request to the Prime Minister for vigorous measures to curtail the sale of drink in Ireland.[76] Other groups such as the Red Cross and the Women's National Health Association also included this type of social service in their contribution to voluntary war work.[77] The establishment of mixed clubs as a meeting place for girls and boys, as an alternative to dark streets and lanes, was advocated by Haslam and Hayden on behalf of the Irish Women's Patrols.[78] Hayden would continue in later years, at the Dominican College Union and the Alexandra Guild, to urge the desirability of mixed clubs.

There were disagreements among suffragists about war relief work, militarism, pacifism and the developing separatist movement. The delay in the implementation of home rule and the increasing interest in a more radical solution to the long drawn out issue of how Ireland should be governed meant that many suffragists became also republicans and placed independence before suffrage in their aims. Cumann na mBan, launched in March 1914 as an auxiliary to the Irish Volunteers[79] which admitted women only in a subsidiary role,[80] was attacked for placing suffrage in second place. Hanna Sheehy Skeffington, who was particularly critical of the Cumann na mBan women, described them as 'animated collecting boxes' for the men.[81] Hayden did not adopt republican views, and she did not mind whether suffrage for women was granted by Westminster or by a home rule parliament. Hayden spoke effectively on the suffrage cause, to the IWRL in an 'interesting and witty' speech, to the Dublin Friends' Institute 'in her usual quiet, rational style', and to the IWFL in a 'masterly address' on co-education.[82]

A new suffrage society appeared in 1915 with the establishment of the Irish Catholic Women's Suffrage Association (ICWSA), an effort to enlist support from Catholic women who had not shown much interest in the movement and had been actively discouraged by statements from some bishops.[83] The prime movers in the new association were Hayden, its chairman, and as its honorary secretary, Mary Gwynn, wife of Stephen Gwynn, MP for Galway, who favoured women's suffrage.[84] The circular announcing the new society appealed to Catholic women to join a league where a Catholic view could be maintained, quoting Pope Leo XIII that it was for Catholics to take the initiative in all true social progress. The Association was inaugurated at a meeting on 23 February 1915 at which Hayden stressed the importance of Catholic women's opinion on the suffrage question. Mary Gwynn described the new society as non-militant and non-party, and hoped to attract working girls and to spread the movement in country districts. The new society received a guarded welcome from the *Irish Citizen* which noted that its promoters were alive to the realities of the political situation.[85] Mary Macken was another member. Its first public meeting, held in the Mansion House, heard among other speakers Professor Arthur Clery who praised the women's courageous denunciation of the evils of the Dublin streets, here articulating the pragmatic support which women's suffrage received from some Catholic quarters, lay and clerical.[86] The first annual report of the ICWSA recorded its co-operation with other suffrage societies in petitions to the government to restrict the sale of drink in Ireland, to demand the inclusion of women in any bill to widen the franchise for men, and to bring back to Ireland its one woman factory inspector transferred to inspect munitions factories in England.[87]

The Easter Monday proclamation of an Irish Republic was addressed to Irishmen and Irishwomen, and guaranteed equality to all citizens. The Rising, the executions and imprisonments occupied the attention of nationalist women, of whom many were also suffragists and satisfied with the statement on equality in the Proclamation. Many women of nationalist views, like Agnes O'Farrelly, Mary Colum, Louise Gavan Duffy, though proclaimed suffragists, had considered the national cause a priority.[88] Nevertheless the *Irish Citizen* claimed Sinn Féin's recognition of women's equality at its convention in 1917 as a 'triumphant vindication of the sound political wisdom of the Irish militants in placing suffrage first' especially during the world war and the trying period since the rebellion.[89] Hayden herself, though a long-time friend of Pearse, MacNeill and other separatists, did not approve of the Rising. Though not a pacifist, she was opposed to militant action. She was critical of the Irish MPs and their leader John Redmond on their attitude to women's franchise. Irrespective of positions on the national issue, suffragists were at one in their belief that votes for women should be included in the political solution, and in March 1917 a meeting presided over by Mary Gwynn made this claim. Hayden was a speaker to the resolution, which also insisted that enfranchisement of women in Britain should be accompanied by equal treatment for women in Ireland.[90]

Achievement of the Parliamentary Franchise

The Representation of the People Bill to enfranchise men aged twenty-one and over who had endured the rigours of the war was now on its way through parliament. A more limited enfranchisement for women was included in the Bill, in recognition of the support for the war effort shown by women in England, and as a response to lobbying by constitutional suffragists like Millicent Fawcett. Public opinion in England had become more favourable than during the earlier militant activity of the Pankhursts and the WSPU. But Irish politicians, both nationalist and unionist, unsuccessfully attempted to delay the application of the Bill to Ireland, fearing the consequences from an increased electorate.[91] However, the Bill was passed in February 1918, giving the parliamentary vote in Britain and Ireland also to women aged thirty[92] (with a property or university qualification).

A further Act entitling women to stand for election and to take their seats in Parliament was passed without difficulty in November, in time for the general election of December 1918.[93] The *Irish Citizen*, now appearing only monthly, had published in October, November and December extracts from letters on the issue of women MPs. Hayden had no doubt that women should be eligible for seats in Parliament and for all positions in the government. She wholly disapproved of a suggestion that women might be co-opted and enter by a 'kind of back door' seeing it as the very essence of parliamentary government that each member be the freely chosen representative of a constituency. Accepting that there might be few women MPs for a considerable time, she believed nevertheless that any special privilege for women in this matter would be contrary to the great principle of the 'feminist movement which stands for equality of opportunity for both sexes'.[94]

In the general election which followed the end of the war, the only woman elected was Constance Markievicz, then a prisoner in Holloway jail. Consistent with the opinion of Hayden and others that women's suffrage was not a party issue, she and Mary Kettle supported an Irish Party candidate; Hanna Sheehy Skeffington supported Sinn Féin, and the ninety years old Anna Haslam declared allegiance to the Conservative (Unionist), Sir Maurice Dockrell – all these candidates being suffragists.[95] The *Freeman's Journal* reported on the procession which accompanied Anna Haslam, the oldest suffragist in Ireland, to the polling station. 'It was a women's celebration apart from national politics, and in the procession were Professor Mary Hayden, Mrs Sheehy Skeffington' and others.[96] Although the vote in 1918 was confined to women over thirty, women played a crucial role in the General Election as voters and party workers, and in the Sinn Féin victory and the virtual annihilation of the Irish Party.[97]

During the Dáil debates in 1922 following the Treaty signed in London in December 1921, efforts to achieve reduction in the voting age for women were unsuccessful, being seen by some as an attempt to destroy the Treaty and by others as usurpation of the powers of the yet to be established Free State. However, Griffith, President of the Dáil, under pressure promised equal voting rights for women in the constitution of the Free State, a promise which was kept.[98] The final suffrage achievement in Ireland, the enfranchisement of all citizens of twenty-one conforming to the declaration on equality in the Easter Proclamation was accomplished in the Free State Constitution of 1922, which in addition to reducing the age for women voters also abandoned the property qualification for men and women included in the 1918 Act.

The question asked by the *Irish Citizen* in 1914, 'Will Ireland Lead?' had now been conclusively answered, and contrary to Hayden's pessimistic expectation; for not until 1928 did Westminster extend the vote to all English women.[99] The introduction in 1922 of full suffrage for women in Ireland has been described as fairly unusual.[100] For instance, in France women did not obtain the parliamentary franchise until the end of World War II.

It is perhaps surprising that, during the years of the campaign, there is practically no mention of the suffrage issue in the Minutes of the National University Women Graduates' Association. (However, after summer 1917 a minute book is not available for some years). This is remarkable since the Association had been founded in 1902 as a pressure group to achieve equality for women in university education, and was later to lead the campaign in opposition to the provisions affecting women in the 1937 Constitution. There may be relevance in the observation that in the context of women's suffrage and other contemporary social issues in England some university women considered discretion advisable from a 'sense of being present on sufferance' and a desire to avoid further negative criticism.[101] Although its President, Hayden, and other members, notably Hanna Sheehy Skeffington, were prominently engaged in the struggle for the parliamentary franchise, the Association's concerns during the years of the campaign, to judge from its Minutes, were directed towards employment opportunities for women graduates particularly in the teaching, medical and legal professions.

Hayden's speeches and writings to suffrage audiences ranged over social, educational and employment issues, where she saw discrimination and injustice as unlikely to be rectified without political influence from women. The demand for voting rights was but one manifestation of the lively spirit of feminism current among some Irish women in the early twentieth century, women who wished for independent responsible roles for themselves and the removal of disadvantage in the lives of women and children of all classes, ambitions requiring fundamental change in society's attitude to women. Suffrage provided a practical issue on which a movement could organise. The struggle itself encouraged political activism by women which was a useful lesson for the future.[102]

Hayden believed in the value of concerted action by, or on behalf of, women workers. The emancipation of women encompassed rights which might have to be obtained for those less able to achieve them by their own efforts. Connections between the suffrage and labour movements were encouraged by the relief work engaged in by the IWRL and other suffrage societies, for instance by Louie Bennett.[103] Hayden encouraged union membership, giving a paper on the need for women's trade unions to the IWFL, and was among the speakers at a meeting of the Irish Women Workers' Union when resolutions were passed on the printing, laundry and dressmaking trades.[104] In another forum she deplored a proposed war bonus for Irish women teachers half the amount paid to men and demanded equal treatment for women teachers.[105]

In spite of her criticism of the Irish Party on its attitude to women's suffrage, Hayden was one of its greatly diminished number of voters in the 1918 election. And on the world war, she described herself as neither anti-British nor pro-German when she joined in the countrywide protests in 1918 against the threatened imposition of conscription, adding that she earnestly desired England and her allies to win the war. (In early 1916, Pearse had noted with disappointment Hayden's support for Britain in the war).[106] But her opposition to conscription prompted a clear expression of her nationalist outlook. 'Ireland has always preserved her entity as a nation, looking back to a national past and forward to a national future.'[107] She was not without sympathy for those who found militant tactics necessary for the good of the cause, as shown by her concern for the militant women imprisoned in 1912, or by her protest at the dismissal of Hanna Sheehy Skeffington from her teaching job. Hayden considered that the women's movement was more significant than any perceived excesses of militant members.[108] Her admiration for the Haslams was unwavering and her participation in the non-militant IWSLGA started by Anna, continued throughout and after the suffrage campaign even though she had become an active member of the IWFL whose founders were impatient of the 'genteel approach' of the older group.[109] Hayden described Anna Haslam as 'one of the pioneers in Ireland of what is called the feminist movement', distancing her from any 'screeching sisterhood'.[110] In her appreciation of Thomas Haslam on his death in 1917, Hayden wrote of his broadminded tolerance and of his belief that the vote was a means rather than an end;[111] her own view also. (The memorial to the Haslams in St Stephen's Green was a project proposed by Hayden in 1924).[112]

Staunchly Catholic and recognising in the foundation of the ICWSA the reservations of many women about the unorthodox views of some in the suffrage movement, she herself had no problem about co-operating with those of other or no religious persuasions. For her the issue of equality was universal, not confined by political allegiance, religion or social class. In her equal respect for and co-operation with the unionist Anna Haslam, the republican Hanna Sheehy Skeffington, the Catholic Mary Gwynn or the labour leader Louie Bennett, she epitomised the inclusiveness of her feminist convictions.

A Significant, if Limited, Achievement

Though there were efforts to spread the suffrage movement more widely in Ireland the demand for the adoption of the local government register of electors with its requirement of a property qualification was seen as a middle-class aspiration, giving rise to the taunt that the objective was votes for ladies rather than votes for women. Hayden was a middle-class woman with a professional career, a social conscience and an ambition to achieve equality of opportunity between men and women. Any qualifications attaching to the franchise should apply, she believed, equally to men and to women – the outcome reached in the 1922 Constitution when all citizens over twenty-one were enfranchised.

The achievement of the two major issues of admission to the university and to the parliamentary franchise meant the removal of inequality in two significant aspects of life, but women were still seen as subordinate beings. Hayden's emphasis on education for women demanded self-awareness, woman's recognition of herself as a distinct, rational individual whose responsible participation was essential for the wellbeing of the society she shared in a complementary, not subservient, way with men. In the remaining decades of her life Hayden would have occasion to articulate this thinking during controversies on jury service, employment, the 1937 Constitution and in addresses to women graduates.

While suffrage provided a unifying issue, feminists were but a small minority whose support did not increase in the aftermath of the suffrage achievement and whose influence was of limited effect in the early decades of the new Irish state. They were radical in the contemporary context of their challenge to the established institutions of church and state, but they were to find that possession of the vote was not of itself sufficient to achieve equal status in a society where the male role was still dominant in most aspects of the law, politics, family, employment and the professions, without much questioning by women. Political disagreements in the efforts to establish a new independent state as a viable and peaceful entity left little room for a minority of forward looking women who sought a more responsible role for women. And feminists themselves were divided politically on the 1921 Treaty settlement. With varying attitudes to the Free State and lacking a common goal, they remained a small minority on the edge of contemporary political events.

NOTES

1   Rosemary Cullen Owens, *Smashing Times: A History of the Irish Women's Suffrage Movement 1899–1922* (Dublin, 1984/1995), p. 20; See also Rosemary Cullen Owens, *A Social History of Women in Ireland 1870–1980* (Dublin, 2005), pp 81–107.

2   Cliona Murphy, *The Women's Suffrage Movement and Irish Society in the Early Twentieth Century* (Hemel Hempstead, 1989), p. 17.

3   Cullen Owens, *Smashing Times*, p. 20.

4   Maria Luddy, *Women in Ireland 1800–1918: A Documentary History 1800–1918* (Cork, 1995), p. 269.

5   J.J. Lee, *Ireland 1912–1985: Politics and Society* (Cambridge, 1989), pp 33–34.

6   Mary Hayden, 'Training of Irish Girls for Citizenship', *Irish Educational Review*, Vol. 2 (October 1908), pp 10–18.

7   *Ibid.*, p. 15.

8   S.M.R., Convent of St Louis, Monaghan, 'Some Thoughts on Woman and her Rights', *Irish Educational Review*, Vol. 2, No. 11, August 1909, pp 653–656.

9   Judith Harford, *The Opening of University Education to Women in Ireland* (Dublin, 2008), p. 123.

10 Margaret Ward, *Hanna Sheehy Skeffington: A Life* (Cork, 1997), p. 47.

11 *Ibid.*, p. 49.

12 Murphy, *The Women's Suffrage Movement*, p. 28.

13 Ward, *Hanna Sheehy Skeffington*, p. 124.

14 Irish Women's Suffrage and Local Government Association, Annual Reports 1906, 1908, 1909.

15 Ward, *Hanna Sheehy Skeffington*, p. 49.

16   Carmel Quinlan, *Genteel Revolutionaries: Anna and Thomas Haslam and the Irish Women's Movement* (Cork, 2002), pp 167–8.

17   Ronan Fanning, 'The Irish Policy of Asquith's Government and the Cabinet Crisis of 1910' in A. Cosgrove and D. McCartney (eds), *Studies in Irish History: Presented to R. Dudley Edwards* (Dublin, 1979), p. 279.

18   Murphy, *The Women's Suffrage Movement*, p. 166.

19   Cullen Owens, *A Social History*, p. 88.

20   Murphy, *The Women's Suffrage Movement*, p. 169.

21   Murphy, *The Women's Suffrage Movement*, pp 51–82.

22   Maria Luddy, *Hanna Sheehy Skeffington* (Dublin, 1995), p. 17.

23   Mary Cullen, 'Women, Emancipation and Politics 1860–1984' in J.R. Hill (ed.), *A New History of Ireland* Vol. VII (Oxford, 2003), p. 849.

24   Ward, *Hanna Sheehy Skeffington*, p. 47.

25   *Ibid.*, pp 70–71.

26   *Irish Citizen,* 25 May 1912.

27   Caitríona Clear, *Women of the House: Women's Household Work in Ireland 1922–1961* (Dublin, 2000), pp 35–36.

28   Patrick Maume, 'Nationalism and Partition: The Political Thought of Arthur Clery', *Irish Historical Studies* (November 1998), p. 224.

29   *Irish Independent,* 1 April 1912. I am grateful to Dr Pauric Travers for this reference.

30   *Irish Citizen,* 8 June 1912.

31   *Irish Citizen,* 15 June 1912.

32   *Irish Citizen,* 29 June 1912. Ward, *Hanna Sheehy Skeffington,* pp 87–91.

33   *Irish Citizen,* 6 and 13 July 1912.

34   *Irish Citizen,* 27 September 1913, quoted in Padraic Yeates, *Lockout: Dublin 1913* (Dublin, 2000), p. 361.

35   *Irish Citizen,* 3 August 1912; reprinted from *Freeman's Journal.*

36   Cullen Owens, *Smashing Times,* pp 60–61.

37   *Ibid.*, p. 68.

38   Printed in full in *Irish Citizen,* 5 October 1912.

39   Maria Luddy, *Prostitution and Irish Society 1800–1940* (Cambridge, 2007), pp 77–87.

40   *Irish Citizen,* 16 November 1912.

41   Murphy, *The Women's Suffrage Movement,* pp 24–37.

42   Cullen Owens, *A Social History*, p. 85.

43   Rosemary Cullen Owens, *Louie Bennett* (Cork, 2001), p. 12.

44   Irish Women's Suffrage Federation Annual Reports 1916, 1917.

45 Cullen Owens, *Smashing Times,* pp 63–65.

46 Murphy, *The Irish Women's Suffrage Movement,* p. 106. Cullen Owens, *Smashing Times,* pp 65–66.

47 *Irish Citizen,* 5 July 1913.

48 *Irish Citizen,* 12 July 1913.

49 Cliona Murphy, '"Great Gas and the Irish Bull"; Humour and the Fight for Irish Women's Suffrage' in Louise Ryan and Margaret Ward (eds), *Irish Women and the Vote* (Dublin, 2007), pp 90–91.

50 *Irish Citizen,* 9, 16, 23 and 30 August 1913.

51 *Irish Citizen,* 18 December 1916.

52 Mary Hayden, 'Women in the Middle Ages', *The Irish Review,* August and September 1913.

53 On medieval women and the vote, see Cullen Owens, *A Social History,* p. 5.

54 Mary O'Dowd, 'From Morgan to Mac Curtain: Women Historians in Ireland from the 1790s to the 1990s' in Maryann Gianella Valiulis and Mary O'Dowd (eds), *Women and Irish History* (Dublin 1997), p. 49.

55 J.B. Lyons, *The Enigma of Tom Kettle* (Dublin, 1983), p. 228.

56 Padraig Yeates, *Lockout: Dublin 1913* (Dublin, 2000), p. 228.

57 Thomas Dillon, 'Early Days in the New University College Dublin', *University Review,* Vol. II (1958), p. 29.

58 Yeates, *Lockout,* p. 423.

59 Paige Reynolds, 'Staging Suffrage: The Events of 1913 Dublin Suffrage Week' in Ryan and Ward (eds), *Irish Women and the Vote* (Dublin, 2007), pp 60–61.

60 *Irish Citizen,* 29 November, 20 December 1913.

61 Mary Clancy, 'It was Our Joy to Keep the Flag Flying: A Study of the Women's Suffrage Campaign in Co Galway', *UCG Women's Studies Centre Review,* Vol 3 (1995), p. 101.

62 *Freeman's Journal,* cited in Murphy, *The Women's Suffrage Movement,* p. 43.

63 *Irish Citizen,* 15 February 1913.

64 Cullen Owens, *Smashing Times,* pp 105–6.

65 *Irish Citizen,* 6, 13 June 1914.

66 *Irish Citizen,* 19 September 1914.

67 *Irish Citizen,* 31 October 1914.

68 Cullen, *op cit,* p. 856.

69 *Irish Citizen,* 28 December 1912.

70 *Irish Citizen,* 10 October 1914.

71 Maria Luddy, *Women in Ireland,* pp 234–5.

72   Ward, *Unmanageable Revolutionaries*, pp 253–54.

73   Cullen, *op cit*, pp 851–52.

74   Seanad Éireann, Garda Síochána Bill, 4 June 1958.

75   Mary Macken 'Women in the University and the College' in Michael Tierney (ed.), *Struggle with Fortune* (Dublin, 1954), p. 147.

76   *Irish Citizen*, 14 November 1914, 2 January, 13 February, 17 April 1915.

77   Eileen Reilly 'Women and Voluntary War Work' in Adrian Gregory and Senia Pašeta (eds), *Ireland and the Great War* (Manchester, 2002), pp 54–55.

78   *Irish Times*, 19 October 1915.

79   Ward, *Hanna Sheehy Skeffington*, p. 136.

80   Murphy, *The Women's Suffrage Movement*, p. 44.

81   Ward, *Hanna Sheehy Skeffington*, p. 137.

82   *Irish Citizen*, 7 February, 7 March 1914, 11 December 1915.

83   Murphy, *The Women's Suffrage Movement*, p. 149.

84   Their son Aubrey, one of the first students to enrol in the new UCD in 1909, became a Jesuit priest and a professor in UCD.

85   *Irish Citizen*, 27 February 1915.

86   *Catholic Suffragist*, Vol. I (1915), p. 95.

87   Luddy, *Women in Ireland*, pp 283–85.

88   Cullen Owens, *Smashing Times*, p. 111.

89   *Irish Citizen*, November 1917.

90   *Catholic Suffragist*, Vol. III (1917) and *Irish Citizen*, April 1917.

91   Cullen Owens, *Smashing Times*, p. 126.

92   Ward, *Hanna Sheehy Skeffington*, p. 219.

93   *Catholic Suffragist* (re-named *The Catholic Citizen* as from February 1918), Vol. V, 1919.

94   *Irish Citizen*, December 1918.

95   *Ibid.*

96   Maire O'Neill, 'The Dublin Women's Suffrage Association and its successors', *Dublin Historical Record* (September 1985), p. 139.

97   Cullen Owens, *Smashing Times*, p. 127.

98   Ward, *Hanna Sheehy Skeffington*, pp 249–252.

99   Cullen Owens, *Smashing Times*, p. 131.

100 Tom Garvin, *1922: The Birth of Irish Democracy* (Dublin, 1996), p. 9.

101 Martha Vicinus, *Independent Women: Work and Community for Single Women 1850–1920* (Chicago, 1988), p. 134.

102 Maria Luddy, 'Introduction' in Ryan and Ward (eds), *op cit*, p. xxi.

103 Cullen Owens, *Louie Bennett*, p. 64.
104 *Irish Citizen*, April 1917.
105 *Irish Citizen*, November 1916.
106 Joost Augusteijn, *Patrick Pearse: The Making of a Revolutionary* (Basingstoke and New York, 2010), p. 302.
107 *Irish Citizen*, May/June 1918.
108 Hayden's speech at the Suffrage Week, *Irish Citizen*, 20 December 1913.
109 Ward, *Hanna Sheehy Skeffington*, p. 46.
110 'Three Notable Irishwomen' handwritten paper read to an 'exclusively feminine audience'. NLI Hayden Papers Ms 24007 Box 14 and listed in NUWGA *First Annual Report* 1929–30. Reference to the Haslam Memorial in St Stephen's Green dates the paper after 1924.
111 *Irish Citizen*, January/February 1917.
112 *Catholic Citizen*, Vol. VI, 15 June 1924.

VIII

THE UNIVERSITY PROFESSOR (2)
1924–1934

UCD continued to function without a break before and during the foundation of the new Irish Free State. Throughout the 1920s it steadily established its position, its graduates contributing 'in no small degree to the building up of a new Ireland'.[1] Hayden continued her work, both in teaching and as a member of the Governing Body, participating in the efforts to achieve a stable, viable existence and a recognised academic reputation for the College. She was later recognised as having 'had a notable share in moulding the growth of the young University and its largest College'.[2] Hayden herself would write of the new Colleges of the NUI that 'their success had surpassed all expectations',[3] an understandable personal comment from one who had experienced the vicissitudes of higher education, and echoed by others, for example J.J. Hogan who wrote of 'the essential greatness of an institution that was outwardly petty'.[4] Hayden was also now embarked on her output of historical writing.

The Governing Body, conscious that staff salaries were poor, attempted to deal with the situation by paying bonuses to some staff, not surprisingly resulting in further representations from the less fortunate. Hayden's chair of Modern Irish History was one of the less well remunerated, a fact recognised when the Governing Body, on receipt of a request from a number of colleagues for an immediate increase in the salaries of the Professorships of Welsh and Modern Irish History as 'more urgent than in other cases', awarded a bonus of £133.6.8 to these two chairs.[5] Professorial salaries were fixed amounts, not scales, and seem to have been based on student numbers. However in 1928 the practice of paying bonuses was ended, salaries overall were increased and the salary for the Chair of Modern Irish History became £750 p.a, while the chairs of History and Early Irish History were each now worth £900.[6] A possible explanation for the differential may have been that the subject Modern Irish History was taken by students as a component of the main subject History, whereas Early Irish History was a separate subject in the area of Celtic Studies. The value of these salaries may be judged by noting the following contemporary prices: comfortable houses in Blackrock, Terenure and Ranelagh were for sale from £550 to £900; Chrysler cars for £400; bed and breakfast in the Gresham Hotel was available from 10 shillings and 6 pence; ladies' coats and men's suits could be bought for £4 and £5.[7] Nor, it seems, were academic salaries out of proportion to those in other professions; a district justice earned £1,300 and a dispensary doctor £300.[8]

The Governing Body was continually concerned about employment for graduates. Students of the 1930s recall that work for graduates was scarce. Teaching in England, temporary clerkships in the Civil Service, secretarial work, or unestablished teaching posts were often the only options, and women who obtained permanent posts in the public sector had to resign on marriage.[9] Employment was a concern also of the Women Graduates' Association (WGA), on whose behalf Hayden in 1926 sought the establishment of an Employment Bureau; one was established in 1928.[10] The WGA also promoted the introduction of a diploma course in Library Training,[11] taken in its earliest years almost entirely by female students. The Association's request to the Governing Body in 1927 that priority be given to graduates of the College may have been the origin of the practice for many years of employing only graduates in the small office staff.

Scholarly Writing

Hayden's commitment to teaching, to the work of the Governing Body and to her feminist activity, did not prevent her from continuing to write. Aside from book reviews, of which there were many, Hayden's other published historical articles were on 'Lambert Simnel in Ireland'[12] (cited by Steven Ellis in 1986–7 on the possible overthrow of Henry VII),[13] 'Prince Charles Edward and his Irish friends',[14] 'Giraldus Cambrensis',[15] (whom she found to be an interesting human being though his work on Ireland was full of errors) and several further articles on women and children. Hayden's involvement in social work in Dublin, her feminist beliefs and her now convinced nationalism, all contributed to her approach to this latter subject in which there is admiration for the Gaelic and the medieval past, optimism for the future and a consciousness of difference in the experiences of rich and poor. Returning to the theme of women and children in historical settings Hayden wrote on 'Women in Ancient Ireland',[16] 'Dublin Workhouse Children in the Eighteenth Century',[17] and the posthumously published 'Charity Children in 18th Century Dublin'.[18] In continuing to write on these subjects she was consciously giving attention to lives not then regarded as significant for the historical record. The latter two articles are alike in both subject and content. The first was published in December 1928, and the second was read to the Old Dublin Society in November 1939 when Hayden acknowledged the use of facts 'borrowed very extensively' from the thesis of Dorothea Casserley. A former student of Hayden's, Casserley gained the MA in 1929 for her thesis on 'Primary Education in Ireland in the Eighteenth Century',[19] on which she would have been working when Hayden wrote the earlier paper. Subsequently Casserley, a Protestant, wrote a *History of Ireland* (1941), a textbook for Protestant schools which became the subject of Protestant criticism for its 'one-sided' (i.e. nationalist) view of Irish History,[20] possibly reflecting the influence of her professor. Hayden's historical studies of impoverished children offer a graphic background to her own charitable work. Her recognition of contemporary Dublin slum children 'who do not get even *one* really warm dress or coat in twelve months' is knowledge gained from her own clothing work among the poor.[21] Citing the philanthropic activity of two eighteenth century women, Lady Arabella Denny and Nano Nagle, Hayden exemplified the contribution to society which she regularly urged contemporary women to make. Both articles conclude with a brief acknowledgement of some improvement in humanitarian attitudes to poor children. The *Alexandra College Magazine* (December 1923) contained Hayden's article on 'The Dublin Streets in the Early Eighteenth Century', an entertaining account of life, people, traffic and spectacle such as street shows, riots, public whippings and executions. No sources are indicated in this article; Hayden seems to have drawn her information from a contemporary account, perhaps a newspaper.

However, the work by which Hayden is most widely remembered is *A Short History of the Irish People* popularly known to generations of students as Hayden and Moonan.

Hayden wrote most of this book, apart from the chapters on the earliest period and on Gaelic literature which were the work of George A. Moonan, a barrister and a lecturer in the Leinster College of Irish (a Gaelic League school to train teachers of Irish). The publishers, the Educational Company of Ireland/Talbot Press, initially planned for a shorter book, titled *The Students' History of Ireland*, to be published in 1917 at a price of 5 shillings, a normal amount for a textbook. When it eventually appeared in November 1921, the work, which had become much larger and more expensive to produce than anticipated, was priced at 20 shillings, the publisher ruefully commenting that it was more likely to 'bring honour and glory to the authors than profit to the publishers', who would have to sell 3000 copies to clear the initial cost.[22] There were several revised editions, and the work continued to be widely used for two decades beyond Hayden's death in 1942. Edmund Curtis, in his textbook (1936), included the *Short History* in his recommendations for further reading.[23] A notice of Hayden's death, in the journal *Irish Historical Studies*, commented that this work during the last twenty years 'has been the most widely used school and college text in Irish history'.[24] However, there were few alternatives. By the 1960s, the *Short History* '... had done duty for decades' as noted by Roy Foster who described it as a didactic tract.[25] It was 'a widely read textbook' according to Joe Lee who dismissed it as 'vintage cowboy and Indian stuff'.[26]

Its authors acknowledged the book to be written 'from a frankly national standpoint' and to be based on their experience in teaching history, making no claim to originality other than in the presentation and treatment of their subject. This approach conformed to the post-colonial emphasis of the new State that the chief aim of teaching Irish history should be 'to inculcate national pride and self-respect'.[27]

The book is, apart from the chapters on literature, a narrative of political events. Hayden had the benefit of the work of W.E.H. Lecky (an author she was reading in 1901) seen as the country's leading historian who also was well thought of in the popular nationalist press. His concern for justice and tolerance, for instance regarding the penal laws against Catholics as indefensible, made him an influential source for later historians including Hayden. His views were attractive to moderate nationalists, a term which would include Hayden, though Lecky did not go so far as to adopt home rule but strongly defended the Union as the home rule claim became coherent.[28] From sources like Stopford Green and Lecky, and with her own background, liberal inclination and now convinced nationalism – which romantically idealised the Irish past without embracing the twentieth century republican aspirations – Hayden produced a textbook which despite its limitations is judged by later historians such as O'Dowd and McCartney to have been a good interpretation of the contemporary research and a reasonable historical narrative.[29]

Hayden's nationalist sympathy is clear in *A Short History*, as advised in the book's preface, but it is not uncompromising. Her historical perspective did not exhibit strong anti-British animosity. Her account is usually mindful of English policy in Ireland which at times she presents as ill-judged or ill-informed rather than deliberately malevolent, for instance in her treatment of the Famine.[30] Her feelings were more chauvinistically expressed in several book reviews published shortly after the appearance of her own textbook, for example when she rejected as inaccuracies, a description of Shane O'Neill as a barbarian and treatments of the Veto controversy of the early nineteenth century. Hayden asserted that O'Neill was a barbarian only in the sense that Raleigh, Drake and Essex were, and she argued that the Irish hierarchy had never accepted the idea of a government veto on Episcopal appointments.[31] While acknowledging Catholicism as the majority religion in Ireland, and herself a committed Catholic, she did not identify nationalism with Catholicism. Her own association with Protestants at school and later, studying for the Royal University examinations, in the literary and language movements and in the suffrage campaign, gave her a wide, non-confessional context in which to consider national issues, both historical and contemporary. For Hayden, modern society was a pluralist concept, an attitude reflected to some degree in her approach to Irish history. Again in 1927, she criticised the prejudiced treatment of Shane O'Neill in contrast to the manner in which the 'brutal and dishonourable deeds' of Walter Raleigh's Irish career are 'lightly passed over' in a work by Eleanor Hull.[32]

There is no suggestion of a feminist agenda in the *Short History*. The preface advised the reader that 'the study of our history is regarded as one of *dynamics* and not of *statics*'. But the dynamism generated by feminist activism of previous decades does not invade this book. Hayden's earlier published articles on women and children did not lead to any treatment of this subject in the *Short History*; nor the admission of women to the university, or the grant of the parliamentary franchise. The inclusion of women in the Local Government franchise in 1898 is noted, but the fact that women for the first time voted in a parliamentary election in 1918, though mentioned in the 1921 first edition, is omitted from later editions of the *Short History*, and the suffrage campaign is ignored. Nor is the inclusion of women noted in the description of the university legislation of 1908. These were not yet subjects of acceptable political history. Hayden's academic life and her public feminist activities were separate, neither hindering the other. Nevertheless, the granting of votes to women was a historic political event, and moreover had ranked ahead of home rule in Hayden's aspirations. But sociological and feminist subjects were peripheral to what has been described as 'the primacy of writing the political history of the new state'.[33] In order to provide the desired new textbook, Hayden conformed to the contemporary academic convention.

Her articles on women in Ancient Ireland and in the Middle Ages were relatively positive about the role of women in those periods, an interpretation influenced as we have seen by the Irish literary revival. Since the late seventeenth century, as she saw it,[34] women's importance in society had greatly diminished to the subordinate situation which she herself had found so galling. However, in Hayden's lifetime women were not seen as relevant to political history. Hayden's feminism was a contemporary issue, signifying the modern emancipation of women. Prudence undoubtedly advised the omission of such subjects, still minority interests, from the narrative. Nor did Professor Mary Donovan O'Sullivan in UCG, a suffragist, allow feminist issues to figure in her historical writing. Some twenty years earlier Alice Stopford Green, pondering on women as writers, had noted how they contrived to adapt and assimilate, and their distrust of originality; the woman writer, she judged, was 'rarely self-forgetful enough for frank expression of her feeling'.[35] Others have noted that many early academic women, 'anxious to establish their credentials in a male-dominated university world, tended towards academic conservatism'.[36] In the *Short History*, Hayden's purpose was to present history as political development interpreted in a nationally acceptable form to a readership still considerably more male than female, or whose thinking was largely male inspired. In writing accessible history she was successful and virtually unrivalled, as the endurance of her book was to show.

The historian Mary O'Dowd considered the merit of the book to be 'that it synthesised, in a more conservative nationalist manner than the publications of Alice Stopford Green, the research on Irish history' completed in the nineteenth and early twentieth centuries. Though based on secondary sources, it was in O'Dowd's view a significant textbook which for several generations substantially influenced Irish people's knowledge of their history.[37] A later more detailed analysis of the *Short History* by Nadia Smith considers that Hayden's textbook, describing themes and events that were still controversial, nevertheless avoided some of the weaknesses attributed to nationalist historians by their critics. Smith's conclusion, that the book narrates a history 'that was acceptable in a post-revolutionary state whose legitimacy was questioned by more radical nationalists', is a judicious comment on a study written and published before the Treaty and the Civil War.[38]

An American critic in 1923 welcomed the book as a first attempt to treat Irish history in its Gaelic context and as an illuminating 'reflection of current thought in Ireland'. He found Irish history interpreted in this work as a conflict between civilizations and the authors remarkably free from prejudice. But the chief defect of the work in his view was the insufficient relation of English policy in Ireland to the European situation. Though sceptical about Moonan's use of sources and not impressed by the workmanlike English in which the book was written, this critic judged the work to be invaluable and progressive in its contemporary context.[39] In the *Irish Independent*, M.R. wrote approvingly of the book, concluding with the comment that it is 'the best and most complete view we have got so far of the history of our country and of the forces that shaped its destiny'.[40] Another reviewer, historian and nationalist Helena Concannon, was more inclined to damn with faint praise, stressing that the work was a textbook. As a closing shot she wrote that Hayden 'has performed the remarkable *tour de force* of writing an up to date' Irish history without mentioning the names of President Griffith or ex-President de Valera, 'and never once includes the words Dáil Éireann'.[41] This review, no less than the book on which it is a comment, must be read in the context of the contemporary Irish political scene. The omissions were rectified in later editions when the work was extended to 1924, as recorded in an obituary note in *Irish Historical Studies*, probably written by R. Dudley Edwards, which referred to Hayden's high degree of objectivity in the original book, and continued that in subsequent editions 'her strong personal feelings on more recent events somewhat obtruded into her narrative'.[42] *Irish Historical Studies*, of which Edwards was joint founding editor, initially precluded publication in that journal of articles referring to Irish politics after 1900.[43] In fact the dissatisfaction of de Valera and his supporters with their treatment by established historians was to result in the encouragement of Dorothy Macardle to write *The Irish Republic*, published in 1937.[44]

Hayden's preference for political action of a non-militant nature emerged at times in her historical writing. She saw Grattan's parliament despite its faults, as a beneficial institution which encouraged industry and trade, with the potential to attract widespread loyalty had it become more representative, particularly of the Catholic landowners and professional classes.[45] In 1922 when reviewing Robert Dunlop's *Ireland from the Earliest Times*, though 'few of our national heroes' received justice, she was pleased to find appreciation of Daniel O'Connell; she advised contemporary young politicians to note the achievements of O'Connell which were currently belittled 'and his political doctrines sneered at'.[46] Two years later she published an article 'History to be Unlearned: A Rapid Survey of the Storm and Stress of a Thousand Years', which read like a brief summary of the *Short History*. Towards the end of the article she wrote of the historic

London treaty of 1921 'with its sorrowful aftermath of domestic woe, due to the impetuous pursuit of ideals'. Concluding by commending Thomas Davis and Arthur Griffith and stressing the need for law and order, she stated her abhorrence of violence, 'no matter how transitory'.[47]

In 1923 Hayden reviewed books by two contemporary historians, Constantia Maxwell and Edmund Curtis, which she estimated as significant works, but in each case with a *caveat* – that Maxwell used insufficient Irish sources and was deficient in her understanding of the native aspect of her subject, and that Curtis had not done justice to the Irish church at the time of the Norman invasion. In both instances Hayden's own awareness of the relevance of native Irish heritage was obvious.[48] (However Maxwell's book quickly became a recommended textbook for Hayden's students). Her appreciation of the importance and the variety of original sources was shown also when she reviewed Helena Concannon's *The Poor Clares in Ireland,* noting that the author had had access to many enlightening documents preserved in convent archives.[49]

Though she had once complained about obscure legal documents which she found unattractive for their lack of human interest, she wrote in the 1920s on 'The Origin and Development of Heads of Bills in the Irish Parliament'. She traced modifications to Poynings' Law from 1570 onwards to allow for initiation of legislation in the Irish Parliament,[50] an expansion of her treatment of the subject in the *Short History.*[51] Though parts of her interpretation were subsequently described by Moody and Edwards as mistaken, confused and misleading,[52] this article was selected by them for mention in the *Irish Historical Studies* obituary where none but the last of her publications on women and children is listed.

Not in the modern sense a researcher of original material, Hayden depended largely on a wide reading of secondary sources. She had had no training in historical research methods. Her postgraduate studies had been in literature and language. Were it not for her failure to gain the Royal University senior fellowship in English, she might not have turned to History as a subject to teach, although her interest was also aroused by the Celtic revival and her growing appreciation of Irish nationalism. The early years of her professorship (1911–1918) were also the most vigorous years of the suffrage campaign. Her teaching and governing role in the University, and the commencement of writing the *Short History* (originally scheduled for publication in 1917) afforded little opportunity to seek and study original source material. Moreover, the statutory duties of UCD professors favoured teaching ahead of research.[53] As a later President recorded, 'the College was understaffed, and teaching was the prime necessity'.[54]

The new approach to 'the advancement of Irish historical learning on scientific principles' launched in the first issue of the journal *Irish Historical Studies* (1938–9)[55] came too late to influence Hayden, who was then aged seventy-six and retiring from her professorship. Continuing to publish book reviews on historical subjects until 1940, she wrote in her customary descriptive manner, not attempting to conform to the new scientific standards adopted by younger scholars.[56] Nevertheless her assistance in the establishment of *Irish Historical Studies* has been acknowledged by the joint editor, R. Dudley Edwards.[57] In her foreword to Edwards's *Church and State in Tudor Ireland* (1935), Hayden had praised the author as unprejudiced, cautious and painstaking in his treatment of evidence; while disagreeing with him in some minor matters, she observed that history is not an exact science, 'and each man is justified, within limits, in forming his own opinions regarding its problems'. Writing that 'modern research has begun to clear away' many misconceptions which formerly clouded the Reformation period in Ireland, she acknowledged the significance of the methods of the new scholars.[58] Edwards has recorded that his lecturers in UCD had had little connection with historical research and had advised him to consult Edmund Curtis of TCD about a research topic.[59] Writing in 1958 T.W. Moody, the other joint founding editor of the journal, included the name of Mary Hayden in his list of seven whom he described as the pioneers of 'that renaissance of Irish history' in which the journal played a worthy part, acknowledging also that these 'scholars worked largely in isolation'.[60] Hayden would again recognise the transition to scientific history when in 1939 she reviewed Moody's book, *The Londonderry Plantation: 1609–41*,[61] where she noted his pioneering work on previously untapped sources and his 'conclusions in conflict with previously held views' – her acknowledgement of the scientific approach to historical research adopted by younger scholars. But in this generally laudatory review she disagreed with Moody on several points, notably his description of Hugh O'Neill and his adherents as 'rebels'. This was a recurring argument for Hayden who repeatedly came to the defence of both Shane O'Neill and Hugh O'Neill. The previous year, in the first issue of *Irish Historical Studies*, in a review of G.A. Hayes McCoy's *Scots Mercenary Forces in Ireland* Hayden had disagreed with the author on Hugh O'Neill as a mere local dynast; in Hayden's perception O'Neill had his sights on a unified Ireland controlled by a 'native government', a view probably not shared by the younger scholars. Traditional and nationalist in her approach to historical writing, she had not lost her sharpness, and while genuinely admiring the output of the more modern writers she felt no awe about their work which she was prepared to question on particular details.

When finally retired from university teaching Hayden did not abandon her subject but continued to write. Her style of reviewing in general had always been to describe the contents of the book, usually though not always, commend the author, and then to take issue on points in the treatment with which she did not agree. The subjects of two books reviewed in 1939 and 1940, *Irish Life in the Seventeenth Century after Cromwell* by Edward MacLysaght and *County and Town in Ireland Under the Georges* by Constantia Maxwell,[62] were themes which had always had an appeal for Hayden since her own early publications on women and children. In Hayden's estimation Maxwell's concentration on the gentry though interesting was not balanced by equal attention to the lives of the poor. Hayden's concluding comments on the enormous difference between the lives of the rich and of the poor then considered 'inevitable' imply her own belief in the possibility of modern reform in social and economic conditions.

Most of Hayden's book reviews throughout her professorship were published in the Jesuit journal, *Studies*, the successor to *Lyceum* and the *New Ireland Review*, and which contained the work of many UCD academics. However Hayden had two reviews published in early issues of the new, more specialised journal *Irish Historical Studies*, the first on the book by Hayes McCoy referred to and the second on G.M. Trevelyan's *The English Revolution 1688–89*.[63] This latter book she described as less concerned with facts than with inferences and explanations, with some of which she then disagreed. She devoted more attention and criticism to the author's eighteen pages on Ireland which seemed to be based on unsatisfactory secondary sources, but she did approve of his 'admirable' paragraph on the results of the penal laws, where his conclusion, that the intention to preserve the English settlement from fear of a French invasion was achieved, 'but at what a cost to the future relations of the English and the Irish peoples', corresponded to her own, derived in some degree at least from her reading of Lecky.

Hayden's approach to historical subjects had not altered to any extent since publication of her own textbook, but she had kept abreast of later works which she judged according to her own standards, one of which was a book's value for students and other readers. The new journal called for co-operation between the historian and the teacher, and aimed to be of service to the specialist, the teacher and the general reader with an intelligent interest in the subject,[64] and, as has been pointed out, the women professors had by their teaching and writing of textbooks conformed to these aims.[65] Hayden showed no sign of being tired of her subject in the closing years of her life. Her final piece of historical work was the posthumously published article 'Charity Children in 18th Century Dublin'.[66] The subject was the type of social history which had often engaged her attention and which in earlier years must have contributed to the corpus of her feminist thinking.

The University Teacher

Hayden's strength was as a teacher of a subject in which popular interest was increasing. A student in the early 1930s recalled her as an effective and competent teacher, and in true teacherly fashion was very particular about practicalities like spelling.[67] She has been described by former students of the 1920s and 1930s as formidable, alert, dominant, with the top floor theatre in Earlsfort Terrace crowded for her lectures.[68] By all accounts Hayden was an accomplished public speaker, clear, witty and incisive, who responded to an appreciative audience[69] and who had no difficulty in presiding over a student debate at the Literary and Historical Society.[70] Debating experience for her had commenced in Alexandra College in the late 1880s.

By the time of her university appointment she was well practised in the skills of both teaching and public speaking. Her great mentor Isabella Mulvany wrote, in support of Hayden's appointment, that to 'her wide knowledge there is added a vivacity and a strong human interest which constitute her a brilliant and eminently successful lecturer'.[71] Some of her most famous students include her UCD successor, R. Dudley Edwards, and the Professor of History in UCC, James Hogan.

Some lecture notes suggest that she spoke to first year honours classes about the use and misuse of sources, and on how to approach examination questions.[72] Her courses ranged from 1485 to 1870. Among recommended textbooks, Alice Stopford Green's *The Making of Ireland and its Undoing*; P.W. Joyce's *A Short History of Ireland*, and W.E.H. Lecky's *History of Ireland in the Eighteenth Century* were constants and, when published, her own *A Short History of the Irish People* and Constantia Maxwell's *Irish History from Contemporary Sources 1589–1610*. Undated press cuttings (in Hayden's papers) of a series of lectures by Charles Oldham on Irish economic history from Grattan's parliament to the end of the nineteenth century suggest him as a useful source for her lectures and her textbook.[73] The syllabus regularly included a special study of the History of the Irish Parliament from 1692 to 1800, and recommendations to read the speeches of Grattan and Curran and *The Last Independent Parliament of Ireland* by George Sigerson. Honours students heard three lectures a week on Irish History, evidently all given by her as there were no other staff. There were also lectures to first year and evening students, amounting to a demanding, wide-ranging teaching programme, and in 1927 she was listed to lecture in a Holiday Course for Foreign Students.[74] As well as day courses, she was still giving two evening lectures a week in session 1932–33.[75] But there was little postgraduate research; only three MAs were awarded in

Modern Irish History during Hayden's professorship. However the record for Master's degrees was no better in either Modern History or Early Irish History, where the Professors, O'Sullivan and MacNeill, had political pre-occupations during the 1920s.[76]

Hayden's appearance was remembered by one student as a 'stocky figure' with 'stocky legs' who mostly wore tweed, without ornament, and by another student as low sized, wearing a plain black jacket which suited her air of efficiency.[77] Her colleague, Mary Macken, described Hayden's short stamping step, her Gladstone bag, short skirts with her father's gold Albert and chain tucked into the waist line.[78] Hanna Sheehy Skeffington recalled that Hayden was one of the first to adopt short hair and tailored costumes, a pioneer in small as in great things.[79] Hayden's short hair is frequently mentioned and there are differing views as to the origin of her nickname among students of her later years – the hairy maiden – whether it referred to her lack of long hair, a suggestion of facial hair, a play on her name, or possibly a combination of all three. Her unadorned no-nonsense suits might be viewed as an early form of late twentieth century power dressing. For instance, Ruth Dudley Edwards, writing of the Gaelic League women such as Hayden, has suggested their unfeminine dress and manner may have been 'an attempt to be taken seriously in a man's world'.[80] A 1906 photograph of the Alexandra Guild shows Hayden the only member without a hat, attired more severely than the other women.[81] Tales survive of her carrying a kettle around to make tea, and of her frying sausages on the open fire in her room on the top corridor at Earlsfort Terrace.[82] The room was furnished as 'a Victorian sitting room with curtains on the windows, a fire in the grate, and a little table with a plush cover and an aspidistra on it'.[83]

Always a strong believer in the value of education for citizenship, particularly for girls whose education in many instances was deficient, she took an interest in students outside of the classroom. Like her colleague O'Farrelly, who founded the Camogie Club (women's hurling) in 1914, Hayden supported the Women Students' Swimming Club, her own swimming evidently continuing well into her old age.[84] She regularly spoke to the new women graduates to encourage them to join the Women Graduates' Association. A graduate of the late 1920s remembered vividly Hayden emphasising the significance of their university education for its broadening of their minds and for their subsequent lives, no matter what their occupation, even in the most essential of tasks such as 'scrubbing a table'.[85] A similar comment had been made in 1911 in an article entitled 'Home Arts' by Margaret A. Gilliland who wanted women to be 'imbued with a deep sense of the worth and dignity of all true work, whether it be scrubbing a floor or construing a crabbed Greek chorus'.[86] The same graduate recalled of Hayden that without shouting about it she was conscious of women's equality with men and felt that they must be so accepted. Hayden's advice to women graduates was not far from the view of Louie Bennett that women should take a more positive attitude to their role within the home 'as a vocation and a social service'.[87]

Social Work

As President of the Dominican College past pupils union since its establishment in 1914, Hayden characteristically had a keen interest in the Union's club for working girls, St Dominic's, though her view that the club should cater also for boys was not accepted.[88] This particular issue was aired by her on occasions as far back as 1915; at the 1937 Alexandra Guild conference she strongly advocated mixed clubs where young people could meet more suitably than in 'dark streets and country roads'.[89] Again in 1939, in a letter to the *Irish Press* on the subject of parish councils, she called for sociable recreation halls where the young of both sexes could meet, under supervision, as an alternative to the 'cheap dance hall'.[90]

However, the social club most directly associated with her name was St Joan's, which she established in UCD and in which women staff and students joined her in caring for working girls and poor children, with food, clothing, entertainment and education; prayers and catechism were taught, and plays were written for the children to act. Hayden's earliest participation as a young woman in social work had been to teach a regular catechism class for poor children, though she had doubts about its value; then she had progressed to visiting and clothing work among the Dublin poor. It was a natural development with her experience of the social work of both the Alexandra Guild and the Dominican past pupils union that she should organise a social commitment to the city on the part of the relatively privileged women in UCD. The club's special events were occasionally noted briefly in the newspapers; at the club's annual display in 1937 there were dancing, songs and sketches, and prizes presented by the Lord Mayor who paid tribute to Hayden and others.[91] Her commitment to social work was marked at her funeral in University Church by the attendance of children from the club with their mothers.[92] Another example of the engagement of academic women with social work in the community was that of Mary Macken in the foundation of the Infant Aid Society.[93] This society, which assisted Dublin Corporation in the organisation of a scheme for the distribution of milk for infants and mothers, worked in co-operation with the Baby Clubs of the Women's National Health Association of Ireland established in 1907 by Lady Aberdeen, wife of the Viceroy. The aims of the WNHAI were to promote hygiene and sanitary improvement, to counter tuberculosis and infant mortality, and to benefit the health of the population at large.[94] The Infant Aid Society was still functioning into the 1950s.

Starting from a background of relative privilege where the concerned woman might dispense charity in various forms to those in need, Hayden had moved towards belief in self-help and self-advancement through education, training and encouragement as the means of escape from poverty and disadvantage. Such thinking was an element of her wider political beliefs that the advancement of woman's role in the community depended upon woman herself having and using her own political voice.

Conscious of the wretched conditions in which many working-class women were employed, Hayden encouraged the establishment of trade unions for their protection. Her belief in the value of union membership extended also to middle-class occupations, notably teaching, and while the Women Graduates' Association was not in the strict sense an association of employees, Hayden saw it as having some functions similar to those of a trade union in protecting and promoting the position of women in middle-class and professional employment, as outlined for instance in her address on becoming President of the Association in 1914.[95]

Beyond the practical questions of living and working conditions, Hayden gave some thought to the wider issue of social equity, as evidenced by her contribution to a discussion at the Alexandra Guild in 1921. Her suggestion of a state bounty at birth for every child, more than twenty years before children's allowances were introduced in Ireland, indicates her awareness of contemporary debate on provision for the needy. Financial support for lone mothers and children was under discussion throughout the 1920s and 1930s.[96] The Irish Women's Citizens and Local Government Association advocated payment of family allowances to mothers.[97] (The Irish Women's Suffrage and Local Government Association had replaced the word 'Suffrage' with 'Citizens' in its title in 1918). When family allowance was introduced in 1944, it was payable to fathers.[98] Hayden proposed also a minimum wage calculated in accordance with the skill of the worker, regardless of sex. James Connolly in 1915 had urged women to insist on minimum wages and war bonuses.[99] War bonuses had been another concern of Hayden's in her general demand for equality. She urged equal training and equal wages for boys and girls, but allowed for compensation of the employer at the expense of the female worker if deprived of her skill on her marriage.[100] While as an attempt to reconcile conflicting interests of employer and employee in the realm of equal pay and equal opportunity this suggestion was impractical and naive, her speech indicates an awakening recognition of the need for a fundamentally altered approach to issues of social justice.

Women's Rights

Nevertheless, the main thrust of Hayden's feminist views for the rest of her life was directed towards civil rights, education and employment, subjects of direct concern to the middle class despite the lack of interest of many. And if rights and freedoms had to be won for middle-class women, so too must the welfare of working-class women be a feminist responsibility. Hayden's concerns here echoed the views of earlier feminists such as Isabella Tod who stressed 'the ability of the middle classes to help those less fortunate than themselves'.[101] Moreover, the exercise of moral power by middle- and upper-class women could identify a social and political role for themselves in Irish society.[102] When educated women of the upper classes made demands on behalf of working women, a successful outcome 'gave the former authority over the latter and a high political profile'.[103]

By her very nature as an authoritative figure, a teacher with a pioneering disposition, Hayden comes into the category of the former. Her high political profile was an asset to the feminist causes she was involved in, but in the 1920s and 1930s the immediate benefits achieved for ordinary women were small. Furthermore Hayden's single status which escaped the cares, chores and distractions of a married woman's life placed her, she felt, apart in a more elevated role. While she stressed the importance of woman's role in the home, her own avoidance of that role exhibited the then conventional attitude which ranked her occupation, one more generally fulfilled by men, as more significant in the hierarchy of work.

Independent minded since her childhood, she remained unconventional throughout her life, but her unorthodoxy did not include what she regarded as impropriety. Writing to Mother Patrick in 1905, she complained of a former Dominican girl 'gossiping for ever so long with usually about half a dozen young men' outside the National Library.[104] Some years earlier she had found a theatrical performance of *The Gay Parisienne* 'so improper, so vulgar and so dull'.[105] Her readiness to challenge society's constraints on what women might do did not extend to moral behaviour, about which she had always been somewhat strait-laced. As a younger woman she had wished that the Crean girls were not 'so fond of risqué topics ... the question of sex is not the only thing in the world surely'.[106] But she could be courageously forthright. When a fracas developed between organised groups of students and a parade of ex-servicemen on Armistice Day 1925 on Earlsfort Terrace, Hayden emerged on the steps to reprimand the students as 'themselves imperialists' and was undeterred by their hostile reaction. This incident is recounted by Mervyn Wall who recalled her as an 'old woman in her academic gown'.[107]

Hayden was then aged sixty-three and held her professorship for another twelve years, years of notable public activity for her in opposition to legislation affecting the lives of women. The Irish Free State was proving unsympathetic to feminist expectations, and by the mid-1920s Hayden was quite prominently involved in increasing opposition to the government's disregard for the citizenship accorded to women in its own Constitution. Moreover, her concept of feminism now envisaged an autonomous role in society for women, where discrimination should have no place.

NOTES

1   T.D. Williams, 'The College and the Nation' in Michael Tierney (ed.), *Struggle with Fortune* (Dublin, 1954), p. 185.

2   *The National Student,* June 1935, p. 67.

3   Mary Hayden and G.A. Moonan, *A Short History of the Irish People* (Dublin, 1927), p. 545.

4   J.J. Hogan, 'The Work of Dr Coffey and Dr Conway 1908–1947' in Tierney, *op cit*, p. 92.

5   UCD Governing Body Minutes, 13 October, 3 November 1925.

6   UCD Statute XIV.

7   All noted in *Irish Independent,* April 1928. This newspaper cost 1 penny per day.

8   Margaret Ó hÓgartaigh, 'Dorothy Price and the Elimination of Childhood Tuberculosis in Ireland' in Joost Augusteijn (ed.), *Ireland in the 1930s* (Dublin, 1999), p. 71.

9   Monica Nevin, 'The 1930s' in Anne Macdona (ed.), *From Newman to New Woman: UCD Women Remember* (Dublin, 2001), p. 12; Peig Roche, 'Coffee, Cream Buns and Civil War', *ibid,* p. 35.

10   UCD Governing Body Minutes, 30 November 1926, 20 March 1928 and 8 May 1928.

11   UCD Governing Body Minutes, 29 March 1927, 10 May 1927.

12   M.T. Hayden, 'Lambert Simnel in Ireland', *Studies,* iv, (December 1915), pp 623–38.

13   Steven Ellis 'Nationalist Historiography and the English and Gaelic Worlds in the Late Middle Ages' in Ciaran Brady (ed.), *Interpreting Irish History: The Debate on Historical Revisionism* (Dublin, 1994), p. 178.

14 Mary Hayden, 'Prince Charles Edward and his Irish Friends', *Studies,* xxiii (March 1934), pp 95–109.

15 Mary Hayden, 'Giraldus Cambrensis', *Studies,* xxiv (March 1935), pp 99–110.

16 Mary Hayden MA, 'Women in Ancient Ireland', *The Catholic Citizen,* Vol. VI, No. 11, 15 November 1920.

17 Mary Hayden, 'Dublin Workhouse Children in the Eighteenth Century', *Alexandra College Magazine* (December 1928), pp 16–19.

18 Mary Hayden MA, D.Litt., 'Charity Children in 18th Century Dublin', *Dublin Historical Record,* V (1942–3), pp 92–107.

19 I am grateful to Maria Luddy for this information. And see Nadia Clare Smith, *A 'Manly Study'? Irish Women Historians, 1868–1949* (Basingstoke, 2006), p. 68.

20 David Fitzpatrick 'The Futility of History: A Failed Experiment in Irish Education' in C. Brady (ed.), *Ideology and the Historian* (Historical Studies XVII, Conference of Irish Historians, 1989), pp 181–82.

21 Hayden, 'Charity Children', *op cit,* p. 100.

22 Educational Company of Ireland to Hayden, 1 December 1921, NAI, Talbot Press Papers, 1048/1/69.

23 Edmund Curtis, *A History of Ireland* (London, 1942), p. 413.

24 *Irish Historical Studies,* Vol. III, September 1943, p. 39.

25 Roy Foster, 'History and the Irish Question' in Brady, *Interpreting Irish History,* p. 141.

26 J. Lee, *Ireland 1912–1985* (Cambridge, 1989), p. 589.

27 R.F. Foster, *Modern Ireland 1600–1972* (London, 1989), p. 518.

28 Donal McCartney, *W.E.H. Lecky: Historian and Politician 1838–1903* (Dublin, 1994), pp 77, 115.

29 Mary O'Dowd, 'From Morgan to Mac Curtain: Women Historians in Ireland from the 1790s to the 1990s' in Valiulis and O'Dowd (eds), *Women and Irish History* (Dublin, 1997), p. 52. Conversation with Donal McCartney, 23 July 2003.

30 Hayden and Moonan, *Short History,* pp 496–498.

31 M.T.H. reviews of '*The Story of the Irish Nation* by Francis Hackett', *Studies,* xiii, No. 3 (September 1924), pp 492–94, and '*The History of Ireland* by Stephen Gwynn', *Studies,* xiii, No. 1 (March 1924), pp 161–63. For the proposed British Government veto on the appointment of Irish bishops, see Daire Keogh, *The French Disease: The Catholic Church and Radicalism in Ireland 1790–1800* (Dublin, 1993), pp 209–13.

32 M.T.H., Review of *A History of Ireland and her People to the Close of the Tudor Period* by Eleanor Hull, *Studies*, June 1927, pp 341–344.

33 O'Dowd, *op cit*, p. 57.

34 Mary Hayden, 'Women and the New Constitution', *Cork Examiner*, 29 June 1937.

35 Alice Stopford Green, *Woman's Place in the World of Letters* (1897) (reprinted as pamphlet, London, 1913), p. 10.

36 Carol Dyhouse, *No Distinction of Sex? Women in British universities 1870–1939* (London, 1995), p. 145.

37 O'Dowd, *op cit*, p. 52.

38 Smith, *A 'Manly Study'?*, pp 70–75.

39 Norreys Jephson O'Conor, *Changing Ireland: Literary Background of the Irish Free State 1889–1922* (Cambridge, 1924), pp 240–245.

40 *Irish Independent*, 5 December 1921.

41 Helena Concannon, Review of Hayden and Moonan, *A Short History of the Irish People, Studies*, XI (March 1922), pp 143.

42 *Irish Historical Studies*, iii (September 1943), p. 402.

43 Ronan Fanning 'The Great Enchantment: Uses and Abuses of Modern Irish History' in Brady, *Interpreting Irish History*, p. 149.

44 Eunan O'Halpin, 'Historical Revisit: Dorothy Macardle *The Irish Republic* (1937)', *Irish Historical Studies*, xxi (May 1999), p. 390.

45 Hayden and Moonan, *Short History*, pp 406–22.

46 M.T.H. Review of Robert Dunlop, *Ireland from the Earliest Times, Studies*, xi (December 1922), pp 642–44.

47 Mary T. Hayden, 'History to be Unlearned' in William G. Fitzgerald (ed.), *The Voice of Ireland: A Survey of the Race and Nation from all Angles, by the Foremost Leaders at Home and Abroad* (Dublin, 1924), p. 56.

48 Constantia Maxwell, *Irish History from Contemporary Sources 1509–1610*, review by Mary Hayden, *Studies*, xii No. 3 (September 1923), pp 507–09. Edmund Curtis, *A History of Medieval Ireland 1110 to 1513*, Review by Mary Hayden, *Studies*, xii, No. 4 (December 1923), pp 668–71.

49 M.T.H., Review of 'The Poor Clares in Ireland by Mrs Thomas Concannon MA', *Studies*, xviii, No. 72 (March 1929), p. 170.

50 Mary T. Hayden, 'The Origin and Development of Heads of Bills in the Irish Parliament', *Royal Society of Antiquaries of Ireland Journal*, LV (1925), pp 112–125.

51 Hayden and Moonan, *Short History*, pp 376–77.

52 T.W. Moody, 'The Irish Parliament under Elizabeth and James', *Proc. RIA*, xlv, Sect. c (1939), p. 69, footnote; R. Dudley Edwards,

T.W. Moody, 'The History of Poynings' Law 1494–1615', *Irish Historical Studies*, Vol. ii, No. 8 (1941), p. 423 footnote.

53 Donal McCartney, *UCD A National Idea* (Dublin, 1999), p. 64.

54 J.J. Hogan, 'The Work of Dr Coffey' in Tierney, *op cit*, p. 97.

55 T.W. Moody and R.D. Edwards, 'Preface', *Irish Historical Studies* 1938–39, rep. in Brady (ed.), *Interpreting Irish History*, pp 35–37.

56 O'Dowd, 'From Morgan to Mac Curtain', p. 53.

57 R.D. Edwards, 'An Agenda', p. 57.

58 Foreword by Professor Mary Hayden M.A. in R.D. Edwards, *Church and State in Tudor Ireland* (London, 1935), pp vii–x.

59 R. Dudley Edwards, 'T.W. Moody and the Origins of *Irish Historical Studies*', *Irish Historical Studies*, xxvi, No. 101 (May 1988), p. 1.

60 T.W. Moody, 'Twenty Years After', *Irish Historical Studies*, xi, No. 41 (March 1958), p. 1.

61 M.T.H., Review of *The Londonderry Plantation 1609–41*, by T.W. Moody, *Studies*, xxviii (September 1939), pp 517–19.

62 M.T.H, Review of *Irish Life in the Seventeenth Century After Cromwell* by Edward MacLysaght, *Studies*, xxviii, No. 112 (December 1939), pp 679–83; M.T.H. Review of *Country and Town in Ireland Under the Georges* by Constantia Maxwell, *Studies*, xxix, No. 116 (December 1940), pp 639–43.

63 Mary Hayden, Review of *Scots Mercenary Forces in Ireland (1565–1603)* by G.A. Hayes McCoy, *Irish Historical Studies*, I, No. 1 (March 1938), pp 86–88; Mary Hayden, Review of *The English Revolution 1688–89* by George MacCaulay Trevelyan, *Irish Historical Studies*, I, No. 4 (September 1939), pp 426–29.

64 *Irish Historical Studies*, Preface, 1, No. 1 (March 1938), pp 1–3.

65 Mary O'Dowd, 'From Morgan to Mac Curtain', p. 53.

66 Mary Hayden, 'Charity Children', pp 92–107.

67 Monica Nevin, conversation with author, 30 March 2000.

68 Monica Nevin, conversation with author, 30 March 2000. Marjorie Quinn, conversation with author, 25 October 2000.

69 Mary Macken, 'In Memoriam Mary T. Hayden', *Studies*, xxxi, No. 123 (September 1942), pp 369–71.

70 John Mowbray, 'The Old Society 1916–23' in James Meenan (ed.), *Centenary History of the Literary and Historical Society of University College Dublin 1855–1955* (Dublin, 2005, 2nd ed.), p. 146.

71 Isabella Mulvany testimonial in Hayden's application to the Dublin Commissioners, NUI Archives.

72 Mary Hayden Papers, NLI, Ms 24007 (1).

73 Mary Hayden Papers, NLI, Ms 23403 (5).
74 UCD Governing Body Minutes, 29 May 1927.
75 UCD Governing Body Minutes, 21 November 1933.
76 Donal McCartney, *UCD A National Idea: The History of University College Dublin* (Dublin, 1999), p. 70.
77 Monica Nevin and Marjorie Quinn, conversations with author.
78 Mary Macken, 'Women in the University and the College' in Tierney, *Struggle with Fortune*, p. 144.
79 'Appreciation' by Mrs H. S. Skeffington, press cutting included in NUWGA Minute Book 1942, UCD Archives, NUWGA 2/21.
80 Ruth Dudley Edwards, *Patrick Pearse: The Triumph of Failure* (London, 1979, 2nd ed.), p. 55.
81 O'Connor and Parkes, *Gladly Learn and Gladly Teach* (Dublin, 1984), p. 68.
82 The latter told to author by Paddy Keogh, longtime head porter in UCD.
83 Mary Semple, 'Going Hatching' in Macdona, *op cit*, p. 13.
84 Mary Macken, 'Women in the University', p. 147; Hayden to Edwards, 16 September (1936?) UCD Archives LA/22/129 (5).
85 Marjorie Quinn, conversation with author, 25 October 2000.
86 Dale Spender (ed.), *The Education Papers: Women's Quest for Equality in Britain, 1850–1912* (London, 1987), p. 316.
87 Cullen Owens, *Louie Bennett*, p. 106.
88 'A Tribute to Professor Mary Hayden, D.Litt.', *The Lanthorn: Yearbook of the Dominican College, Eccles Street, Dublin,* 1942, p. 351.
89 *Irish Times,* 26 April 1937.
90 *Irish Press,* 15 November 1939.
91 *Irish Press,* 12 July 1937.
92 Mary Macken, 'In Memoriam: Mary T. Hayden', p. 371.
93 *Report of the President UCD 1949–50,* p. 41.
94 The Marchioness of Aberdeen and Temair [Lady Aberdeen] 'Health and Happiness in the Homes of Ireland' in FitzGerald, *The Voice of Ireland,* pp 438–39.
95 Minutes, 20 March 1914, UCD Archives, NUWGA 2/2.
96 Caitríona Clear, *Women of the House: Women's Household Work in Ireland 1922–1961* (Dublin, 2000), p. 51.
97 Caitriona Beaumont, 'Women and the Politics of Equality' in Valiulis and O'Dowd, p. 176.
98 Clear, *Women of the House,* pp 52–56.
99 Margaret Ward, *Unmanageable Revolutionaries: Women and Irish Nationalism* (London, 1995), p. 253.

100 *Alexandra College Magazine,* June 1921, p. 20.

101 Maria Luddy, 'Isabella M.S. Tod (1836–1896)' in Mary Cullen and Maria Luddy (eds), *Women, Power and Consciousness in 19th Century Ireland* (Dublin, 1995), pp 205–6.

102 Maria Luddy, *Women and Philanthropy in Nineteenth-Century Ireland* (Cambridge, 1995), p. 8.

103 Caitríona Clear, 'The Women Can Not be blamed: The Commission on Vocational Organisation, Feminism and Homemakers in Independent Ireland in the 1930s and 1940s' in Mary O'Dowd and Sabine Wichert (eds), *Chattel, Servant or Citizen* (Belfast, 1995), p. 184.

104 Quoted by E. Breathnach, 'A History of the Movement for Women's Higher Education in Dublin 1860–1912' MA thesis, UCD, 1981, p. 130, cited in McCartney, *UCD,* p. 77.

105 Hayden Diary, 17 November 1897.

106 Hayden Diary, 5 March 1899.

107 Mervyn Wall, 'New Beginnings 1922–30' in Meenan, *Centenary History,* pp 178–79.

IX

THE ACTIVE FEMINIST
1922–35

In the new Irish Free State, despite the achievement of the
parliamentary franchise, women experienced restrictions
affecting their employment and career prospects, their
right to sit on juries, and in general a denial of the wide
equality guaranteed to them in the Constitution. Hayden
was one of the minority of women who protested at these
measures, seeing them as the expression of a reactionary
and paternalist attitude to women by the new and very
conservative State. This attitude did not change with the
change of government in 1932.

Political Environment
Party politics had never held particular interest for
Hayden. Her sympathies lay with the Irish Parliamentary
Party and their expectation of Home Rule, but she was by
no means an uncritical supporter of the Irish MPs. Despite
long-time friendship with people like Patrick Pearse, Eoin
MacNeill and Agnes O'Farrelly, Hayden had not identified

with their separatist ambitions; but, as during the suffrage campaign, her sympathetic understanding extended to individuals with whose actions she might not agree. Her sympathy expressed to Pearse's mother, Margaret, after his execution has been noted, and in later years she wrote of him as 'a young schoolmaster of great literary talent'.[1] In the case of Eoin MacNeill she had co-operated in keeping the chair vacant while he was imprisoned. Hayden was one of many who sent appeals to the British authorities to seek reprieve of the death sentence on Kevin Barry, a medical student arrested for participation in an IRA ambush in 1920.[2]

Rejoicing in the achievement of the parliamentary franchise for women in 1918, Hayden when casting her vote remained loyal to the Irish Party. In 1919 she was one of the signatories to the launch of the Irish Dominion League led by Sir Horace Plunkett to advocate 'self government for Ireland within the Empire'. Other prominent members included Stephen Gwynn, Mary Kettle, Viscount Gormanston, the Earl of Fingall and Colonel R. Pope Hennessy.[3] The League aimed for the support of middle-class Ireland for a dominion settlement to include Ulster, as a moderate alternative to both unionism and extreme nationalism,[4] but it had little impact. Hayden's association with an organisation like this may have made her suspect in later years, although the League, having dissolved itself in November 1921, was in December to claim the Treaty as 'the most conspicuous vindication of the Irish Dominion League'.[5] Hayden's instincts were for a measured approach, as in the Irish Dominion League, or the 1913 Industrial Peace Committee, or the 1907 proposal for a modest devolution of government powers. Now, in the latter years of the second decade, she was writing her nationalist history of Ireland.

Hayden never had any objection to an association with Britain. A tendency identified by Senia Pašeta for educated

Irish nationalists to become entwined in a British middle-class culture of respectability, professional advancement and social refinement,[6] might in some degree apply to Hayden while not discounting her commitment to her native language, history and heritage. Her constitutional convictions and objection to militant methods placed her in the majority favouring the 1921 Treaty which she considered offered more than any Home Rule Bill.[7] A weakening of the connection with Britain had not been of major concern to her; what was important in political terms was that Irish affairs should be governed by an Irish parliament. The new independent State was quite acceptable, offering, as she and others had hoped, prospects for development in civil, social, educational and economic affairs, the new parliament representing its people, as she wrote, 'in a far broader and truer sense than the old Parliament which the Union destroyed ever did'.[8] Hayden's optimism about the Irish Free State hoped for a more radical approach than either the government or the population were prepared for. Even for Hayden herself the sentiment was somewhat visionary. She was in essence a realistic pragmatist.

Following the republican rejection of the Treaty and withdrawal from the Dáil (1922), the country was drifting into civil war. The anti-Treaty Irregulars had occupied the Four Courts in Dublin, which they intended to destroy as they vacated it. Efforts were made to save the material held in the Public Record Office located there. Eoin MacNeill, then Minister for Education, went to the building to plead for the preservation of the records.[9] Thomas Morrissey, an Assistant Keeper of the PRO (and later Secretary of the Department of Education) was another who expressed his concern and sought to remove the records to safety; his daughter understood that he was accompanied on his mission by Mary Hayden and possibly also Eoin MacNeill.[10] The importance of these precious records was immense, but the building was mined and its contents 'lovingly accumulated by scholars were distributed in tiny fragments all over the city' as far as the Hill of Howth.[11] Another intermediary in the cause of the records had been Seamus Ó Ceallaigh, a medical practitioner and Gaelic scholar who was sympathetic to the republican position.[12] In Hayden's own words the loss of 'many documents which had never been transcribed' left 'Ireland for all future time the poorer'.[13] Yet again, as well as major concern for the preservation of the irreplaceable material is an instance of her belief in the value of dialogue with those with whose actions she did not agree, apart also from some courage in the face of possible physical danger.

The Irish state in the aftermath of the War of Independence and the Civil War was faced with major tasks in the restoration of law and order and in the maintenance of security in a population containing many still adhering to republican aspirations who disputed the very existence of the Irish Free State. It was a post-revolutionary as well as a post-colonial state, under threat, in its early years, of political or military anarchy.[14] Hayden was one who criticised the execution without trial of leaders of the anti-Treaty Irregulars; she considered that 'their lives were justly forfeit' but it was neither just nor wise for an established government to indulge in reprisals.[15] In economic terms the new government had to manage an impoverished country, cut off from the more industrialised northeast of the island, during a period of deepening world recession. Furthermore, repair of the material damage of the previous years and compensation costs placed an immense burden on the exchequer.[16] While the Treaty involved membership of the British Commonwealth and dominion status, the Irish Free State stressed that national sovereignty had been attained, for instance by joining the League of Nations as early as

1923.[17] Delays in the establishment of the Boundary Commission as provided in the Treaty, and in 1926 disappointment that the border remained unaltered were but one pre-occupation. The establishment of an unarmed police force and of an army loyal to the state were crucial achievements in the development of a stable society. The abandonment of abstention and the entry to the Dáil in 1927 of de Valera and his newly-formed Fianna Fáil party was a significant event in the establishment of parliamentary democracy, followed by the peaceful transfer of power in 1932 with the general election defeat of W.T. Cosgrave's Cumann na nGaedheal party who had been in government since independence. Such was the broad canvas of the early years of the Irish Free State, a canvas on which feminist issues occupied but small spaces in the view of the legislators and of the public in general. Stability and reconstruction were the goal, a pre-occupation which did not encompass radical thinking.

Women in the Free State

The 1920s and 1930s in Ireland were to prove disappointing to feminists. The idea of women having political power was unwelcome to those, both men and women, who viewed prominent suffragists, members of Cumann na mBan and women participants in 'the Troubles' of 1916–23 as unnatural, untypical of the generality of women. Though the opposition to the Treaty by six women members of the Dáil was not representative of feminists as a totality, it contributed to the distrust of women in political life in the succeeding years.

Successes in the university and franchise issues were optimistic auguries for women at the establishment of the new Irish State in 1922. In a 1920s paper read to the Women Graduates' Association, Hayden spoke of the three early feminists whom she greatly admired, Anna Haslam, Alice Oldham and Isabella Mulvany. Haslam had died in 1922 in her ninety-fourth year. Oldham and Mulvany had taught Hayden in Alexandra and in 1884 had been among the first women graduates of the Royal University. They became the first and second Presidents of the IAWGCG (Hayden being the third) and had been lifelong advocates of equality for women in education at secondary and university level. Hayden told her audience that her object was to explain by what labours the rights which they now tranquilly enjoyed had been won, and she concluded with a statement of the aims for women's opportunities in public life, education, employment and ownership of property.[18] These were middle-class aspirations, addressed to a middle-class audience.

The new Irish Free State adopted its Constitution in 1922. During the debates on the text, concern was expressed by some women about the position of women. A proposed statement in the draft that 'men and women have equal rights as citizens' was modified to 'men and women have equal political rights'. This provoked letters to the *Freeman's Journal* from Hayden and Hanna Sheehy Skeffington.[19] Hayden wrote of her 'indignant amazement' at the Dáil debate. The speeches were incongruous in an Irish Free State 'whose formation was as much facilitated – one might almost say was rendered possible – by the generous exertions and unflinching courage of Irish women'. She unhesitatingly acknowledged the efforts of republican and other women. Hayden pointed out that to confine the guarantee of women's equality to political matters only allowed for the introduction of limitations in other areas, which as she saw it, was intended by President Cosgrave who looked forward to the time when women would 'go out of' public life.[20] Dismissing as absurd the explanations by Kevin O'Higgins, Minister for Home Affairs, Hayden's concern was for equal citizenship and equal opportunity in public affairs and employment. She concluded with a reminder that sex equality was a plank of the Free State platform at the last election, and there could soon be another election. This was Hayden at her political best engaging head-on with the legislators of a government which in principle she supported. She was now concerned with party politics as the context in which the position of women had to be established and defended. She had become an incisive critic, discarding the irrelevancies of her opponents' arguments. Similarly, Hanna Sheehy Skeffington invoking the Proclamation of 1916, 'the Irish charter of liberty inspired by James Connolly',[21] called on women to make clear to the male legislators that they had no mandate to restrict women's rights of equal citizenship and equal opportunity.

In the end the disputed provision was omitted entirely. Women's position was provided for in Article 3 on citizenship and domicile, with the statement that:

> Every person, without distinction of sex ... is a citizen of the Irish Free State and shall ... enjoy the privileges and be subject to the obligations of such citizenship.

O'Higgins considered that political rights were obvious as women had the vote and the right to be elected, and any existing restrictions or qualifications could be repealed by law.[22] Hayden objected to the word 'privilege' instead of 'right'; as events were to show, several detrimental items of legislation affecting their equality would be passed during the lifetime of the Free State Constitution. In one instance a threat from women to challenge the constitutionality of an Act contributed to its non-implementation; but in others the Constitution did not prevent the imposition of measures to which feminists strenuously objected.

However, at the time, the inclusion of women in Article 3 which conferred the privileges and obligations of citizenship, without distinction of sex, was acceptable to the majority of women. The reduction of equal rights, first to equal political rights, and finally to the privileges and obligations of citizenship, applied equally to men and women, and the Free State Constitution was to be vehemently defended in 1937 by a concerted campaign of women objecting to the discriminatory provisions of de Valera's new Constitution.

Issues for Feminists

In the succeeding two decades feminists in Ireland appear in a more defensive role, resisting attempts to impose, or re-impose, restrictions on existing freedoms and rights. Though there was some small success in modifying these fresh impediments to their role in society, in general feminists were fighting a losing battle. The status of independent citizen bestowed by the Constitution was not seen in practice as meaning equal roles in society, as had been shown in the debate on the citizenship provision. The feminist protests were significant, despite their lack of success. The political divisions of the post-Treaty years fractured the women's movement, nor could it extend its appeal to any extent beyond its educated middle-class adherents in those years of economic deprivation and political insecurity. These feminists were radical in that their thinking was far-sighted, perceiving fundamental threats in the actions of the new State in regard to women, threats which were not apparent to the population as a whole in a State which was fundamentally conservative despite its revolutionary origins. The new rulers were, in the words of one of them, Kevin O'Higgins, 'probably the most conservative minded revolutionaries that ever put through a successful revolution'[23] and Irish society in 1923 resembled what existed before 1914.[24] Hayden is an example of the non-republican feminist whose support was available to the new State but whose feminist concerns were ignored by the conservative government. Continuing to pursue feminist issues these women were often criticised, after the advent of the Fianna Fáil government in 1932 as anti-government, anti-national and pro-British.

The extension by Westminster at the end of World War I of the parliamentary franchise to women aged thirty had been followed by the Sex Disqualification (Removal) Act in 1919 which opened the legal and accountancy professions to women and made them liable for jury service. In 1924 the Dáil legislated to allow women to opt out of this duty in an Act presented by Kevin O'Higgins who, in reforming the working of the jury system, thought to get rid of 'the unwilling woman juror'.[25] In fact, and as Hayden would later point out, men were equally unwilling, to judge from a newspaper report of fines imposed on jurors who failed to answer their names at Green St Court in December 1921. Half of the seventy-five defaulters were men.[26] A more organised opposition developed in 1927 when another Juries Bill was introduced by O'Higgins (now Minister for Justice). In his continued endeavours to simplify the administration and reduce the costs of the jury system, O'Higgins proposed to remove women entirely from liability for this duty, arguing that none but a few 'advanced propagandist women' wanted the obligation. He subscribed also to the widely held belief that women's primary obligations were in the home rather than in the courtroom.[27] His paternalistic attitude was that he and the government knew what was best for women.[28] Similarly, some in the Catholic church considered jury service to be inconsistent with women's domestic duties and in conflict with female modesty.[29] Much press coverage was unfavourable to the women, for instance seeing them as 'a few ladies who have nothing else to do but gad about, and who dearly love the limelight'.[30] Many women's organisations protested at the proposal as contrary to the principle of equality proclaimed in the Constitution, and there were letters to the newspapers making this and other arguments such as the positive contribution which women could make to the work of juries, particularly in cases involving women and children. It was pointed out, for instance by Sheehy Skeffington, that women were regularly challenged and excluded when they attended for jury service.[31] Hayden contributed a letter[32] in which she acknowledged that most women did not welcome the liability for jury service but added neither did most men. It was an irksome public duty, but a duty nevertheless of a citizen so that the ends of justice be served. She pointed out that those women who wished to be exempted were provided for by the 1924 Act. The new bill proposed to exclude all women, which would doubtless please many of them; if men could then be similarly exempted, the satisfaction among them also would be even greater. But would 'justice gain thereby?' asked Hayden in her characteristically pragmatic approach. She saw no good reason why the public duties of women citizens should differ from those of men citizens.

Among the organisations voicing opposition was the Irish Women's Citizens and Local Government Association of which Hayden was now Chairman. It sent a deputation to the minister to urge amendment of the 1924 Act to make the grounds for exemption identical for men and for women. The deputation included Jennie Wyse Power, who was a strong opponent in the Senate of the new bill, and Hayden's academic colleague Mary Macken. There were also protests from the Irish Women's Equality League, the Irish Women's International League and the Irish Women Workers' Union.[33]

The Juries Act (1927) as finally passed contained an amendment reluctantly included by O'Higgins which while maintaining the exclusion of women from jury service allowed a woman, by volunteering, to have her name included on the register of jurors. This provision, opposed by women's groups, remained in force until 1976 when the Supreme Court found the exclusion of women to be unconstitutional; effectively it meant that very few women served on a jury during this period.

Although the women's campaign in 1927 was unsuccessful, it was for them a learning experience and did force the government to retreat from its original proposal to exempt women completely from jury service.[34] The jury service responsibility had applied to women for less than a decade and meant little to most of them. Apart from the feminist minority, there was no great desire among women to retain this onerous novelty, which makes the feminist opposition the more significant in its recognition of this civic duty as an element of full citizenship. The virtual removal of the duty was seen as a dilution of the equal status only recently granted. Further interference with that concept was to follow.

Employment for Women in the 1920s and 1930s

Unemployment was increasing in the 1920s and though Patrick McGilligan, Minister for Industry and Commerce, considered it 'not the function of the government to provide work',[35] it was nevertheless expedient to preserve jobs for men by discouraging women from the workforce where in the conservative thinking of the period women were out of place. Employment for graduates was a regular concern of both the UCD Governing Body and the Women Graduates' Association. The 1920s and 1930s were decades of economic recession, exacerbated in the 1930s by an economic war against Britain. Though Fianna Fáil would achieve some increase in industrial employment from 1932, unemployment remained 'a chronic problem'.[36] It affected all levels of the population, and in this context women were unwelcome in the workforce.

Between the two Juries Acts there had been controversy about employment opportunities for women in the civil service. Contrary to the Civil Service Regulation Act 1924, which entitled both men and women to compete for appointments, examinations from which women were excluded were advertised for junior executive and junior administrative posts. When challenged as illegal the advertisements were withdrawn. An amending bill was introduced in 1925 to empower the Civil Service Commissioners arbitrarily to exclude women from any examination; the bill also provided for some appointments without an examination. The amending proposals aroused widespread opposition. Two letters[37] on behalf of the IWCLGA, signed by Mary Hayden, Chairman, and Ethel MacNaughten, Honorary Secretary, deplored the attempt to introduce an element of sex discrimination into the regulations, and in the name of the fully enfranchised women of the Irish Free State urged the members of the Dáil to vote against the bill. There is a conciliatory tone in the first letter's acknowledgement that to the credit of the Free State Government there had been no element of sex discrimination in regard to the original (1924) Act. Feminist optimism about the new state persisted in some degree – or the desire not to arouse its antagonism. The second letter stated that legal opinion obtained by the Association advised that the bill was unconstitutional. The writers dismissed the assurances of Minister Blythe that the Act would not be misused. They repeated that women had proved their efficiency in the civil service and called on all fair-minded deputies to oppose the bill.

Opposition to the Civil Service Regulation (Amendment) Bill was not confined to women. Its possible unconstitutionality was pointed out by T. O'Shea, Secretary of the Civil Service Federation, and by speakers in the Dáil debate including Alfred Byrne and Professor William Magennis.[38] A leading article in the *Irish Times* noting the narrow margin of five votes by which the second reading of the bill was carried in the Dáil, favoured examinations, honestly conducted, to achieve an efficient civil service.[39]

On 15 December 1925 the National University Women Graduates' Association held a protest meeting in Dublin which condemned the bill as reactionary and called on the Senate to reject it. Agnes O'Farrelly, presiding, said the bill was not receiving much attention in the country which was pre-occupied with other matters such as the Boundary Commission and partition. Hayden, proposing a motion of protest, referred to the old argument about woman's place being in the home and asked whether offering no temptation to leave it was the only way to keep her there. There was, she said, no shortage of women who could stay at home, but some women needed to support themselves and their dependents and should not be restricted in their earning opportunities. A second motion proposed by Mary Macken called on the Senate to reject the bill, and Hayden and Macken were appointed as a deputation to interview Lord Glenavy, Senate chairman.[40] The Dublin University Women Graduates' Association was also active in the opposition to the bill.[41]

The bill was strongly opposed in the Senate by Jennie Wyse Power and Eileen Costello. Costello (née Drury) had been born and spent her early life in London where she joined the Irish Literary Society and the Gaelic League. From her marriage in 1903 she lived in Ireland and during the War of Independence became active in Sinn Féin. She supported the Treaty and was elected to the first Free State Senate where she regularly opposed discrimination against women. The arguments advanced by Wyse Power and Costello were largely responsible for the rejection by the Senate of the Civil Service Regulation (Amendment) Bill.[42] The adoption of the Act was thus delayed for a year, but the regulations for which it provided were never issued owing to doubts about its constitutionality.[43] The interview became increasingly important from 1929 in competitions for the administrative grade, and women were no longer successful.[44] Mary Kettle, in a paper to the Women

Graduates' Association, noted this injustice, saying the interview had replaced the examination because women were beating men in the examination,[45] a legitimate assumption. Likewise, Hayden wrote that when the attempt to exclude women from the examinations for the higher posts had foundered, a selection board was established which achieved the end sought,[46] the preservation of the senior posts for men.

Following the General Election in 1932 Éamon de Valera's Fianna Fáil government denoted no change in the attitude of the State towards women in public life or employment. Though Sean T. O'Kelly had, during the election campaign, proclaimed Fianna Fáil's belief in 'the duty of the state to provide work',[47] that duty did not appear to extend to women. Employment for women was a major issue for Hayden, and she often expressed her views on working women, married and single, as she did in a paper composed in reply to a pamphlet, *The New Woman*, published in 1934 by Alice Curtayne.[48]

Curtayne, some forty years younger than Hayden, was in the early stages of a long life as a journalist and writer on religious and historical subjects. Her public lecture, 'The Renaissance of Woman', in October 1933 considered it timely to review the achievements of feminism, noting that admission to education, the professions, business and suffrage had been won by secular feminism of the previous hundred years, but she considered that Catholic feminism was a distinct and much older phenomenon, citing as examples, the cult of Our Blessed Lady and, in the Irish context, St Brigid, seen by Curtayne as inspirer of a definite intellectual movement, and the Brehon Laws which secured women's property rights long before the 1870 Act giving married women possession of their earnings. She decried the suffrage achievement and secular feminists' 'false ideal' which inspired competition and 'even conquest' between the sexes, leading to the evil effects of unemployment and the detachment of women from family life, their choice of career becoming superior to marriage or domesticity. Her assertion that hardly one woman in a thousand could be truly content without entering religion or marriage was a repetition of the Victorian constraints against which Hayden had struggled for most of her life. Curtayne wanted Catholic women to maintain their distinctiveness; she credited the Irish church particularly with the most advanced thought on woman's intellect, freedom and dignity. Curtayne's views on women's emancipation were current in some Catholic publications of the period.[49] The emphasis was on the family, headed by the breadwinning father.[50] The grant of female suffrage in many countries after the First World War was an achievement for feminism, which experienced a shift in direction towards the promotion of improved conditions for mothers in the 1920s and 1930s.[51] Combined with the importance of protecting jobs for men, this thinking produced the context in which Curtayne's strictures were expressed. Her harking back to Gaelic Ireland and an idyllic era for women was reminiscent of the work of Hayden, Stopford Green, Helena Concannon and other women writers; but her criticism of secular feminism provoked Hayden to compose a detailed reply in which she disagreed with Curtayne's assertion that woman's liberty in social life was now complete, pointing to restrictive legislation and regulations in professions and industries, and warning of further threatened enactments, which is probably a reference to the Conditions of Employment Act 1935/36. Hayden defended the life and independence of the working woman, whether she worked from choice or from necessity. On marriage, Hayden protested that the feminist movement in which she had been involved 'to some extent' for more than forty years had never denigrated it in favour of a career. However she conceded that a married woman's duties could be 'serious obstacles to the concentration demanded for high class work', and continued that there are persons, male and female, whose characters do not fit them for married happiness. There were, she wrote, women and men who deliberately choose not to marry and who substitute their careers for family life.[52]

These latter sentiments describe Hayden's own position at seventy-three reflecting on a life in which independence and a career had been paramount. This somewhat superior attitude may be detected also in Curtayne's article, for instance where she pities London office girls; the article is a defence of traditional conservative Catholicism, is printed with an episcopal *imprimatur*, and in effect calls for a halt to further feminist claims. Curtayne's satisfaction with woman's position was more in tune with establishment attitudes of contemporary Irish society than was the sceptical attitude of Hayden, whose typescript article does not appear to have been published.

Hayden would not have disputed Curtayne's opening statement that the emancipation of women was an outstanding and complete change of the social order, but unlike Curtayne she believed there was much more to be accomplished. The two women – middle class, Catholic, thoughtful, perhaps somewhat prescriptive – differed in their response to the conservative society in which they lived. Hayden was a proponent of feminism without qualifications such as 'secular' or 'Catholic'. Her feminism was non-sectarian, inherited from nineteenth century non-conformists like the Haslams. Whereas Curtayne thought the extravagant hopes of the suffragists had proved to be a delusion, Hayden, though without examples to cite from the Dáil, pointed out the beneficial influence of women's suffrage on legislation by the British Parliament affecting women, children, the aged and the poor.

Jobs for women were the most immediate concern. In 1936 the advertisement of a post of assistant inspector of fisheries (male) drew protests from the Women Graduates'

Association. The WGA considered the express exclusion of women candidates as indefensible and a violation of the Constitution, adding that an exactly similar post had been for many years successfully filled by a woman graduate.[53] A few weeks later Hayden herself wrote to protest about unequal pay for government posts, citing recent advertisements including those for a legal assistant in the Office of Charitable Donations and Bequests and a medical inspector in the Department of Public Health. She pointed out that although a woman appointee would receive a lower salary, her hours would not be shorter nor her duties lighter; her training had been as long and as costly and her qualifications were the same as those of a male candidate. This discrimination was an injustice, a violation of the principle of equality of men and women in the Constitution, and an insult to the learned professions, wrote Hayden, calling it also an injustice to men that persons of equal qualifications might be employed at a cheaper rate – what in industry would be denounced by trade unions as blacklegging. Hayden then continued that women in the Irish Free State had grievances enough. In the Civil Service sex seemed to count for promotion rather than merit where the 'Appointments Board, like the Star Chamber of old, is governed by no known rules in its decisions'. The banks, the diplomatic service and the police were also at fault. She concluded with the hope that this new development of inviting women to undersell men by performing the same duties for a lower salary would be noted and opposed.[54] 'Letters to the Editor' was not a major feature of the *Irish Times* then, and no response to Hayden's letter appeared. A much earlier instance of her concern about equal pay occurred at the NUI Senate in 1920 when she seconded a proposal by Patrick McGilligan that a pay increase for a typist should be at the same rate as the civil service scale for male clerks. The Senate accepted the proposal on a show of hands, although the Vice-Chancellor (then Dr Coffey) asked to be recorded as disagreeing.[55] The same Patrick McGilligan was in 1935 one of the few to argue against the restrictions on women's employment in industry during the Oireachtas debates on the Conditions of Employment Bill,[56] though the government of which he was a member in the 1920s had attempted to legislate against women's opportunities in the Civil Service.

Protection of jobs for men in years of economic depression was one reason for the series of restrictions imposed on women's employment opportunities in the 1920s and 1930s. Supportive of this justification were the beliefs, then widely held by men and women, that woman's natural place was in the home, caring for husband and family rather than competing with men in employment and challenging them in public life. The arguments displayed a belief that there were jobs for women, but careers were for men.[57] The prevailing mood, as in Europe, stressed the role of women in the home, an attitude re-enforced by the teachings of the Catholic and Protestant churches.[58] The addition of the entire adult female population to the electorate had little impact on the economic or social thinking of Dáil members who, for the most part, were conservative. In the male-dominated society which they represented the fact that some women had participated effectively for over twenty years in local and municipal government did not signal any major incursion by women into representative politics on a national level, even to the mind of the average woman. Hence the comparative ease with which restrictions to women's employment opportunities were imposed. However, many women were forced by economic necessity to take up paid employment, poorly paid in most cases, and many others sought fulfilment in occupations which exercised their abilities and allowed them to participate in some degree in the world beyond the confines of the home.

From the early 1930s, women in the civil service and in primary teaching were required to retire on marriage. Similarly in England a marriage bar on women's employment in teaching and other areas was increasingly common. And throughout Europe the numbers of women in employment were also being limited.[59] In Ireland in 1935 women's employment in industry was curtailed by the Conditions of Employment Act introduced by Sean Lemass, Minister for Industry and Commerce, to improve working conditions in industry, and which empowered the minister to limit or prohibit the employment of women in a particular industry as he thought fit. This bill particularly affected working-class women, as the earlier legislation had restricted opportunities for middle-class women. In both instances opposition was expressed by the small minority of women, active feminists, dismayed by the erosion of the principle of equal citizenship. The proposed constraints on women's employment in industry aroused the explicit opposition of Louie Bennett, leader of the Irish Women Workers' Union (IWWU) which ran a campaign against the Conditions of Employment bill.[60] A vigorous meeting organised by the IWCLGA and the National Council of Women of Ireland (NCWI), heard Dorothy Macardle warn that the tendency to relegate women to the background could affect all their laws and institutions.[61]

A protest meeting organised by the IWWU was held in the Mansion House on 20 November 1935. Attended by several hundred women and some men, it was a lively event with cheers and heckles at which strong opinions were expressed. Louie Bennett proposed a resolution against the infringement of the principle of equality and the bill's arbitrary limitation of the employment of women. Dr Ethna Byrne, lecturer in UCD, joined the protest as a delegate from the Irish Federation of University Women. Hayden, representing the NCWI, said that to impose the misery of unemployment on women in order to provide work for men would merely aggravate poverty and unemployment. As an alternative, the meeting should urge the government to provide more work for men by initiating public works of national utility. She said that no other country would attempt so sweeping a measure to the detriment of women.[62] Later, Hayden was to note also the doubtful legality of this controversial measure,[63] and to draw attention to the inclusion of the Free State on a League of Nations blacklist of countries which legislated contrary to women's interests.[64]

The leader of the opposition to the Conditions of Employment Bill, Louie Bennett, was one of many with whom Hayden had worked during the earlier suffrage campaign. There are interesting similarities between the lives of these two feminists. Both came from comfortable, middle-class Dublin families – one professional and Catholic, the other business and Protestant. Both had attended Alexandra College, though not at the same time; Bennett was the younger by twelve years, and she did not undertake university studies. Public campaigning for women's rights began for Hayden and Bennett as each approached the age of forty. For Bennett, the issue was woman's suffrage, as she joined the IWSLGA and in 1911 was a founder of the IWSF.[65] Becoming leader of the IWWU, she worked to improve employment conditions for working-class women, a cause with which Hayden was in sympathy. Bennett, however, was less concerned about the situation for middle-class women, as would be demonstrated in 1937 when she stood back from the later stages of women's opposition to the new Constitution. And Bennett and Hayden were alike in their conservative views on married women, whose normal role, they believed, was more properly in the home. Equal pay for women, which they continually pressed for, to avoid the employment of women as cheap labour, and adequate pay for men to support their families, were issues which both women promoted. Feminist arguments for rights and services for women varied between their political and civil equality with men or their difference from men, a dilemma faced by all feminists of the period.[66] These two lines of argument go back to nineteenth-century emancipationists whose claims for women were based on both her individual, rational human nature, like men's, and her contribution to society, different from that of men but equally essential.[67]

For now, the Conditions of Employment Bill, which contained threats to the employment of working-class women, completed its passage in the Dáil, the minister thanking the Labour Party and other members of the Opposition for their contribution to its improvement.[68] The NCWI had established a standing committee on legislation to study existing and proposed legislation affecting women, their rights and interests. This committee made representations to members of the Senate to try to have the objectionable provisions deleted from the Bill, a motion for which was duly proposed by Senator Kathleen Clarke,[69] and defeated. Kathleen Clarke was a committed republican whose husband Tom had been executed in 1916. Prominent in both Cumann na mBan and Sinn Féin and elected to the Dáil in 1920, she had fiercely opposed the Treaty. Having lost her Dáil seat she became a Senator in 1929. A protagonist of women's rights she became, in 1939, the first female Lord Mayor of Dublin. Clarke and Jennie Wyse Power strongly opposed the Conditions of Employment Bill, which was accepted by the Senate. The Conditions of Employment Act in general was welcomed by male workers and their unions,[70] providing as it did for workers in industry a reduced working week of forty-eight hours, a statutory one-week holiday entitlement and protection against exploitation of young workers, as well as the power to protect jobs for men. Apart from the contentious clauses, the Act has been described by Mary E. Daly as 'otherwise a progressive piece of legislation'.[71]

Feminist Perceptions

The feminist protesters in all these issues were mainly middle-class educated Dublin women, a small, active, courageous minority 'undaunted by sneers, jibes and derision'.[72] At this remove it may be difficult to appreciate quite how unusual was their vision in being so acutely conscious of the implications of measures inherently paternalistic, to which nevertheless many women saw no reason to take exception. The Juries Acts, the ban on married women in the civil service and primary teaching, the Conditions of Employment Act, were pragmatic responses by the new State to some of its economic and social problems, a State moreover preoccupied with political issues and where women workers were seen as a threat to the scarce employment prospects for men. To later generations these measures read as attacks on women's rights and status as independent citizens, which is how the actions of the State were seen by contemporary feminists. The 'desire to restore traditional order and hierarchy, the need to consolidate power' and reaction to republican women's opposition to the Treaty, are in retrospect cited as reasons for the gender legislation of the 1920s and 1930s.[73] Society was complacent, its structure not open to question in the independent, conservative Free State and the reinforcement of the stereotypical image of woman as subordinate and domestic was a concomitant of its efforts to establish an orderly, viable identity for itself.

For the patriarchal society to be changed its existence had first to be acknowledged, but as yet many men and women were not conscious of the paternalistic ethos of the society in which they lived. However, it has been argued that these attacks on women's role though substantial were 'piecemeal and inconsistent'.[74] And the danger of overstating the repressive nature of the new Irish state has been pointed out by Mary E. Daly who cautioned against allowing the issues of the late twentieth-century influence our interpretation of women's lives in the earlier period.[75] As another historian, Ronan Fanning, has commented in another context, 'for the historian the present is essentially an enemy obstructing a proper perspective on the past'.[76] In hindsight the challenges mounted by the feminists appear unexceptionable. To many of their contemporaries these women were perceived as abnormal, atypical and, at times, eccentric. In the context of early twentieth-century Ireland they were undoubtedly courageous and radical.

At a debate in the Alexandra College Students' Union in 1903 Hayden and another speaker, both opposing a motion about conformity and society, had argued that if the fear of being thought eccentric were a universal deterrent the world would be at a standstill.[77] Almost four decades later, Hayden was one of the oldest among these feminists, whose eminence was acknowledged by her appointment as President of the NCWI established in 1924 to promote co-operation among women, feminist or not, on social issues.[78] An obituary in 1942 would describe her attitude on women's rights as 'eminently reasonable and consistent'.[79] A similar comment had been included in the account of her career placed before the NUI Senate in 1935 when it decided to confer on her the honorary degree of D.Litt; the statement referred to Hayden's:

> two great devotions – education and a uniformly consistent and reasoned attitude as to the advancement of the public opportunities and rights which women should receive in all educational and other departments of activity.[80]

Another contemporary comment confirms the perception of her as an acknowledged and respected feminist:

> She has remained the champion in and out of the University of her sisters' rights. The revolution which has changed so greatly the position of women in public life in Ireland owes

much of its success to her quiet but persistent effort and example.[81]

The words 'reasonable', 'quiet', 'persistent', give an impression of an effective, non-aggressive protagonist. She was well-regarded even by those who might not have shared her enthusiasm for women's rights. A 'viable and visible public role in the Irish Free State' was what Hayden and other feminists sought.[82] For Hayden, women and men should fulfil equal but complementary roles in society. Women had different perceptions to bring to public issues, perceptions which were no less significant than the exclusively male vision which still dominated. The most immediate example was that of jury service, but on a broader scale women's participation in the decision-making process would bring a new dimension to thinking on health, welfare, education, family and indeed on all aspects of life. Hayden herself was both positive and optimistic. She saw that much had changed since her own childhood when the only two options were domesticity or the convent,[83] but Hayden frequently urged confidence in the future on younger women. Age did not diminish her resolution, as her 1930s activities bear witness.

The conservative, often reactionary, attitude to the role of women through the 1920s and 1930s was unaffected by the change of Government in 1932. Control, rather than equality, seemed to be the aim in what has been described as an 'increasingly coercive society'.[84] The growing alarm of feminists led to the formation of two groups to scrutinise and express women's views on future legislation – the Standing Committee (of the NCWI) on Legislation affecting Women, previously referred to, and the Joint Committee of Women's Societies and Social Workers (an umbrella group to include women's organisations such as the IWCLGA, the Mothers' Union, the Central Association of School Mistresses, the NUWGA and others).[85] Louie Bennett was chairman of the Standing Committee and

Mary Kettle of the Joint Committee. The next struggle was to be about the 1937 Constitution, a struggle led by the Women Graduates' Association presided over by Hayden and joined by the other organisations of women.

NOTES

1   Mary Hayden and G.A. Moonan, *A Short History of the Irish People* (Dublin, 1927 ed.), p. 548.

2   M.A. Doherty, 'Kevin Barry and the Anglo-Irish Propaganda War', *Irish Historical Studies,* XXXII, No 126 (November 2000), p. 222.

3   R. Pope Hennessy, *The Irish Dominion League: A Method of Approach to a Settlement* (London, 1919), p. 32.

4   Senia Pašeta, 'Ireland's Last Home Rule Generation: The Decline of Constitutional Nationalism in Ireland 1916–30' in Mike Cronin and John M. Regan (eds), *Ireland: The Politics of Independence 1922–49* (London, 2000), pp 22–24.

5   Printed slip 7 December 1921 inserted in *The Irish Dominion League: Official Report* (Dublin, 1921).

6   Senia Pašeta, *Before the Revolution: Nationalism, Social Change and Ireland's Catholic Elite, 1879–1922* (Cork, 1999), p. 3.

7   Hayden and Moonan, *Short History,* 1921/1927 editions, p. 562.

8   *Ibid,* 1927 ed., p. 574.

9   David Edwards, 'Salvaging History: Hogan and the Irish Manuscripts Commission' in Donnchadh Ó Corráin (ed.), *James Hogan: Revolutionary, Historian and Political Scientist* (Dublin, 2001), p. 118.

10 Monica Nevin (daughter of Thomas Morrissey), conversation with author, 30 March 2000.

11 Tom Garvin, *1922: The Birth of Irish Democracy* (Dublin, 1996), p. 130. *Fifty-fifth Report of the Deputy Keeper, Public Record Office* (Dublin, 1928), p. 4.

12 Niamh Whitfield, 'My Grandfather, Dr Seamus Ó Ceallaigh 1879–1954', Foreword in Seamus Ó Ceallaigh, *Gleanings from Ulster History* (Draperstown, 1994, new ed.), p. xix.

13 Hayden and Moonan, *Short History,* 1927 ed., p. 567.

14 R.F. Foster, *Modern Ireland 1600–1972* (London, 1989), p. 524.

15 Hayden and Moonan, *Short History,* 1927 ed., p. 569.

16 Ronan Fanning, *Independent Ireland* (Dublin, 1983), p. 39.

17 F.S.L. Lyons, *Ireland Since the Famine* (Glasgow, 1973, 2nd ed.), p. 550.

18 Mary Hayden, 'Three Notable Irishwomen', NLI Hayden Papers, MS 24007 Box 14, and listed in NUWGA *First Annual Report 1929–30*.

19 *Freeman's Journal*, 29 September 1922, 2 October 1922. I am grateful to Tom Mohr for this reference, and for bringing this debate to my attention.

20 Mary Hayden letter, *Freeman's Journal*, 29 September 1922.

21 Hanna Sheehy Skeffington letter, *Freeman's Journal*, 2 October 1922.

22 *Freeman's Journal*, 19 and 26 October 1922.

23 Quoted in J.J. Lee, *Ireland 1912–1985*, p. 105.

24 John M. Regan and Mike Cronin, 'Ireland and the Politics of Independence 1922–49: New Perspectives and Reconsiderations' in Cronin and Regan (eds), *Ireland: The Politics of Independence 1922–49*, p. 2.

25 Maryann Valiulis, 'Defining their Role in the New State: Irishwomen's Protest against the Juries Act of 1927', *Canadian Journal of Irish Studies*, 18 (July 1999), p. 43; See also Rosemary Cullen Owens, 'The Machine Will Work Without Them: Kevin O'Higgins and the Jury Bills 1924 and 1927' in Myles Dungan (ed.), *Speaking Ill of the Dead* (Dublin, 2007), pp 41–66.

26 *Irish Times*, 8 December 1921.

27 Maryann Valiulis, 'Engendering Citizenship: Women's Relationship to the State in Ireland and the United States in the Post-Suffrage Period' in Maryann Valiulis and Mary O'Dowd (eds), *Women and Irish History* (Dublin, 1997), p. 165.

28 Mary Cullen, 'Women, Emancipation and Politics, 1860–1984' in J.R. Hill (ed.), *A New History of Ireland*, Vol VII (Oxford, 2003), p. 869.

29 Edward Cahill SJ, 'Social Status of Woman', *Irish Monthly*, January 1925, cited in Maryann Valiulis, 'Neither Feminist nor Flapper: The Ecclesiastical Construction of the Ideal Irish Woman' in Mary O'Dowd and Sabine Wichert (eds), *Chattel, Servant or Citizen?* (Belfast, 1995), p. 171.

30 Valiulis, 'Defining their Role in the New State', p. 53.

31 *Ibid.*, p. 48.

32 *Irish Times*, 15 February 1927.

33 *Irish Times*, 22 February 1927.

34 Valiulis, 'Defining their Role in the New State', p. 55.

35 Lee, *Ireland 1912–1985*, p. 127.

36 *Ibid*, p. 195.

37 *Irish Times*, 18 and 24 November 1925.

38 *Irish Times*, 19 November 1925.
39 *Ibid.*
40 *Irish Times*, 16 December 1925.
41 Annual Report of Irish Federation of University Women 1931. UCD Archives, Bridget Stafford Papers, P 63/4.
42 *Irish Times*, 18 December 1925.
43 Belinda Finnegan, 'The Democratisation of Higher Education and the Participation of University Women in the Labour Force 1920–50' (MA thesis, UCD, 1985). UCD NUWGA 3/35 p. 137.
44 *Ibid*, p. 85.
45 UCD NUWGA 2/21, Minutes 13 March 1935.
46 Hayden, 'Women and the New Constitution. Hard won rights to be lost', *Cork Examiner*, 29 June 1937.
47 Lee, *Ireland 1912–1985*, p. 169.
48 Alice Curtayne, *The New Woman* (Dublin, 1934).
49 Caitríona Clear, *Women of the House: Women's Household Work in Ireland 1922–1961* (Dublin, 2000), p. 36.
50 Finola Kennedy, *Cottage to Crèche: Family Change in Ireland* (Dublin, 2001), p. 188.
51 *Ibid.*, p. 91.
52 Mary Hayden, The New Woman: A Reply (1935), Typescript, NLI Hayden papers, MS 24011.
53 *Irish Times*, 23 May 1936.
54 *Irish Times*, 15 June l936.
55 NUI Senate Minutes, 5 March 1920.
56 Astrid McLaughlin, 'Received with Politeness, Treated with Contempt: The Story of Women's Protests in Ireland Against the Regressive Implications of Sections of the Conditions of Employment Act 1936 and the Irish Constitution of 1937' (MA thesis UCD, 1996. UCD Women's Education, Research and Resource Centre), p. 24.
57 Finnegan, 'The Democratisation of Higher Education', p. 133.
58 Cullen, *op cit*, p. 863.
59 Carol Dyhouse, *No distinction of Sex? Women in British Universities 1870–1939* (London, 1995), p. 243; Rosemary Cullen Owens, *A Social History of Women in Ireland 1870–1970* (Dublin, 2005), pp 265–66.
60 Rosemary Cullen Owens, *Louie Bennett* (Cork, 2001), pp 84–85.
61 *Irish Times*, 6 and 7 November 1935.
62 *Irish Times*, 21 November 1935.
63 *Irish Independent*, 16 December 1937.
64 *Irish Times*, 22 June 1937.

65 Cullen Owens, *Louie Bennett*, pp 11–12.

66 Caitríona Clear, 'The Women Can Not Be Blamed: The Commission on Vocational Organisation, Feminism and Home-makers in Independent Ireland in the 1930s and 1940s', *Chattel, Servant or Citizen* (Belfast, 1995), p. 186.

67 Cullen, *op cit*, p. 827.

68 *Irish Times*, 22 November 1935.

69 *Irish Times*, 10 December 1935.

70 *Irish Times*, 30 May 1936.

71 Mary E. Daly, 'Women in the Irish Free State, 1922–39: The Interaction between Economics and Ideology' in Joan Hoff and Moureen Coulter (eds), *Irish Women's Voices: Past and Present/ Journal of Women's History*, Winter/Spring 1995, p. 110.

72 Valiulis, 'Defining their Role in the New State', p. 56.

73 Maryann Valiulis, 'Free Women in a Free Nation: Nationalist Feminist Expectations for Independence' in Brian Farrell (ed.), *The Creation of the Dáil* (Dublin, 1994), p. 88.

74 Clear, *Women of the House*, p. 5.

75 On feminists and historical perspective, see Daly, 'Women in the Irish Free State', pp 99–100.

76 Ronan Fanning, 'Mr de Valera Drafts a Constitution' in Brian Farrell (ed.), *De Valera's Constitution and Ours* (Dublin, 1988), p. 33.

77 *Alexandra College Magazine*, December 1903, p. 42.

78 Caitriona Beaumont, 'Women and the Politics of Equality: The Irish Women's Movement, 1930–1943' in Valiulis and O'Dowd (eds), *Women and Irish History*, pp 176–77.

79 *Report of the President, University College Dublin*, December 1942, p. 15.

80 NUI Senate Minutes, 21 March 1935.

81 *The National Student*, June 1935, p. 67.

82 Valiulis, 'Power, Gender and Identity in the Irish Free State' in Hoff and Coulter (eds), *Irish Women's Voices*, p. 130.

83 Ward, *Hanna Sheehy Skeffington*, p. 306.

84 Cullen Owens, *A Social History*, p. 257.

85 Beaumont, 'Women and the Politics of Equality', pp 178–79.

X

THE ROLE OF MARY HAYDEN AND THE WOMEN GRADUATES' ASSOCIATION IN THE OPPOSITION TO THE 1937 CONSTITUTION
1936–37

When the draft of a new Constitution proposed by Éamon de Valera was published in 1937 it was seen by feminists to contain several propositions detrimental to the equal citizenship of women. This possibility had been anticipated by the articulate women who had protested at discriminatory measures during the 1920s and 1930s. Though some concessions were obtained, efforts to achieve satisfactory amendments to the draft were unsuccessful. A campaign led by the National University Women Graduates' Association urged the rejection of the entire Constitution, and although the campaign was not successful, its vigour seemed to surprise de Valera. As NUWGA President, Mary Hayden had a prominent role.

The Irish Free State Constitution, adopted in 1922 and written in accordance with the terms of the Anglo-Irish

Treaty, included items which committed republicans found repugnant, such as an oath of allegiance to the Crown and an office of Governor General. The 1922 Constitution had moreover been subject to many amendments throughout the 1920s, some of a technical nature, and has been described as having a moth-eaten look.[1] De Valera, in government from 1932, embarked on a series of amendments, and then decided to introduce a totally new Constitution based on the authority of the Irish people, to replace that which derived its authority from the Treaty with Britain.[2]

Nevertheless the Proclamation of 1916 and the Irish Free State Constitution of 1922 had been regarded by women as satisfactory guarantees of their status as citizens and of their rights to equality in the new state.[3] The 1916 Proclamation addressed to 'Irishmen and Irishwomen' stated: 'The Republic guarantees religious and civil liberty, equal rights and equal opportunities to all its citizens ...' In the 1922 Constitution, Article 3 read:

> Every person without distinction of sex domiciled in ... the Irish Free State ... is a citizen of the Irish Free State and shall, within the limits of the jurisdiction of the Irish Free State, enjoy the privileges and be subject to the obligations of such citizenship.

Furthermore the parliamentary franchise granted by Westminster in 1918 to women aged thirty and over was extended by the 1922 Constitution to women over twenty-one and the property qualification was abolished.

The 1916 and 1922 statements on equal citizenship were often cited during the feminist resistance to the unacceptable legislation of the new State. In spite of the active participation of many of their number (though not Hayden) in Irish revolutionary politics, women after 1922 were 'dutifully expected to revert to the conventional role of housewife and homemaker'.[4] Nora Connolly O'Brien, daughter of James Connolly, writing in *An Phoblacht* in

1932, regretted that Irishwomen 'having won the right to share in the dangers of war ... have relinquished their right to share in the dangers of peace'.[5] Early hopes of a significant political contribution by Irish women to the new and evolving State proved groundless.[6] Hanna Sheehy Skeffington in a paper in 1936 on 'Woman: Has She Advanced?' expounded her view that progress had slowed or ceased during the previous ten years. She contended that women in Ireland had stood still since 1923 and that women were allowing the privileges so hardly won to be filched from them.[7]

In the context of the 1920s, 1930s and 1940s, domesticity and patriarchy pervaded the climate in which women's lives were experienced. But those lives were not necessarily lives of unremitting hardship. In spite of serious attacks on their rights and opportunities, women had citizenship and the franchise; they could, to an extent, take up paid employment, obtain education and live varied public lives. There was also privation, and women in the home often endured ill health and ceaseless hard work. But in some aspects women's lives were slowly changing for the better.[8] For many of these women, arguments about issues of women's rights were of little concern, as would be seen during the short campaign against the 1937 Constitution. In another context, Irish feminists are judged to have been 'sadly out of touch ... with the concerns of the majority of women'.[9] This was one of the reasons for the failure of their campaign against the Constitution, conducted by a minority of women, conscious of their rights, fearful of retrogression of their position in the community, and predominantly middle class. Hayden was a typical member of this class.

Foreboding about a New Constitution

Various women's groups, particularly alert to the possibility of erosion of the position achieved less than twenty years earlier, felt concern on the subject of women's place in a new Constitution. The committee of the National University Women Graduates' Association in November 1936 joined a protest organised by the Joint Committee of Women's Societies against the refusal of de Valera to meet a deputation. When on 30 January 1937 the requested meeting finally took place, the discussion did not encourage the women or allay their forebodings.[10]

The text of the proposed new Constitution, drafted in spring 1937 and published on 1 May, drew speedy reaction from the NUWGA. As early as 4 May, Hayden, with Mary Kettle, proposed a meeting of all women graduates to consider the threats to the status of women implied in certain provisions of the draft document. Anxiety focused on the omission of Article 3 of the 1922 Constitution (which guaranteed equal citizenship), and on certain provisions of Articles 40, 41 and 45 of the draft which were perceived to threaten woman's place in society and in the workplace.[11] Furthermore, Article 16 on voting rights and membership of Dáil Éireann did not contain the phrase 'without distinction of sex' and seemed to allow for removal of the franchise in the future from women on grounds of disability or incapacity. The three provisions, 40, 41 and 45, were read as the relegation of women to a domestic role, and they seemed to be a culmination and a legitimising of the various particular restrictions imposed on women in the preceding years since the establishment of the Free State. The implication that women's activity should be limited to the domestic sphere prompted much of the criticism of the articles from feminists who were mostly middle-class women.[12]

Before the Constitution was finally adopted by the Dáil, discrimination on grounds of sex was prohibited in the provisions on citizenship and voting rights (Articles 9 and 16), but of the other three unacceptable Articles, only Article 45 would be amended. Efforts to secure amendments to Articles 40 and 41, with their references to 'social function', to woman's 'life within the home' and to the 'duties in the home' of mothers, were not successful. In the opinion of a legal scholar the provisions may be regarded as either protective of women or as grossly offensive to their dignity and freedom.[13] The latter was the interpretation taken by the women opponents. But in the ensuing debates, de Valera insisted that the intention was to protect women.

Article 45.4.2 which originally read:

> The State shall endeavour to ensure that the inadequate strength of women and the tender age of children shall not be abused, and that women and children shall not be forced by economic necessity to enter avocations unsuited to their sex, age or strength.

was amended by deletion of the phrase 'the inadequate strength of women' (replaced by 'the strength and health of workers, men and women'), and the alteration of the term 'women and children' to 'citizens'.

Efforts to Secure Amendments to the Draft

The Women Graduates' Association led the campaign against these unacceptable provisions and was joined by the Joint Committee of Women's Societies and Social Workers, the NCWI, the IWWU and other women's organisations. The campaign developed in two stages, the first being an effort to secure deletion or amendment of the objectionable articles, an effort in which, as noted above, some success was achieved.

The special meeting of women graduates, held on 10 May in 86 St Stephen's Green with Hayden in the chair, was described in newspaper reports as 'largely attended'. The meeting unanimously decided, as proposed by Agnes O'Farrelly, to ask for the deletion of the clauses referring to women in Articles 40, 41 and 45, and for the re-insertion of Article 3 of the Free State Constitution or the declaration of equality in the Proclamation of 1916. The meeting was of the view that the clauses complained of would open the way for reactionary legislation against women. The principle was stressed of a woman's right to work, to choose her own work, and to equal pay. An emergency committee was formed, and plans were made for further action, for a fighting fund, pamphlets and posters, and for a deputation to seek a meeting with the President of the Executive Council, Éamon de Valera.

According to a statement supplied by the Association and published in newspapers,[14] there were speeches also from Eileen McCarvill, Anne Kane, Angela Russell, Eileen Davitt and Hanna Sheehy Skeffington. Eileen McCarvill (née McGrane) and Anne Kane (née Humphries) were lecturers in English and Zoology respectively in UCD.[15] Angela Russell was a medical doctor particularly concerned with public health and the welfare of children,[16] and Eileen Davitt, daughter of Michael Davitt, was a teacher in the Holy Faith Convent Secondary School at Haddington Road, Dublin.

Hayden, as President of the NUWGA, was a significant figure in the campaign, revered by the younger women, and joined by her longtime associates, O'Farrelly, Macken and Sheehy Skeffington. All four played leading roles, writing and speaking on the issues, which brought them together once again on the public platform. Sheehy Skeffington and to a lesser extent O'Farrelly had, over the years, participated in national politics, and their names were known in several contexts. Hayden and Macken were the professors who brought their learning to bear on feminist issues, while on the whole maintaining their detachment from the party political controversies of the recent decades. The NUWGA decided to co-operate with other women's organisations for the more effective fighting of the reactionary clauses. The emergency committee met frequently during May and June, planning approaches to members of the Dáil, both Government and opposition, letters to newspapers and efforts to rally support and subscriptions from all women graduates.

The *Irish Independent* had published on 7 May an article by journalist Gertrude Gaffney entitled 'A Woman's View of the Constitution: How it Affects the Principle of Sex Equality'. Critical of de Valera as a reactionary where women were concerned, she wrote of rights and opportunities for women in the workplace. Gaffney acknowledged that de Valera was conscious of the nightmare of unemployment, but she suggested that equal pay for women would, by depriving employers of cheap female labour, be the way to improve employment prospects for men, an argument advanced in previous years by both Hayden and Bennett.

Gaffney's suggestion that the objectionable proposals would thrust women back to their status in the middle ages gave Hayden the opportunity for a response.[17] She agreed with most of the article criticising women's position under the proposed new Constitution, except the author's reference to the middle ages. In Hayden's view, women would be well content with a public position such as they held in Ireland, and in most European countries, during the middle ages, allowing for changed modern conditions (views she had expressed over twenty years previously). Departing then from historical analogies, Hayden warned against empty promises and vague declarations about the value of women's life within the home. A woman's opportunities of earning, her civil status and her position as a citizen would depend on the judgement of perhaps a single minister or a single State department as to her 'physical or moral capacity'; and Hayden commented that even ministers and departments are not always infallible or unprejudiced.

A meeting sought with de Valera took place on 14 May. The NUWGA delegation included Hayden, Macken,

O'Farrelly and McCarvill. He informed the women graduates, and also deputations from other women's organisations received separately on the same date, that while he did not share their apprehensions, he would nevertheless give careful consideration to the issues of possible discrimination against women in the matters of citizenship and franchise.[18] A detailed report by Mary Macken on this meeting with de Valera was given to the Association on 18 May, with Hayden again in the Chair. Over two hours had been spent with him, and his assurances had been received about clauses to safeguard the political rights of women to be inserted in Articles 9 and 16. However he had given no hope of amending or deleting the clauses in Articles 40, 41 and 45, which the Association regarded as threatening the status of women.[19] Eileen McCarvill then reported on a deputation to Helena Concannon, a member of both the NUWGA and the Dáil for the NUI constituency,[20] who had told the deputation that as a disciplined member of Fianna Fáil she could not propose any amendments to the draft constitution.[21]

A lobbying and letter writing campaign, a Women's Party, and plans for a public meeting were all discussed. Among those addressing the Women Graduates' Association were two speakers from TCD,[22] one of whom, Edna C. Fitzhenry, previously in the *Irish Independent* had referred to de Valera's wish to protect women's rights, and pointed out that women did not ask for protection, but for equality of rights, opportunities and wages.[23] The Dublin University Women Graduates' Association supported the other women's societies in protests against the discriminatory clauses in the draft Constitution.[24]

Another member of the Association, Mary Kettle, writing in her role as Chairman of the Joint Committee of Women's Societies, had two letters published in the *Irish Press* on 11 May and 13 May. On each date the letters were accompanied by an editorial strongly refuting her charges about the intentions of the Government and suggesting that her assertions were merely borrowed from others. Much of the response to the women's campaign, particularly in the *Irish Press*, repeated the old patronising assertion that political activity was too difficult for women's understanding, despite the evidence to the contrary shown by feminists' perceptive analysis of the contentious provisions. The *Irish Press*, established in 1931 by de Valera to support the Fianna Fáil party and counter its unfavourable coverage in other newspapers, was particularly incensed about the issues raised by the women, which it insisted had no validity and must be politically inspired. On the other hand the *Irish Independent*, which generally supported the Fine Gael party, welcomed the women's criticisms as an opportunity to oppose the Fianna Fáil government and object to the draft Constitution. Concerns about the provisions affecting women were also expressed by Louie Bennett, Secretary of the IWWU, who foresaw a possibility of fascist legislation; her letters published in the *Irish Press* on 12, 15 and 18 May also merited editorial comment. The editorials were defensive, seeing Bennett's comments as based on misconceptions about the character of the draft Constitution.

Letters to the newspapers continued. Dorothy Macardle, usually a supporter of de Valera, wrote that the relevant clauses of the Constitution 'although no doubt framed with excellent intentions ... open the way to legislation prejudicial to women in industry and in public life', and seem to invite invasion of women's rights.[25] Also in the *Irish Press* on the same day, Mary Kettle and the editorial were again locked in combat.[26] Another contribution to the correspondence on the objectionable Articles came from the IWCLGA (the renamed suffrage association).[27]

The Catholic social teaching on which the draft constitution was seen to be based was proclaimed in

Catholic newspapers such as *The Standard* and the *Irish Catholic*, and reported in the national press.[28] Notably a statement from An Ríoghacht, a Catholic Action association founded in 1926, warned against un-Christian liberalism.[29] A founding member of An Ríoghacht, the Jesuit priest Edward Cahill, had submitted an amount of material to de Valera during the drafting of the Constitution, but a more influential adviser was John Charles McQuaid, then President of Blackrock College. McQuaid had a good deal to do with early drafts of Articles 40, 41 and 45, and he wrote of 'the law and fact of nature that woman's natural place is in the home'. McQuaid also noted that 'the feminists are getting angry ... stung by the suggestion that the normal place for a woman is in the home ... Their thoughts are very confused.'[30] However McQuaid's comments were in private communications to de Valera. An Ríoghacht, in its statement issued by its President and Secretary, both lay men, claimed that the Catholic Church had always been the champion of the rights, dignity and true interests of women, and quoted from papal encyclicals, from which they stated the draft Constitution derived its inspiration.[31]

An Ríoghacht's statement drew a long letter to the newspapers from Mary Macken. She defended Catholic women critics from the charge of disagreement with the principles of the encyclicals and deprecated the manner in which these documents were being used, disputing An Ríoghacht's interpretation. She pointed out the difference between a Constitution and an encyclical. The first was a charter of rights and liberties on which a citizen could vote, which was amenable to interpretation in a court of law, and which implied legislation the effect of which might not be foreseen. An encyclical on the other hand was 'an exhortation by the Holy Father to the faithful' on certain situations in matters of morals, economics, education and so on, which would be studied with devout attention as expressing the care of Mother Church for the spiritual and temporal wellbeing of her children.[32] Macken's analysis of the separation of state and church in the context of the Constitution was an impressive contribution to the debate, and no doubt owed something to her previously noted study of Catholicism in Germany. Further correspondence ensued on this issue, including a letter from Professor Kathleen Mulchrone of UCG, who came to the defence of Macken.[33] Hayden drew attention to a recent memorandum from the International Union of Catholic Women's Leagues, as outlined in *The Standard* of 28 May 1937 which she saw as upholding the principles for which Irish women were contending. According to Hayden the memorandum recognised a woman's right to work and to equal pay, but also advocated the economic conditions in which the father's work should suffice for the support of the family.[34]

This latter belief, that the father should be able to maintain the household – the motif also of the statement from An Ríoghacht – had been expressed by de Valera in the Dáil on 17 May 1937, and it was the view of feminists like Hayden and Bennett. They, however, saw de Valera as using it as an excuse to exclude women from the workforce. For their part, they advocated equal pay for women as a deterrent to their employment as cheap labour, and Hayden in particular feared further legislative curtailment of employment opportunities for women. Decisions whether women should work outside the home were not for the State to make in Hayden's view which she found endorsed by the 'enormous body of Catholic feminine opinion'.[35] It will be recalled that in the suffrage campaign Hayden had been firm that her feminist beliefs and her adherence to Catholicism were not in conflict. Paternalism, whether of state or church, she disliked, but its existence did not alienate her from either state or church. Those institutions would be the better, she considered, for a recognition of the individuality and equality of women. Alice Curtayne's version of Catholic feminism she had dismissed as deficient, and Hayden's final publication on the role of women (1940) would be written to dispute reactionary statements on women in the modern world by a Jesuit priest, Hunter Guthrie.

De Valera was defended against the charge of anti-feminism by Jennie Wyse Power, who politically approved of his approach to the Constitution;[36] but Hester Sigerson Piatt (Hayden's longtime friend) wrote of 'grave uneasiness at the prospect of further curtailing of women's liberty as Irish citizens', both letters in the *Irish Press*.[37] There were also letters sent directly to de Valera, such as two (25 and 27 May) from women writers 'of many political and religious opinions', concerned about the contentious Articles and listing over forty names which included Mary Hayden, Christine Longford, Patricia Lynch, Dorothy Macardle and Nora Connolly O'Brien.[38] A feminist organisation in England, The Six Point Group (founded in 1921 to seek the abolition of legal inequalities), wrote to de Valera praising the recognition of equality in the earlier Irish Free State Constitution but expressing dismay at the new proposals based on a fascist and slave conception of woman as 'a non-adult person'.[39] There had been some newspaper coverage of the issues in England.

A further attempt by the Women Graduates' Association to persuade de Valera was made in a memorandum, signed by Mary T. Hayden, President, NUWGA, UCD, and Mary J. Hogan, Hon. Secretary,[40] and presented by 'Members of a University in which perfect equality of rights and opportunities has been enjoyed by women both in theory and practice since its foundation in 1908'. The memorandum referred to the assurances from the President about Articles 9 and 16 but viewed 'with alarm' menaces to citizens' right to work of their choice and was concerned about the possibility of future legislation 'worsening the economic and social status of women'. Dealing specifically with Articles, 40, 41 and 45, the memorandum decried interference by the State in the affairs of the family. It concluded that the remedy for the unemployment of men and the exploitation of women would be the application of the fundamental principle of social justice, equal pay for equal work.

The opposition members of the Dáil, both Fine Gael and Labour, and the University representatives, were approached.[41] The NUWGA emergency committee considered amendments to the three objectionable clauses which Fine Gael might be asked to put forward at the report stage of the Dáil procedure, and Mary Macken was deputed to consult Patrick McGilligan, a Fine Gael deputy elected by the NUI constituency, about the form of these amendments.[42] There were three women deputies in the Dáil. Margaret Pearse, Fianna Fáil, did not speak in the debate. Helena Concannon, Fianna Fáil, elected by the NUI constituency, mentioned the concerns of the women graduates,[43] but she supported the new Constitution and was unwilling to propose any amendments. Bridget Redmond, Fine Gael, put forward amendments, which were then proposed by other speakers.[44]

Opposition in the Dáil to the controversial clauses had some success.[45] Amendment to Article 45, 4.2. was achieved with the inclusion of men within its scope and the deletion of the words 'the inadequate strength of women'. Also adopted were the insertion of the phrase 'without distinction of sex' in Article 16, and a similar amendment in Article 9, as agreed by de Valera with the NUWGA and other women's deputations. Opposition contributors to the debate included John Costello, Cecil Lavery, Patrick McGilligan, John Marcus O'Sullivan, Ernest H. Alton, Vincent Rice and Robert J. Rowlette.[46] De Valera had insisted that the phrase 'without distinction of sex' was 'altogether unnecessary'[47] but his subsequent decision to include it in Article 16 was an achievement for critics in and beyond the Dáil.[48]

Campaign to Defeat the Constitution

The Constitution was passed by the Dáil on 14 June. Realising this inevitability, the emergency committee of the NUWGA had since early June been planning a campaign of posters, newspaper advertisements and an open meeting to muster opposition to the referendum by which the Constitution would be put to voters on 1 July, the date also of a general election. The second stage of the women's opposition now began. The campaign took no particular stance on most of the provisions of the draft Constitution which were not feminist issues, but the only escape now from the objectionable Articles was to defeat the Constitution as a whole, which meant appealing to the electorate to vote against it in the referendum. The Women Graduates' Association embarked on this wider endeavour, with the Joint Committee of Women's Societies and the NCWI continuing as active partners in the campaign. But Bennett and the IWWU withdrew from participation, being fairly satisfied with the amendments which had been secured.

A public meeting, with Mary Macken in the chair, took place on 21 June in the Round Room of the Mansion House, and was widely reported.[49] The attendance was noted as 1200 in the Association's Minute Book and 1500 in the *Irish Independent*. Gertrude Gaffney wrote:

> It was wonderful. They kept coming in droves, old women, middle-aged women, young women, working women, professional women, girls from the Sweep and the Civil Service, girls out of shops and offices ... They filled every seat in the Round Room, they thronged the balconies, they sat on the steps of the stage ... and some had to stand all the time.[50]

The first resolution, condemning the retention of certain sections of Articles 40 and 41 and the inadequately amended section of Article 45, was proposed by Mary Hayden in a sturdy defence of the economic interests of women and their right to work. Mary Kettle, Eileen Davitt, Dr Kathleen Lynn and others spoke to the resolution which was passed unanimously. A resolution was also passed advising all women voters to vote against the Constitution. A final resolution, proposed by Hanna Sheehy Skeffington and seconded by Anne Kane, called for the formation of a woman's party with branches throughout the country to safeguard the interests of women in every sphere of activity. This proposal, carried unanimously, had been a previous suggestion at the Women Graduates' Association and would be put into effect in the aftermath of their campaign.

Letters of support were read to the meeting from Kathleen Clarke and Kate O'Callaghan, both prominent republicans and founders of Cumann na mBan. Clarke had been a strong opponent in the Senate of the Conditions of Employment Bill. However, Cumann na mBan as a whole did not support the campaign against the Constitution. Adhering to the ideal of the Republic, they considered discussion of the Constitution, either the 1922 or 1937 versions, as implicit acceptance of the Treaty and a betrayal of that ideal. But individual republican opponents of the new proposals could refer to the statement on equality in the 1916 Proclamation; and even Hayden who had not approved of the Rising would cite the Proclamation in support of her case for women's rights. The *Irish Press* in a sub-leader entitled 'More Feminine Logic' refuted the criticisms by the women, and did 'not accept the high estimate which some of these women graduates have of themselves as constitutional lawyers', suggesting that they learn some simple logic, and ending with a swipe at the curriculum of the NUI.[51]

A leaflet from the Association addressed to 'Women Voters!' contrasted the existing and the proposed new constitutional status of women, asking 'Do you realise your rights are being filched from you under the New Constitution?' and advised them to 'Vote Against'.[52] A cartoon on the cover of the June issue of *Dublin Opinion* was reproduced for circulation on the suggestion of Hanna Sheehy Skeffington;[53] this cartoon, titled 'A Dream of Fair Women' shows de Valera, dreaming that he was being threatened by Queen Maeve and Grainne O'Malley '... about those Articles in the New Constitution?' Another *Dublin Opinion* cartoon[54] depicted a woman surrounded by household chores and demanding children while her husband explains her position under the new Constitution.

Hayden was the author of one of three articles on women and the new Constitution published in the *Cork*

Examiner; the other two were written by Anne Kane and Hanna Sheehy Skeffington.[55] Hayden commenced by distancing the issue from party politics, and proceeded to historical analogies, as in the *Irish Independent* on 12 May, to show that women's status in the past was often superior in Ireland to that in other countries, until the late seventeenth century when a great division arose between rich and poor women. This idealising of the Gaelic past had been a regular theme in Hayden's writing since the early years of the suffrage campaign. The nineteenth century beginnings of the movement for women's suffrage, leading to the great victory of the parliamentary franchise in 1918, the civil and religious liberty affirmed in the Easter Proclamation and the Free State Constitution are all mentioned in her *Cork Examiner* article. But, continued Hayden, the rights of female citizens began to be restricted soon afterwards, and she cited women's exclusion from jury service, from higher posts in the civil service, and restrictions on women's employment in the Conditions of Employment Act, until as she put it 'to crown all' there is this new Constitution with all its possibilities of injustice, 'its mixture of flattery and insult'. This exasperated comment is, yet again, her rejection of the notion of protection, which de Valera and others were proclaiming as the intention of the provisions relating to women.

Throughout, the NUWGA endeavoured to conduct its campaign without engaging in party politics.[56] Its circulars were addressed to all women graduates, and the Mansion House meeting was open to all women. In her speech at that meeting Hayden received applause for her statement that they did not stand for any particular government, they stood for women.[57] Supplied statements from the Association, published in several newspapers,[58] included the claim that the campaign organised by the NUWGA 'despite all attempts at misinterpretation, is entirely non-political'. Newspaper advertisements published by the

NUWGA immediately before the referendum advised women to vote in the general election on the same date for Fianna Fáil, Fine Gael, Labour or Independent 'as they chose', but to vote against the Constitution.[59] Avowed Fianna Fáil supporters such as Dorothy Macardle and Kathleen Clarke declared their support for the campaign against the controversial articles. Macardle in a personal letter to de Valera wrote that anyone with advanced views on the rights of women could not support the Constitution, thus posing a 'tragic dilemma for those who have been loyal and ardent workers in the national cause'.[60] Hayden pointed out that the current campaign included many supporters of the present Government, and she referred to her advice to the organisers that there should be no condemnation of the Government as a whole at the public meeting.[61]

Failure of Women's Endeavour

In the referendum held on 1 July, the Constitution was accepted by 685,105 votes in favour with 526,945 against, that is a majority of 57% of those who voted;[62] it was estimated that 31% of the electorate did not vote. The high rate of abstentions in the referendum is believed to have included many republicans who were unwilling to give tacit recognition to the Irish Free State by voting.[63] The five constituencies in which there were majorities against the Constitution were Dublin Townships, Dublin County, Cork County West, Sligo, Wicklow.[64] The NUWGA was mainly Dublin based; a writer to the *Irish Independent* who approved of the campaign but considered it insufficient, had asked that the women graduates should hold meetings in the provinces.[65] Women had gone about the campaign with organised thoroughness, given lack of funds[66] and shortness of time. The initial expectation had been that satisfactory amendments might be achieved before conclusion of the Dáil debate.

Various explanations have been advanced for the failure of the campaign. Traditional party loyalties and the Catholic social principles expressed in the Constitution were factors which influenced voters[67] despite the insistence of the campaigners that women's rights were a completely separate, distinct, issue. The opponents were mostly educated middle-class women whose arguments did not impinge on the average woman throughout the country with concerns focused on keeping hearth and home together. Anne Kane had written that women countrywide 'do not realise the dangers ahead'.[68] Popular sympathy, including female sympathy, inclined more to de Valera's view than to that of the women graduates.[69] That the majority of women at the time were not interested in politics was the view of C.S. Andrews who, in an interview in 1984, saw the women opponents as a small number of agitators who would always be 'campaigning against something'.[70] On the other hand the interviewer, McGinty, comments elsewhere in the same work that the:

> scale and persistence of their protest took many people by surprise, including de Valera, who found himself on the defensive, both in the Dáil and on election platforms, whenever the issue of women's rights was raised.[71]

During the campaign de Valera devoted considerable attention to refuting the arguments advanced by the women critics, protesting that the intention was to give women 'a special position of privilege'.[72] He did not underestimate the ability of women but seemed surprised that his well-intentioned paternalism could be so unwelcome and, as it appeared to him, so misunderstood. No more than most of his contemporaries he had no real understanding of feminist thinking or any appreciation of its long-term significance. Feminist protests during the 1920s and 1930s had been for the most part ineffective. De Valera seems to have believed that in the Constitution he was bestowing benefit on women by protective provisions which detached them from the grosser realities of a man's world. While allowing for their membership of the legislature, he did not envisage any significant role there for women, knowing that in the contemporary state of public opinion, few would be elected.[73] The feminist concept of woman as a responsible, self-determining individual did not square with the traditional paternalism of contemporary society, either state or church. The feminist response to the Constitution, rejecting protection and seeking equality no matter how onerous it might prove to be, was a reiteration of Hayden's argument in 1927 that women should be liable for jury service on the same terms as men and of her earlier approach to the responsibilities of the parliamentary franchise. However, these were middle-class attitudes. As commented by one historian, 'for many women, equality was an abstract concept which had little to do with the everyday necessities of life'.[74] Similarly, another historian asks 'How many women were aware of Article 41.2 in the 1937 Constitution?'[75] Moreover, what middle-class feminists saw as a right to work outside the home, could be experienced by working-class women as an onerous obligation.[76] The trade unionist and feminist, Helena Molony, was later to write that the women's movement 'passed over the heads of Irish working women and left her untouched'.[77]

Even the IWWU, representing women employed in industrial and non-professional work, dropped out of the campaign when its leader Louie Bennett felt satisfied by the amendments made to the original proposals.[78] While supportive of the campaign for full rights of citizenship and employment, she considered that a women's trade union owed its first loyalty to the trade union movement as a whole and needed to persuade the men's trade unions in favour of the principal of equality in pay, opportunities and privileges for women and for men. She also saw, in the emphasis on woman in the home, a possibility of claims for higher wages, homes for mothers and children, adequate widows' pensions and a family allowance payable to mothers.[79] Widows' pensions had been introduced in 1936, and children's allowances would in fact be introduced for the first time in 1944, but payable to fathers. Bennett, like Hayden, saw homemaking as the more likely occupation for many women.[80]

Nor were the issues of major concern to the male electorate. For example, a *Cork Examiner* leading article supportive of the women's campaign nevertheless regarded it as entirely their affair, saying that if the women graduates can convince two-thirds of their non-graduate sisters, the 'fate of the Constitution will be decided'.[81] Mary Kettle believed that the defeat of the Constitution in certain constituencies was largely owing to the fight by women;[82] but objections to provisions other than those disturbing women opponents may well have contributed to these votes, though the political opposition to the Constitution has been described as 'a rather lack-lustre affair' in contrast to the 'vigour and determination' of the campaigns by the women and the press.[83]

The concerns of the women campaigners were but one element of the opposition to the Constitution. In the Dáil debates on the draft, more attention was given by the Fine Gael and Labour critics to the role of the President, the freedom of the press, and the link with the British Commonwealth. But the electorate in general remained unmoved by these issues.[84] It has been suggested that the vote in the referendum was 'heavily influenced by party political loyalties' and that 'the overwhelming majority of Protestants' voted against the Constitution.[85] The *Irish Press* in a second leader entitled 'Last Reserve called up' accused Fine Gael of making use of the women's issue,[86] and Sean T. O'Kelly in an election speech accused women of using the issue as a useful stick with which to beat the

Government in order to help the opposition party which they supported.[87] De Valera, in a speech in Carlow in which he dealt at length with the position of women, said that the whole issue was started as a political move by John Costello, the ex-Attorney General.[88] Similar accusations were levelled at Costello throughout the campaign, stemming from his article in early May in the *Irish Independent* headed 'New Constitution Curtails Women's Rights: Disclosures by Mr Costello: Threats to Liberty of Subject and Press'. The article, which was the first of a series by legal and other experts, was a full-page critique of the draft, in which, despite the headline, just two paragraphs were devoted to the status of women.[89]

It is also accepted that many voters, women as well as men, did not disagree with the assumption of the Oireachtas in its legislation both before and after 1937 that women would normally be occupied in the home. Yvonne Scannell has commented that de Valera was not 'consciously anti-woman'; his views on women's rights were 'those of most people in Irish society at the time'. Later in the same article on 'The Constitution and the Role of Women' she wrote that by these provisions of the Constitution 'women were guaranteed equality before the law, tempered with regard to differences of capacity' and that 'the Constitution seemed to contemplate ... some preferential treatment for women citizens',[90] a possibility envisaged by Bennett, as noted. Mary E. Daly, commenting on the constitutional emphasis on the importance of woman's role within the home at a time when 'the overwhelming majority of Irish women – married, widowed, and single – were based within the home', suggested that the Constitution can be viewed as 'giving status to many members of Irish society who were otherwise ignored'.[91] Scannell, quoted above, nevertheless described the Constitution as 'rooted in a patronising and stereotyped view of womanhood'.[92] Feminist thinking itself at the time included some who argued for the moral superiority of woman and consequent recognition of her home-making and motherhood role.[93] Another commentator, Finola Kennedy, has made the point that in the 1930s, an era of conservatism and economic depression, policies, and the political ideologies on which they were based, to encourage women to stay in the home and rear children were not peculiar to Ireland.[94] Máire Cruise O'Brien, then a student at UCD, and her peers were not engaged by the issues.[95] But irrespective of interpretation, the effect of the Constitution, as observed by Scannell, was to relegate women to a life of domesticity and powerlessness.[96]

There is no reference to the referendum result in the NUWGA Minutes when meetings resumed in October. However in January 1938, there was a proposal from Mary Kettle and Hayden that the Association apply for registration as a nominating body for the new Senate. The Senate, having shown itself to be an obstructive body, had been abolished by de Valera in 1936, and thus had no role in passing the new Constitution. A new form of Senate was established by the new Constitution, with provision for university representation, no longer included in the Dáil. Hayden, Kettle and the Hon. Secretary were to prepare the application for registration. Prior to the publication of the new Constitution, various women's groups had, without success, sought increased representation for women in the new Senate.[97] In 1954 the NUWGA was to apply, unsuccessfully, for inclusion on the Educational and Cultural Panel of Senate nominating bodies.[98]

Although the referendum had resulted in favour of the Constitution, the agitation arising from its provisions affecting women was not over. Following proposals during the campaign for a political party for women, the NUWGA arranged a meeting, held on 24 November 1937, at which the Women's Social and Political League was established as a non-party, non-sectarian organisation to promote and protect the political, social and economic status of women.[99] Hayden, who presided at the meeting and proposed the formation of the new party, was a longtime advocate of independent women candidates for the Dáil specifically to promote the interests of women, having spoken to this effect in 1923.[100] Mary Kettle, an early advocate of a women's party, seconded the proposal, to which other speakers included Dorothy Macardle, Agnes O'Farrelly, Hanna Sheehy Skeffington and Mary Macken. Hayden spoke of the need for women in public life, free from party obligations in order to promote the best interests of women. Elaborating on the different view which women could bring to public affairs, she said that men were better at grasping main principles, and women at detail.[101] Feminist experiences in Ireland in the 1920s and 1930s had convinced women like Hayden that direct engagement with the political system was the way for women to strive for their rightful status in the community. So far, the women members of the Dáil had not shown themselves as campaigners for women's rights, an attitude which the new party would try to change.[102] However, within a few years the new League had evolved as 'another small, Dublin-based feminist society'.[103]

Whether or not the formation of the women's party had anything to do with it, the controversy about the Constitution continued. At a Fianna Fáil meeting in Glynn, Co Wexford, Dr J. Ryan, Minister for Agriculture, again criticised women's interpretation of the Constitution. This meeting concluded with the chairman, Reverend P. Murphy, attributing the opposition to the new Constitution to a number of noisy women and politicians.[104] Sean T. O'Kelly, Minister for Local Government, addressing a meeting on the Constitution in Wynn's Hotel, Dublin, queried the nationalist credentials of the organisers of the women's opposition who, he said, would rather the country to be still 'under the Union Jack'.[105] His annoyance at the temerity of the women critics ignored the presence among them of acknowledged republican activists like Lynn, Macardle and Kathleen Clarke.

In response to these two speeches, both Hayden and Mary Hogan had letters in the newspapers in December. Hayden defended again their interpretation of the controversial clauses, and referred specifically to the Conditions of Employment Act of 1935 regarded when passed as of doubtful legality but now with the new Constitution 'perfectly legal' (which may have been de Valera's intention, in the view of a later historian).[106] Hayden cited recent advertisements of posts with higher pay for men, married and single, though equal qualifications were required from all candidates. Ending with a reference to the reverend gentleman who spoke of 'noisy women', Hayden commented that silence is scarcely the way to obtain redress of grievances. Hogan pointed out that O'Kelly's charges had previously been refuted in a statement from the Emergency Committee published in the newspapers on 25 June. These two letters were published in the *Irish Independent* as a news item with the heading 'Critics of Constitution: Women Reply to Ministers'[107] and on the following day the *Irish Press* had a leading article titled 'Women Graduates Again'. This leader again accused women of misrepresenting the implications of the constitutional articles. The leader-writer hotly disputed the allegations by Hayden, and concluded by advising the women of the country to 'pray to be saved from the advocacy of the academic group who have constituted themselves their champions'.[108]

In the contemporary context this latter view was a weakness of the women's opposition. Though it attempted to attract all women and did include various women's groups, this campaign was led mainly by the NUWGA, by definition a small and select group. Even with the Joint Committee of Women's Societies and other associates, articulate feminists were still 'a small and unrepresentative minority'.[109] Heirs of the earlier struggles for women's emancipation in the areas of education and the franchise, they were unable to persuade the beneficiaries and potential beneficiaries of these achievements of the significance of feminist objections to the Constitution.

However, the campaign should not be seen as a total failure. It had achieved amendments which secured the equal citizenship and voting rights of women from the possibility of modification, as, for instance, the right to serve on juries had been modified almost to extinction. The failure was in regard to women's place in society and in employment, where feminists saw women being excluded as they had been in the past. The emphasis on woman's 'life within the home' and her 'duties in the home', which remained unchanged, was particularly disturbing to the women graduates who were the kind of women who might think of professional careers and vocations in various spheres of employment. And of course the older among them, like Mary Hayden, Mary Macken and Agnes O'Farrelly did have such careers, achieved with some difficulty, which they thought should not impede later generations of women. The employment opportunities for women graduates had been a regular concern of the NUWGA throughout its existence. But the paternalism of the new State, and the belief in separate spheres for men and women, were to persist. The opposition to the Constitution was the last major campaign of Hayden's life, and one in which she had trenchantly stated her understanding of women's citizenship, an evolving concept of individuality, autonomy and responsibility, derived from her own experience.

" I may seem old-fashioned, but I must say I agree with the President Woman's place is in the home."

NOTES

1   Michael Gallagher, 'The Constitution' in John Coakley and Michael Gallagher (eds), *Politics in the Republic of Ireland* (Dublin, 1993, 2nd ed.), p. 51.

2   Ronan Fanning, *Independent Ireland* (Dublin, 1983), pp 116–18.

3   Caitriona Beaumont, 'Women and the Politics of Equality' in Maryann Valiulis and Mary O'Dowd (eds), *Women and Irish History* (Dublin, 1997), p. 173.

4   Dermot Keogh, *Twentieth Century Ireland: Nation and State* (Dublin, 1994), p. 38.

5   Quoted in Margaret Ward, *In Their Own Voice: Women and Irish Nationalism* (Dublin/Cork, 1995/2001), p. 175.

6   Maurice Manning, 'Women in Irish National and Local Politics 1922–77' in Margaret Mac Curtain and Donncha O'Corrain

(eds), *Women in Irish Society: The Historical Dimension* (Dublin, 1978), p. 92.

7   Minute Book, 19 February 1936, NUWGA 2/21 UCD Archives.

8   Caitríona Clear, 'Women in de Valera's Ireland 1932–48: A Reappraisal' in Gabriel Doherty and Dermot Keogh (eds), *De Valera's Ireland* (Cork, 2003), pp 104–6.

9   Caitríona Clear, *Women of the House* (Dublin, 2000), p. 212.

10   Sean A. Faughnan, 'De Valera's Constitution: The Drafting of the Irish Constitution of 1937' (MA thesis, UCD, 1988), pp 103–4.

11   Minute Book, 4 May 1937, NUWGA 2/21, UCD Archives.

12   Finola Kennedy, *Cottage to Creche: Family Change in Ireland* (Dublin, 2001), p. 83.

13   Yvonne Scannell, 'The Constitution and the Role of Women' in Brian Farrell (ed.), *De Valera's Constitution and Ours* (Dublin, 1988), p. 124.

14   *Irish Press*, 11 May 1937; *Irish Times*, 11 May 1937; *Irish Independent*, 11 May 1937.

15   *Report of the President UCD, 1983–84*, p. 141.

16   Margaret Ó hÓgartaigh, *Quiet Revolutionaries: Irish Women in Education, Medicine and Sport, 1861–1964* (Dublin, 2011), p. 105.

17   *Irish Independent*, 12 May 1937.

18   National Archives S.9880 Women and the Constitution 1937. Department of Taoiseach. *Irish Press, Irish Times, Irish Independent*, 15 May 1937.

19   Minute Book, NUWGA, UCD Archives, NUWGA 2/21(1).

20   Mary Clancy, 'Aspects of Women's Contribution to the Oireachtas Debate 1922–37 in the Irish Free State' in Maria Luddy and Cliona Murphy (eds), *Women Surviving: Studies in Irish Women's History in the 19th and 20th Centuries* (Dublin, 1989), p. 231.

21   Minute Book 18 May 1937, UCD Archives, NUWGA, 2/21(1).

22   *Irish Independent*, 20 May 1937.

23   *Irish Independent*, 13 May 1937.

24   *Irish Times*, Trinity College Notes, 7 June 1937.

25   *Irish Press*, 17 May 1937.

26   *Irish Press*, 17 May 1937.

27   *Irish Times*, 22 May 1937.

28   *Irish Press*, 14 May 1937; Maria Luddy, 'A "Sinister and Retrospective Proposal": Irish Women's Opposition to the 1937 Draft Constitution', *Transactions of Royal Historical Society*, 15 (2005), pp 184–85.

29 *Irish Press*, 20 May 1937.
30 McQuaid to de Valera, undated, cited in Sean A. Faughnan, pp 108, 109.
31 *Irish Press*, 20 May 1937.
32 *Irish Press*, 27 May 1937; *Irish Times*, 27 May 1937; *Irish Independent*, 26 May 1937.
33 *Irish Press*, 29 May 1937; *Irish Independent*, 3 June 1937.
34 *Irish Independent*, 3 June 1937; *Irish Times*, 3 June 1937.
35 *Irish Times*, 3 June 1937; *Irish Independent*, 3 June 1937.
36 Marie O'Neill, *From Parnell to de Valera: A Biography of Jennie Wyse Power 1858–1941* (Dublin, 1991), p. 177.
37 *Irish Press*, 17 May 1937.
38 National Archives S.9880 Women and the Constitution 1937. Department of Taoiseach.
39 National Archives S 9880 Letter 14 June 1937, in Women and the Constitution 1937. Department of Taoiseach.
40 National Archives S.9880 Women and the Constitution 1937. Department of Taoiseach.
41 *Irish Independent*, 14 and 24 May 1937.
42 Minute Book, 4 June 1937, UCD Archives, NUWGA 2/21.
43 *Dáil Debates,* 12 May 1937.
44 *Dáil Debates,* 28 May, 2 June, 4 June l937.
45 Clancy, 'Aspects of Women's Contribution', p. 224.
46 Alton and Rowlette had been elected by Dublin University, and McGilligan by the NUI. Costello and Lavery represented Dublin County, O'Sullivan, Kerry and Rice, Dublin Borough North.
47 *Dáil Debates,* 11 May 1937.
48 Mary Clancy, 'Aspects of Women's Contribution', p. 224.
49 *Irish Times,* 22 and 25 June 1937; *Irish Press,* 22 June 1937; *Irish Independent* 22 and 25 June 1937.
50 *Irish Independent,* 25 June 1937.
51 *Irish Press*, 25 June 1937.
52 UCD Archives, NUWGA 1/51.
53 Margaret Ward, *Hanna Sheehy Skeffington: A Life* (Cork, 1997), p. 327.
54 Reproduced in *The Capuchin Annual,* 1940, p. 90.
55 *Cork Examiner,* 26, 29 and 30 June l937.
56 For example, Anne Kane, 'Women and the New Constitution', *Cork Examiner,* 26 June 1937.
57 *Irish Press,* 22 June 1937.
58 UCD Archives, NUWGA 1/51.

59   *Irish Independent,* 30 June 1937.
60   National Archives S.9880. Letter 21 May 1937 in Women and the Constitution 1937. Department of Taoiseach.
61   *Irish Press,* 25 June 1937.
62   John A. Murphy, *Ireland in the Twentieth Century* (Dublin, 1975), p. 92.
63   Ward, *Hanna Sheehy Skeffington,* p. 327.
64   *Irish Press* 17 July 1937.
65   *Irish Independent,* 23 June 1937. Letter from Mrs T. McKee, Sligo.
66   Hilda Tweedy, quoted in Mary C. McGinty, 'A Study of the Campaign For and Against the Enactment of the 1937 Constitution' (MA thesis, UCG, 1987), p. 302.
67   Beaumont, 'Women and the Politics of Equality', p. 184.
68   Kane, 'Women and the New Constitution'.
69   J.J. Lee, *Ireland 1912–85: Politics and Society* (Cambridge, 1989), p. 208.
70   McGinty, 'A Study of the Campaign', p. 302.
71   *Ibid.,* p. 279.
72   *Irish Press,* 1 July 1937.
73   Sean A. Faughnan, 'De Valera's Constitution', p. 104.
74   Beaumont, 'Women and the Politics of Equality', p. 184.
75   Clear, 'Women in de Valera's Ireland', p. 106.
76   Carol Dyhouse, *Feminism and the Family in England 1880–1939* (Oxford, 1989), p. 187.
77   Nell Regan, *Helena Molony: A Radical Life, 1883–1967* (Dublin, 2017), p. 208.
78   Margaret Ward, *Unmanageable Revolutionaries: Women and Irish Nationalism* (London, 1995), p. 242.
79   *Irish Press,* 22 June 1937.
80   Rosemary Cullen Owens, *Louie Bennett* (Cork, 2001), p. 90.
81   *Cork Examiner,* 26 June 1937.
82   *Irish Times,* 25 November 1937.
83   McGinty, 'A Study of the Campaign', p. 349.
84   *Ibid.,* p. 302.
85   J.J. Lee, *Ireland 1912–1985,* pp 210–211. That people's views on the Constitution as a whole would have been influenced by party political affiliations is also the view of McGinty, 'A Study of the Campaign', p. 303.
86   *Irish Press,* 8 May 1937.
87   *Irish Independent,* 23 June 1937.
88   *Irish Press,* 26 June 1937.
89   *Irish Independent,* 6 May 1937.

90   Scannell, 'The Constitution and the Role of Women', pp 123, 127.

91   Mary E. Daly, 'Women in the Irish Free State 1922–39: The Interaction Between Economics and Ideology' in Joan Hoff and Mooreen Coulter (eds), *Irish Women's Voices: Past and Present/Journal of Women's History,* 6, 4 (1995), pp 111–112.

92   Scannell, 'The Constitution and the Role of Women', p. 134.

93   Richard J. Evans, *The Feminists: Women's Emancipation Movements in Europe, America and Australasia 1840–1920* (London, 1977), pp 233–4.

94   Finola Kennedy, 'Family Life' in K. Kennedy (ed.), *From Famine to Feast* (Dublin, 1998), p. 132; Kennedy, *Cottage,* pp 90–91.

95   Máire Cruise O'Brien, *The Same Age as the State* (Dublin, 2003), p. 141.

96   Scannell 'The Constitution and the Role of Women', p. 127.

97   Owens, *Louie Bennett,* p. 91.

98   NUWGA 2/53 UCD Archives.

99   *Irish Independent,* 25 November 1937; *Irish Times,* 25 November 1937.

100 *Irish Times,* 28 September 1923.

101 NUWGA 1/51, UCD Archives.

102 Mary Cullen, 'Women, Emancipation and Politics, 1860–1984' in J.R. Hill (ed.), *A New History of Ireland,* Vol. VII (Oxford, 2003), p. 877.

103 Beaumont, 'Women and the Politics of Equality', p. 185.

104 *Irish Independent,* 6 December 1937.

105 *Irish Independent,* 14 December 1937.

106 Clear, 'Women in de Valera's Ireland', p. 108.

107 *Irish Independent,* 16 December 1937.

108 *Irish Press,* 17 December 1937.

109 Rosemary Cullen Owens, *A Social History of Women in Ireland 1870–1970* (Dublin, 2005), p. 278.

FINAL YEARS
1934–42

At the age of seventy-six Hayden, with some reluctance, retired from her professorship. She continued to write on historical and feminist topics. And she was still active in the Women Graduates' Association until a few months before her death.

Once her diaries cease in 1903, there is practically no source material on Hayden's personal life, apart from what might be gleaned from records of her professional and public doings. She lived in lodgings or rented accommodation at various addresses in Dublin until her death at 26 Cambridge Road on 12 July 1942. The landlady there was Mrs Annie Reeves with whom the two Haydens had lived at several addresses in the Rathmines area for over twenty-five years. Perhaps this was the devoted family referred to by Agnes O'Farrelly amongst whom Hayden 'lived for a great part of her life'.[1] Hayden's friend, Lilian Green, had in 1901 married a dentist named Samuel Reeves who may have been a connection of the same family. Also living at that address were Hayden's cousin, Percy Hurley, for whom Hayden had taken on some responsibility, and Eileen Taylor, both beneficiaries of Hayden's will. Taylor, in codicils dated 1937 and 1942, was bequeathed £400 'in recognition of her kindness to my late brother, my cousin and myself'. Taylor dated back to the Stamer Street address, where she was the landlady to whom Hayden paid rent.[2] Others living in the Rathmines vicinity included Hanna Sheehy Skeffington and Kathleen Lynn, both well known to Hayden.

John Hayden had returned to Dublin after some years abroad, and lived with his sister until his death in 1936. He was one of a list of students of the Catholic University of Ireland on whom NUI degrees were conferred by decision of the Senate in recognition of their having for conscientious reasons (i.e. the Catholic hierarchy's objection to both the Queen's Colleges and TCD) refrained from attending institutions where they could have obtained a university degree and had attended instead at the Catholic University which had no authority to grant degrees. The degrees were conferred by Denis Coffey in his capacity as Pro-Vice-Chancellor at a ceremony on 30 March 1915.[3] John is thereafter described as barrister and LL.D. But he was not engaged in legal practice. He seems to have occupied himself writing poetry which was published fairly regularly in the *Irish Monthly* up to 1926. Shortly after his death his sister published a slim volume of his poetry as he had requested.[4] It is possible that John was the J.J. Hayden who was remunerated by the NUI in 1919 for setting a paper and reading the script for a matriculation examination in Portuguese, as he might have added that language to his accomplishments during his years abroad, but this is speculation.[5] He had moved around; in 1903 he was in Los Angeles. Mary Hayden had been in America in 1905, visiting Philadelphia, New York,

Washington and moving on to Los Angeles where John possibly still resided.[6]

Retirement

By the mid-1930s Hayden was close to her retirement. The terms and conditions of professorships in UCD provided for tenure to age sixty-five with the possibility of annual extension in office for a further five years. In 1932 the Governing Body made statutory provision to alter this five years to seven in the case of the initial appointments made by the Dublin Commissioners.

Hayden had been recommended annually by the Governing Body for extension in office, but there may have been some doubt about her exact age as she did not retire on reaching the age of seventy-two on 19 May 1934. She was corresponding with Robert Dudley Edwards, her former student, about possible employment for him and she informed him of her earnest desire to see him 'in the College in any capacity – as the thin end of the wedge'; but she thought the proposal should be put to the President by someone with more influence than she had, such as Professor MacNeill.[7] She seems to have suggested an assistantship appointment for Edwards.[8] Edwards, now returned from postgraduate work at the Institute of Historical Research in London, was seeking employment; in 1934 he had been recommended by Hayden as a well-trained student for work on a proposed History of the Irish Parliament, a major project which at the time did not materialise.[9] In a testimonial in 1935 for a post at Carysfort Teacher Training College, Hayden wrote that Edwards showed '... a quite singular enthusiasm for research work, the result of which appears in his lately published volume on the Reformation in Tudor Ireland'.[10]

Hayden was still lecturing in session 1937–38, as is clear from her letters to Edwards,[11] and seemed reluctant to retire. In a mistake in the formal procedure by which statutory staff could be continued in office by the University Senate, Hayden had been recommended by Dr Coffey for continuance for a further academic year, 1937–38. Presumably Coffey then discovered his error; according to a graduate student who noted Hayden's unease, she had had 'a protracted interview with Dr Coffey, the then President, regarding her retirement'.[12] The University Senate, having in early December approved of Hayden's continuance, at its next meeting in January noted that the continuance in office of Professor Hayden 'was due to a misunderstanding' and the Registrar was directed so to inform her.[13] Hayden's services were retained in a non-statutory (i.e. unestablished) role for the current session. On 31 March 1938 the President informed the Governing Body that Hayden had resigned as from 30 September 1937; and a statute then under consideration and finally adopted in June contained a specific provision retrospectively terminating her tenure of the Professorship of Modern Irish History on that date.[14] But she was still lecturing to the second and third year pass classes in the autumn term 1938.[15] Earlier in 1938 Hayden had been authorised to bring Edwards in to give some lectures, but delayed about informing him, either through misunderstanding or reluctance.[16] According to some of his own students, Edwards believed she had been unenthusiastic about his appointment and would not allow him a key to the history professor's room.[17] What is likely, from the correspondence and events described, is that she simply did not want to face the fact of her own retirement. The same statute which specified her retirement placed the professorship in temporary abeyance and established a lectureship in Modern Irish History, to which R. Dudley Edwards was later appointed and in which he took up office on 1 January 1939.

Financial worries may have been part of Hayden's problem. She had been one of eight professors who signed an application to the Governing Body in December 1936 for an increase in salary on grounds of their long service at very low salaries.[18] Five (including Hayden, Macken and Degani) of the eight signatories were eventually awarded an increase of £50 bringing their salaries to £800 p.a. rather than the £900 requested by them.[19] Payable from 1 January 1937 the increase must have benefited Hayden's final nine months in office and her pension.[20] However, her pension became the subject of an appeal from her colleagues, submitted to the Governing Body by Agnes O'Farrelly, requesting addition to Hayden's years of service in view of her distinguished service to the College. It was then decided to add five further years to increase her pensionable years to thirty-five.[21] Thus concluded the university career of a woman who may with fairness be described as a pioneer. Is it ironic that she who found it so hard to get in, may in the end have been somewhat difficult to remove? A few years later, Constantia Maxwell in TCD was similarly worrying about her pension as her salary had always been very small.[22]

Now past her mid-seventies, Hayden was still active. In the years 1931–33 she had held office as President of the Irish Federation of University Women, the co-ordinating body for the individual associations in the different institutions. At the annual dinner of the NUWGA in December 1937, in a speech welcoming new graduates and referring to unlimited opportunities for women of the future, she said that women had no desire to be regarded as the rivals of men in public life; their aim was merely to work in conjunction with them for the general good of humanity and the advancement of social and economic interests throughout the world,[23] once again eschewing confrontation, but calling for recognition of women's autonomous role. On a specific issue like the provisions of the 1937 Constitution, she had been prepared to engage in outright confrontation but, in the wider perspective of feminism and women's identity, dialogue and reasoned argument were her preferred approaches. As a strong-minded woman, her avoidance of combat was not a sign of weakness, rather she was estimated as an authoritative figure by both feminists and critics. She was the initiator of a discussion at the Association in 1938 on 'Openings for women graduates in country towns in Ireland', a discussion which found the medical profession to offer the best prospects for women.[24] Though she indicated in January 1939 her wish to resign from its Presidency, the committee unanimously asked her to remain as honorary President of the Association, and appointed a chairman, Eileen Davitt, to preside at meetings. Hayden remained involved, attending, speaking and on occasion presiding, as for instance in 1941 when she opened the discussion on the exclusion of women from a special course for the training of teachers of Irish advertised by the Department of Education.[25] On 10 February 1942 Hayden took the chair for the annual general meeting and on 3 March for a committee meeting, which is the last record of her attendance.

Final Publication

Aside from the posthumous article, Hayden's last publication, perhaps fortuitously but fittingly was on a feminist rather than a historical subject. Her final writing on the position of women, 'Woman's Role in the Modern World',[26] was in response to an article with the same title by Hunter Guthrie SJ which blamed women for what he saw as the faults of the contemporary world, its youth and its society; his belief that women should be domestic, holy and suffering was a conventional Victorian concept of women. Hayden wrote a sturdy refutation of Guthrie's arguments. On Guthrie's disapproval of the feminist movement, she pointed to the influence of female suffrage on British legislation, listing in an Appendix some of the laws passed since 1918 to the benefit of women and children. As always she applied the same standards to women's conduct as to men's – if violence by suffragettes was regrettable, she wrote, so too was violence in the land agitation and in the achievement of needful reforms in other countries. Hayden did not deny some of Guthrie's criticisms of modern society, for which, she insisted, society and its education were to be blamed, not women. The female brain was no different from the male, and modern life no longer required women to be totally occupied with domestic responsibilities. While accepting as generally correct that 'the home is woman's sphere', Hayden employed her understanding of logical reasoning to deem as unjustifiable the reverse assertion that 'woman's sphere is the home'. Mechanical appliances and prepared food (i.e. baker's bread or canned provisions) had reduced the chores of housekeeping, though more so for the urban than for the rural housewife. And with her children reared, a woman of forty-five had many years still in which to engage in useful social work or remunerative occupation without damaging the home life where she 'has not nearly enough to do'.

Hayden acknowledged that she was thinking, though not exclusively, of the 'comparatively well-off'. Responding to Guthrie's complaints about woman's intrusion into man's world of the professions and business and, as he saw it, her consequent reluctance to marry, Hayden defended the modern woman's freedom to marry from choice rather than economic necessity. Women could now support themselves by means other than marriage, though much of the work was, she recognised, monotonous and poorly paid. She admitted the existence of a small minority of women so fascinated by their professional, scholarly or cultural occupations that they would be reluctant to abandon them for domesticity. This latter observation is a fair description of Hayden's own feelings in her youth, and is her implicit rejection of the separation into public and private of the respective roles of men and women. However, she acknowledged that the vast majority of women, like the vast majority of men, worked in unattractive conditions to secure a tolerable living. Nor did Hayden absolve the modern woman from a share of responsibility for the failings of contemporary life, but she saw it as the task of Christian women to strive for a better world to be achieved by rejecting obsolete conventions and promoting 'the ideas which are essential and eternally true'. Hayden had high expectations of the educated woman. Previously she had queried the result of women's higher education – was she a happier, more useful citizen, a more elevated spirit? In how far had the educated woman repaid her debt to her sex, her country, or humanity in general for the advantages enjoyed over the majority of women?[27]

Again, in her response to Guthrie, Hayden was restating her belief that educated middle-class women should lead the way to an estimable and independent life for all women. She did at times seem to feel somewhat superior to the average married woman. Another of the earlier feminists, Isabella Mulvany, was forthrightly described by Enid Starkie, a pupil in Alexandra in the early years of the century:

> Like most feminists, like most women who have struggled hard for intellectual liberty and recognition, [Mulvany] had a profound and unacknowledged contempt for women and much preferred the company of men. She often made mothers feel perfect idiots, when they went to enrol their daughters at the school.[28]

This recollection in 1941 by Starkie, an Oxford academic, may have been coloured by a not very happy childhood and her sense that at Alexandra she 'was considered far below the average intellectually'[29] but Mulvany was undoubtedly a formidable figure, as also though less intimidating was Hayden. Another scholarly woman, Alice Stopford Green, was admired for her historical writing by Mary Colum who however felt Green did not take her seriously, 'in fact she seldom took women seriously at all and often had a whole dinner party composed exclusively of men'.[30] A similar comment has been made about another contemporary woman, Lady Augusta Gregory that she 'had very little time for women'.[31] These educated women had found a more stimulating intellectual environment than that offered among conventional circles of women's occupations. They were in their different ways penetrating the world of men, the realm of power and influence, and they had the determination needed to do so.

But Hayden certainly, though conscious of her own intellect and status, was not dismissive of women, as shown by her constant encouragement to students and others. Perhaps she was more radical in having arrived at a perception of a world which would encompass and value the role, the experience and the intellect of women as essential components of a true society. Possibly Hayden's involvement in issues other than the academic, particularly social work among the poor, gave her greater tolerance for life beyond the classroom. Her sympathy for the plight of many women was genuine, and so it seems was her belief that it was for educated feminists like herself to defend and improve the lives of their less fortunate sisters. The process of self-definition for women required a particular self-awareness to be achieved by education. Otherwise, women's sense of themselves received little if any encouragement from the male-dominated society, which often seemed to view women as either failed men or grown-up children.

Hayden's sense of superiority was in matters intellectual. Even as a child she had at times despised the unscholarly interests of her contemporaries, both female and male; in her maturity she knew she was among a minority of highly educated women. She saw her role as educator beyond as well as in the classroom, and as champion of women who had not had her advantaged life. Experience had shown her that education and reasoned argument had achieved considerable improvements in conditions affecting women's lives since her childhood. But by this date, 1941, there had been a succession of legislative acts by the Irish Free State to which feminists had strongly objected. The 1920s and 1930s had halted the advance of emancipation for women, which feminists of earlier years wanted to see continued. The struggle was far from over for the recognition of women as responsible individuals with a role as genuinely equal citizens. Nevertheless women's emancipation had come a long way in Hayden's lifetime, despite many setbacks, and she remained hopeful. Within four months of her last appearance at the Women Graduates' Association, she died on 12 July 1942

Conclusion

Mary Hayden's life as a whole shows her as not untypical of other contemporary feminists. From an early age she felt impatient with the constraints of female life, which she could contrast with the attractions available to her only sibling, John. For Hayden, one of the earliest Irish women to benefit from the late nineteenth century developments in secondary and university education, these opportunities provided an escape to a challenging, more fulfilling life, offering examinations, prizes, university degrees and a fellowship, for all of which she was in competition with men. Earning a living by teaching and writing then afforded Hayden more satisfying prospects than domesticity. It was education which allowed women like Hayden to establish their equality and to begin to see themselves as independent, self-determining individuals.

The second half of Hayden's life coincided with the emergence of more organised groups of women, starting for her with the Irish Association of Women Graduates and Candidate Graduates followed by the campaign for women's suffrage. Unlike some among the women graduates, Hayden saw admission to the university as but a start for women on the way to a significant role in society, and under her presidency the Association turned its attention to educational, employment and professional opportunities for women graduates. While it was established in pursuit of fundamental change for women in the realm of university education, the Association during its first two decades remained otherwise modest in its demands and in its methods. Notably the Association did not participate in the demand for the parliamentary franchise; Hayden and Sheehy Skeffington both exercised their deep commitment to the campaign through various suffrage societies without involving the IAWGCG.

In the 1920s and 1930s Hayden spoke and wrote on many subjects which had aroused the concern of feminists. She was one of the relatively small number of women who identified ominous prospects in much of the legislation of the new State, foreseeing a consequent curtailment of women's role and rights. Her distinction as a veteran of the university issue and as a university professor made her an important and noteworthy participant, and something of a mentor also in the women's organisations. Hayden was still President in 1937 when the National University Women Graduates' Association played its most prominent public role in mounting a campaign against the new Constitution. Though aged seventy-five and surrounded by many committed campaigners, Hayden herself was clearly quite energetically involved.

While the term 'career woman' was not current in Hayden's youth, her career had satisfied much of the undefined yearnings of her formative years. However, in her view which did not change, marriage and the home was the destiny for the majority of women. In her younger days Hayden had sometimes been quite critical of, and at times pitied, some married women of both middle and working classes. Occasional statements by her in later years which reiterated these criticisms might be read as displaying a lofty detachment from the lives of ordinary women – that the housewife had not enough to do or that the workman's wife fed her family 'from cans'.[32] This negative and glib view of working-class women as bad housekeepers was shared by many educated women, including the historian Helena Concannon.[33]

In spite of herself Hayden at times exhibited the traditional male attitude to woman's role in the home; unpaid work did not rank in the same scale as men's occupations. But she also, and for this reason, urged that women should aspire to better themselves in their domestic role, in both performance and attitude. Hayden was by no means unusual even among her feminist contemporaries in seeing the home as the more desirable occupation for very many women.[34] She recognised that for working-class women paid employment was frequently a necessity, imposed by poor wages paid to men, and she believed that a man's earnings should be enough to support his family. A woman's work outside the home should then be her choice, freely made, appropriate to her abilities and qualifications, and rewarded on the same scale as men in the workplace. Furthermore, while she believed strongly in employment opportunities at all levels for women, single and married, she also saw marriage as a possible diversion of a woman's attention from her professional advancement, a perception which owed something to her own single status.[35] Here, there is a suggestion of élitism in her personality. Her privileged life had allowed her to indulge her aspirations in ways not open to the majority of contemporary women.

Her social work, a continuation of the philanthropic work in which she and her predecessors had engaged in the nineteenth century, had a notable content of educational endeavour. Though detail is scant about the social club, St Joan's, which Hayden founded, its work with poor children included educational and cultural events, as well as the provision of food and clothing. Unconsciously she was here in a small way exercising the domestic responsibilities which she had so deliberately eschewed as her main role in life.[36] While much of Hayden's thinking was concentrated on women of the middle class, their education and occupations, her social conscience, evident in her girlhood, extended in very practical ways to the less privileged during the years of the suffrage campaign through her association with the work of the IWRL. The League's activities brought her face to face with the Dublin poor, their living and working conditions, and with the problems of drunkenness and prostitution aggravated by the circumstances of World War I.

She also encouraged the organisation of unskilled women workers in trade unions. In joining in the opposition to the Conditions of Employment Act 1936 with its restrictions on women's employment in industry, Hayden and other feminists were acutely conscious of the threatening implications which they perceived in the accumulation of constraints on women's place in society, though this latest measure did not affect middle-class women. Nor were the practical results for working-class women of major significance, but the issue was seen by feminists as symptomatic of the State's attitude to women.[37] Hayden's comment that the Irish Free State Government had been placed 'on a black list at Geneva' as a result of this Act is one of the most frequently quoted references to her.[38]

Hayden was a significant figure of twentieth-century feminism in Ireland, one whose youthful instincts gradually evolved as a coherent belief in women's equality and in the necessity of its recognition in all aspects of life, family, education, employment opportunities and pay. While there is no evidence that she knew of Mary Wollstonecraft's *A Vindication of the Rights of Woman* (1792), that author's argument as described by Mary Cullen 'that women were rational human beings as men were and as such should be educated to become self-determining adults who took responsibility for their own lives'[39] accurately represents Hayden's convictions. Her stature as a professional woman and a university professor made her a formidable exponent of feminist thinking. This status, represented also by other academic feminists, emphasised the middle-class tenor of the movement, giving rise for instance during the campaign against the Constitution to jibes about 'learned ladies'.

Even within the middle class, feminists were a minority and 'the mass of Irish women were untouched by feminism'.[40] Feminism might have been expected to extend its influence following the achievement of the parliamentary franchise and the establishment of a new independent State, but as we have seen this did not happen. Most women were as conservative as most men in that society, a fact which distinguishes feminists, a minority, as remarkable, radical thinkers and activists. And in recognition of the efforts of the feminists, we may note Caitríona Clear's comment, 'the very fact that women's rights were constantly being debated, defined and defended indicates that they were very much alive'.[41]

Though now less well known than some of her peers, Hayden was, in her time, an influential figure whose contribution was important for the example of her own achievements, for her outspoken articulation of her feminist attitude and for her constant encouragement to other, particularly younger, women to see themselves as individuals, as citizens with rights and opportunities, duties and responsibilities in no way inferior to those of the male members of the community. Writing sixty-four years after Hayden's death, the historian Nadia Smith described her as 'one of the most prominent feminists in the Irish Free State'.[42] Uninterested in national or party politics in her early life, Hayden had gradually developed sympathy for the nationalist cause, a sympathy informed by her interests in the Celtic revival, the Irish language, the history and heritage of the country. It is accurate to describe her as a nationalist, but it is also clear from a study of her life and writing that her feminist beliefs and aspirations took precedence in her thinking; this was the cause nearest to her heart in the words of Agnes O'Farrelly.[43]

In her time Hayden was a scholar of some repute. The articles on medieval literary texts included among her earliest writings were learned works. Her education in the classics and later her interest in the revival of the Irish language led her to the study of Old Irish in which she had at least one respected publication.[44] The textbook on Irish history and the articles and reviews in that subject were her major output, all the work of her later years. As a historian she is now hardly known except to other historians for whom she is outdated. During the years when she was teaching and writing Hayden was a respected authority from whom several generations in schools and universities acquired their knowledge of Irish history. Her textbook proved, as intended by its two authors, to be a widely acceptable account of its history for those living in the newly-independent State, despite the misgivings of a few republican critics,[45] and was not superseded until well into the second half of the century.

Why was this singular woman almost forgotten? For much of the twentieth century the history of Irish women was dominated by the nationalist agenda and the women of Inghinidhe na hÉireann and Cumann na mBan.[46] The many issues of equality for women which Hayden and her contemporaries pursued were not accorded their place in the conventional history of the period. And more widely beyond feminism, women's experience in general in the political, social and economic movements of the past is only slowly being recognised as a legitimate and significant ingredient of mainstream history. In his consideration of the journal *Irish Historical Studies* of the mid-twentieth century, Joe Lee has written 'History was essentially the study of institutions, mainly political and ecclesiastical, rather than of society or of mentalities'.[47] In a wider context, the comment might be borrowed and applied to the absence of the very existence of women from the subjects of study in the discipline.

Hayden had no involvement in party politics and, unlike for instance Jennie Wyse Power or Louie Bennett, never held public office or a public appointment. The offices which Hayden held in the university world though prestigious were of less popular significance. There were many factors to place her in an unfavourable light when viewed by the rulers of the Irish Free State, particularly once the Fianna Fáil party came to power in 1932; one could cite her disapproval of militant republicanism and her emphasis on women's suffrage ahead of nationalism, her earlier sympathy for the Irish Parliamentary Party, or her association with some unionist sympathies in the short-lived Irish Dominion League and with organisations which included Ladies Fingall, Arnott, Dockrell and so on. Taunts about being anti-national were directed at Hayden and other women campaigners against the Constitution in 1937. As one historian has commented the universities had been 'not entirely without reason, seen as bastions of unreconstructed unionism and of pro-treaty partisanship'.[48] In the 1920s Hayden's acceptance of the

Treaty and the government led by W.T. Cosgrave was recognised by her nomination by that government on three successive occasions to the Governing Body of UCD, a valued appointment. She was not however, either then or later, inhibited from criticism of government measures inimical to women's interests.

The opposition to the Treaty by all six women members of the Dáil is seen as one reason for the subsequent exclusion of women from political life, but many other women including Hayden accepted the Treaty and were satisfied to work with the new State to which they wished to make their contribution. Their disappointment in these expectations has been recounted. Another possible reason for the omission of women from the historical record was resentment at the intrusion of women into the male world of power and influence, and those women who were intelligent, educated and articulate were particularly to be feared as posing the greatest threat.

Hayden was optimistic about women's advancement, however slow the progress might be, having experienced in her own lifetime changes which would have been unimaginable to the Victorian girl of the 1870s. Feminist women, though a minority, became increasingly confident about adopting a public stance from which to argue their particular concerns and to engage in debate with men. While Hayden took no part in the Easter Rising and subsequent republican activities, she knew many women who did. During the early years of the Irish Free State the tide of emancipation expected by feminists was halted, but feminist protests at constraints on women's lives continued until in 1937 women launched a vigorous public campaign against the adoption of the new Constitution proposed by Éamon de Valera. The view of women as subordinate individuals was still widespread, but women like Hayden were prepared by challenging that view to demonstrate that they no longer accepted it, as she for one had done in her girlhood. Women remained a marginalized group throughout Hayden's life, but much had been achieved in breaching the boundaries which separated, as public and private, the roles assigned respectively to men and to women.

As she moved towards adulthood in the 1880s and 1890s Hayden had admired the personalities and abilities of Oldham, Mulvany and Haslam, whom she came to recognise as significant individuals in the advances towards women's recognition of a distinct, emancipated identity for themselves, as described in her talk to the Women Graduates' Association in the 1920s. Hayden's own life provided a credible model for the next generation, the young women of the early twentieth century. Equality with men had been the only exemplar of freedom, as in the demands for university education and the franchise. Hayden and other women had arrived at the belief that equal citizenship for women implied an autonomous role for them as not identical but complementary to men in a society of equal participants. Women no less than men were agents of that society.

Having achieved for herself the sort of life she had wanted, Hayden's hope was that in time every woman would have the opportunity to fulfil her individual potential, whatever it might be, and that the significance of woman's role, both public and private, would be acknowledged. As a feminist, Hayden remained patiently optimistic.

NOTES

1   Agnes O'Farrelly, 'Mary Hayden', *Alexandra College Magazine*, (December 1942).
2   Hayden Diary, 26 March 1901.
3   NUI Senate Minutes, 21 May 1915.
4   John J. Hayden LL.D., *Poems: Original and Translated* (Dublin, 1938).
5   NUI Senate Minutes, 21 May 1919.

6   Hayden to Pearse, 14 March 1905, NLI, Patrick Pearse Papers, Ms. 21050.

7   Hayden to Edwards, 4 August (1936?), UCD Archives, Edwards Papers, LA 22/129/(4).

8   Hayden to MacNeill, 27 September (1936?), NLI MacNeill Papers, Ms 10,881.

9   Edith Mary Johnson, 'Managing an Inheritance: Col JC Wedgewood, the *History of Parliament* and the Lost History of the Irish Parliament', *Proceedings Royal Irish Academy*, Vol. 89, Section C, No 7 (1989), p. 179. (cited in O'Dowd, 'From Morgan to Mac Curtain', p. 298, n. 89).

10   UCD Archives, R.D. Edwards correspondence, LA 22/83.

11   UCD Archives, Edwards Papers, LA/22/146.

12   Thomas A. Burke to R.D. Edwards, 21 January 1941, UCD Archives, Edwards Papers, LA/22/131(15).

13   NUI Senate Minutes, 9 December 1937 and 13 January 1938.

14   UCD Statute XXIII, 1938, Chap. I.

15   Hayden to Edwards, 8 November 1938, UCD Archives, Edwards Papers, LA/22/146(18).

16   A. Conway to Edwards, 4 February 1938. UCD Archives, Edwards Papers, LA/22/146 (10). Hayden to Edwards, 4 February 1938, *ibid*, 146 (11).

17   Author's conversations with Donal McCartney and Kevin B. Nowlan.

18   Governing Body Minutes, 1 December 1936.

19   Governing Body Minutes, 23 February 1937.

20   UCD Statute XXVI, Chap. I, Section 8, 1939.

21   Governing Body Minutes, 15 November 1938.

22   Nadia Clare Smith, *A 'Manly Study'? Irish Women Historians, 1868–1949* (Basingstoke, 2006), p. 103.

23   *Irish Times,* 13 December 1937.

24   UCD Archives, NUWGA 2/21 Minutes, 15 March and 27 April 1938.

25   UCD Archives, NUWGA 2/2 Minutes, 17 and 27 January 1941.

26   Mary Hayden, 'Woman's Role in the Modern World', *Irish Monthly,* LXIX, No 818 (August 1941), pp 392–402.

27   Mary Hayden, 'A Few Thoughts on Women in Universities and on University Women', *The National Student*, June 1935, p. 71.

28   Enid Starkie, *A Lady's Child* (London, 1941), p. 183.

29   *Ibid*, p. 191.

30   Mary Colum, *Life and the Dream* (Dublin, 1966, rev. ed.), p. 244.

31   Colm Tóibín, *Lady Gregory's Toothbrush* (Dublin, 2002), p. 112.

32 Hayden, 'Woman's Role in the Modern World', *The Irish Monthly* (August, 1941), p. 398.

33 Caitríona Clear, 'No Feminine Mystique: Popular Advice to Women of the House in Ireland 1922–54' in Maryann Valiulis and Mary O'Dowd (eds), *Women and Irish History*, p. 190; Nadia Clare Smith, *A 'Manly Study'?*, p. 128.

34 Mary Cullen and Maria Luddy (eds), 'Introduction', *Female Activists: Irish Women and Change 1900–1960* (Dublin, 2001), p. 5.

35 Mary Hayden, 'The New Woman: A Reply', Typescript, NLI. Hayden Papers Ms 24011.

36 Mary Macken, 'In Memoriam; Mary T. Hayden', *Studies*, (September, 1942), p. 370.

37 Rosemary Cullen Owens, 'Louie Bennett' in *Female Activists*, p. 52.

38 *Irish Times*, 22 June 1937.

39 Mary Cullen 'Making Argument Work: The Case of Feminism' in Toner Quinn (ed.), *Desmond Fennell, His Life and Work* (Dublin, 2001), p. 105.

40 Cullen Owens, *Smashing Times*, p. 134.

41 Caitríona Clear, 'Women in de Valera's Ireland 1932–48: A Reappraisal' in Gabriel Doherty and Dermot Keogh (eds), *De Valera's Ireland* (Cork, 2003), p. 108.

42 Smith, *A 'Manly Study'?*, p. 65.

43 Agnes O'Farrelly, 'Mary Hayden', *Alexander College Magazine* (December, 1942).

44 'The Songs of Buchet's House', *Zeitschrift fur Celtische Philologie*. See above Chapter 5.

45 See above Chapter 8.

46 Carmel Quinlan, *Genteel Revolutionaries: Anna and Thomas Haslam and the Irish Women's Movement* (Cork, 2002), p. x.

47 J.J. Lee, *Ireland 1912–1985: Politics and Society* (Cambridge, 1989), p. 593.

48 Eunan O'Halpin, 'Historical Revisit: Dorothy Macardle, *The Irish Republic* (1937)', *Irish Historical Studies*, XXXI, 123 (May, 1999), p. 390.

PUBLISHED WRITINGS OF MARY TERESA HAYDEN (*chronologically arranged*)

The Diaries of Mary Hayden 1878–1903, edited and annotated by Conan Kennedy (Killala, 2005), 5 volumes.

'Religious Poetry', *The Lyceum,* 1, 7 (March 1888).

'Biographies of Words', *The Lyceum,* 1, 8 (April 1888).

and Lilian Green, 'Greek Peasant Girls, and How they Live', *The Girl's Own Paper,* 4 June 1892, pp 564–565.

'Medieval Etiquette', *New Ireland Review,* 6 (October 1896), pp 86–102.

'Maria Edgeworth', *National Literary Society of Ireland Journal,* 1 (1900), pp 15–42.

'The Irish Language Movement and the Gaelic League', *Alexandra College Magazine* (December 1903), pp 3–9.

Ní Aodáin, Máire, 'The Golden Mean', *An Claidheamh Soluis,* 7 and 14 January 1905.

Ní A, M. 'Living for Ireland', *An Claidheamh Soluis,* 25 January 1908.

'Children in the Middle Ages', *Alexandra College Magazine* (December 1906), pp 20–32.

and Hanna Sheehy Skeffington, 'Women in Universities: A Reply', *Irish Educational Review,* 1, 5 (February 1908), pp 272–83.

and Hanna Sheehy Skeffington, 'Women in Universities: A Further Reply', *Irish Educational Review,* 1, 7 (April 1908), pp 410–18.

'Training of Irish Girls for Citizenship', *Irish Educational Review,* 2, 1 (October 1908), pp 10–18.

Facts About the Irish Language and the Irish Language Movement (Dublin, 1910).

'The Congress of Historical Studies', *Studies,* 2 (June 1913), pp 99–102.

'Report of Debate in the Parliament of Amazonia on the Representation of the People (Men) Bill', *Irish Citizen,* 9, 16, 23 and 30 August 1913.

'Women in the Middle Ages', *The Irish Review,* 3 (August 1913), pp 282–358 (September 1913), pp 344–58.

'Lambert Simnel in Ireland', *Studies,* 4 (December 1915), pp 623–38.

and George A. Moonan, *A Short History of the Irish People* (Dublin, 1921).

'The Dublin Streets in the Early Eighteenth Century', *Alexandra College Magazine* (December 1923).

'History to Be Unlearned' in William G. Fitzgerald (ed.), *The Voice of Ireland (Glór na hÉireann): A Survey of the Race and Nation from All Angles, by the Foremost Leaders at Home and Abroad* (Dublin, 1924), pp 47–56.

'The Origin and Development of Heads of Bills in the Irish Parliament', *Royal Society of Antiquaries of Ireland Journal,* 55 (1925), pp 112–25.

'Dublin Workhouse Children in the Eighteenth Century', *Alexandra College Magazine* (December 1928), pp 16–19.

'Prince Charles Edward and his Irish Friends', *Studies,* 23, 89 (March 1934), pp 95–109.

'My Recollections of Pádraig Pearse' in Mary Brigid Pearse (ed.), *The Home Life of Pádraig Pearse as Told by Himself, his Family, and Friends* (Dublin, 1979, 2nd ed. [First published 1934]), pp 113–6.

'A Few Thoughts on Women in Universities and on University Women', *The National Student,* 12, 1 (June 1935), pp 70–77.

'Giraldus Cambrensis', *Studies,* 24 (March 1935), pp 99–110.

'Women and the New Constitution: Hard Won Rights to be Lost', *Cork Examiner,* 29 June 1937.

'Dublin Ladies of the Eighteenth Century', *Alexandra College Magazine,* 91 (1938), pp 3–13.

'Woman's Role in the Modern World', *The Irish Monthly,* 59 (August, 1941), pp 392–402.

'Charity Children in 18th Century Dublin', *Dublin Historical Record,* 5, 3 (1943), pp 92–107.

PRIMARY
Dublin Diocesan Archives (DDA)
Archbishop Walsh papers.

National Archives of Ireland (NAI)
Talbot Press papers.
Department of Taoiseach. Women and the Constitution 1937.

National Library of Ireland (NLI)
Diaries of Mary Hayden (NLI, Ms. 16,627–16,683).
Eoin MacNeill papers (NLI MS 10,881).
Hanna Sheehy Skeffington papers (NLI Ms 22,667 (i)).
MacIomaire papers (NLI Ms 24,043).
Mary Hayden papers (NLI Mss 23,403–23,404, 24,407, 24,009–24,013).
Minute books of the National Literary Society, Dublin, 1892–
1911(NLI Ms 645–6).
P.H. Pearse papers (NLI Mss 21,050, 21054 (4), 21,059).

National University of Ireland (NUI)
Minutes of the Senate of the National University of Ireland.
Minutes of the Senate of the Royal University of Ireland.

Trinity College Dublin (TCD)
Hayden to Pearse, 4 June 1903, 2 June 1904 (TCD, Ms. 8265/154,182).

University College Dublin Archives (UCDA)
Bridget Stafford Papers (UCDA P 63/4).
Papers of the National University Women Graduates' Association
(NUWGA 1–2/21).
R. Dudley Edwards papers (UCDA, LA 22/129).
R. Dudley Edwards correspondence (UCDA LA 22/83).
University College Dublin, Governing Body Minutes
(UCDA/C/GBMIN).

University College Dublin Library
Catholic Graduates and Undergraduates Association, Minutes of
Committee Meetings (UCD Library, Curran papers, CUR Ms 25).

Research Theses

Faughnan, Sean A., 'De Valera's Constitution: The Drafting of the Irish Constitution of 1937' (MA thesis, UCD, 1988).

Finnegan, Belinda, 'The Democratisation of Higher Education and the Participation of University Women in the Labour Force 1920–50' (MA thesis, UCD, 1985).

McGinty, Mary C., 'A Study of the Campaign For and Against the Enactment of the 1937 Constitution' (MA thesis, UCG, 1987).

McLaughlin, Astrid, 'Received with Politeness, Treated with Contempt: The Story of Women's Protests in Ireland Against the Regressive Implications of Sections of the Conditions of Employment Act 1936 and the Irish Constitution of 1937' (MA thesis, UCD, 1996).

Newspapers

An Claidheamh Soluis
An Macaomh
Catholic Suffragist (re-named *The Catholic Citizen* from February 1918)
Cork Examiner
Freeman's Journal
Irish Citizen
Irish Independent
Irish Press
Irish Times
The Leader
The Sphere

Electronic Sources

Dictionary of Irish biography (http://dib.cambridge.org)
Directory of Sources for Women's History in Ireland
(http://www.nationalarchives.ie)
Oxford Dictionary of National Biography (http://oxforddnb.com)
Women in 20th-Century Ireland, 1922–1966: Sources from the Department of the Taoiseach (http://www.nationalarchives.ie)

Printed Primary Sources

First Report of the Royal Commission on Trinity College, Dublin, and the University of Dublin, 1906 (Cd. 3174, 3176), lvi, 601; Final Report 1907 (Cd. 3311–2), xli, 1[Fry].

First Report of the Royal Commission on University Education in Ireland]: 1902 (Cd. 825–6), xxxi, 21; Second Report 1902 (Cd. 899–900), xxxi,

459; Third Report 1902 (Cd. 1228–9), xxxii, 1; Final Report 1903 (Cd. 1483–4), xxxii, 1. [Robertson].

Royal University of Ireland, *Calendar* (Dublin, 1883–1909)

University College Dublin, *Report of the President* (Dublin, 1909–)

SECONDARY

[Anon.], 'A Tribute to Professor Mary Hayden, D.Litt.', *The Lanthorn: Yearbook of the Dominican College, Eccles Street, Dublin, Christmas 1942* (Dublin, 1942), pp 349–351.

[Anon.], 'Report of Students' Union Debate', *Alexandra College Magazine* (December 1900), pp 101–2.

Aberdeen, John Campbell Gordon (1847–1934), 7th Earl of and 1st Marquess of Aberdeen and Temair and Ishbel Gordon, Marchioness of Aberdeen and Temair, *We Twa: Reminiscences of Lord and Lady Aberdeen* (London, 1925), 2 volumes.

'Health and Happiness in the Homes of Ireland' in William G. FitzGerald (ed.), *The Voice of Ireland (Glór na h-Éireann): A Survey of the Race and Nation from all Angles by the Foremost Leaders at Home and Abroad* (Dublin, 1924), pp 434–39.

Andrews, C.S., *Dublin Made Me* (Dublin, 1979).

Augusteijn, Joost, *Patrick Pearse: The Making of a Revolutionary* (Basingstoke, 2010).

Beaumont, Catriona, 'Women and the Politics of Equality: The Irish Women's Movement 1930–43' in Maryann Valiulis and Mary O'Dowd (eds), *Women and Irish History: Essays in Honour of Margaret Mac Curtain* (Dublin, 1997), pp 179–88.

Berg, Maxine, 'A Woman in History: Eileen Power and the Early Years of Social History and Women's History' in Mary O'Dowd and Sabine Wichert (eds), *Chattel, Servant or Citizen? Women's Status in Church, State and Society* (Belfast, 1995), pp 12–21 (Historical Studies, XIX).

Boland, John P., *Some Memories* (Dublin, 1928, private circulation).
Irishman's Day: A Day in the Life of an Irish M.P. (London, c. 1944).

Brady, Joseph, 'Dublin at the Turn of the Century' in Joseph Brady and Anngret Simms (eds), *Dublin Through Space and Time* (Dublin, 2001), pp 221–81.

Breathnach, Eibhlin, 'Women and Higher Education in Ireland (1879–1914)', *The Crane Bag*, 4, 1 (1980), pp 47–54.

'Charting New Waters: Women's Experience in Higher Education, 1879–1908' in Mary Cullen (ed.), *Girls Don't Do*

Honours: Irish Women in Education in the 19th and 20th Centuries (Dublin, 1987), pp 55–78.

Bunkers, Suzanne L., '"Faithful Friend": Nineteenth Century Midwestern American Women's Unpublished Diaries' in Dale Spender (ed.), *Personal Chronicle: Women's Autobiographical Writings* (New York, 1987), pp 7–17.

Cameron, Charles A., *History of the Royal College of Surgeons in Ireland and of the Irish Schools of Medicine* (Dublin, 1916).

Clancy, Mary, 'Aspects of Women's Contribution to the Oireachtas Debate in the Irish Free State, 1922–37' in Maria Luddy and Cliona Murphy (eds), *Women Surviving: Studies in Irish Women's History in the 19th and 20th Centuries* (Dublin, 1989), pp 206–32.

'"It was our Joy to Keep the Flag Flying": A Study of the Women's Suffrage Campaign in County Galway', *UCG Women's Studies Centre Review*, Vol. 3 (1995), pp 91–104.

Clear, Caitríona, '"The Women Can Not Be Blamed": The Commission on Vocational Organisation, Feminism and "Homemakers" in Independent Ireland in the 1930s and 1940s' in Mary O'Dowd and Sabine Wichert (eds), *Chattel, Servant or Citizen? Women's Status in Church, State and Society* (Belfast, 1995), pp 179–86 (Historical Studies, XIX).

'No Feminine Mystique: Popular Advice to Women of the House in Ireland 1922–54' in Maryann Valiulis and Mary O'Dowd (eds), *Women and Irish History: Essays in Honour of Margaret Mac Curtain* (Dublin, 1997), pp 189–205.

Women of the House: Women's Household Work in Ireland 1922–1961: Discourses, Experiences, Memories (Dublin, 2000).

'Women in de Valera's Ireland 1932–48: A Reappraisal' in Gabriel Doherty and Dermot Keogh (eds), *De Valera's Irelands* (Cork, 2003), pp 104–14.

Colum, Mary, *Life and the Dream* (1947/1966).

Cooper, Joanne E., 'Shaping Meaning: Women's Diaries, Journals and Letters: The Old and the New' in Dale Spender (ed.), *Personal Chronicles: Women's Autobiographical Writings* (New York, 1987), pp 95–9.

Coulter, Carol, *The Hidden Tradition: Feminism, Women and Nationalism in Ireland* (Cork, 1993).

Cullen, Mary and Maria Luddy (eds), *Women, Power and Consciousness in 19th Century Ireland: Eight Biographical Studies* (Dublin, 1995).

'Anna Maria Haslam' in Mary Cullen and Maria Luddy (eds), *Women, Power and Consciousness in 19th Century Ireland: Eight Biographical Studies* (Dublin, 1995), pp 161–96.

and Maria Luddy (eds), *Female Activists: Irish Women and Change, 1900–1960* (Dublin, 2001).

'Making Argument Work: The Case of Feminism' in Toner Quinn (ed.), *Desmond Fennell: His Life and Work* (Dublin, 2001), pp 100–116.

'Women, Emancipation, and Politics, 1860–1984' in J.R. Hill (ed.), *A New History of Ireland Vol. VII: Ireland 1921–84* (Oxford, 2003), pp 826–91.

Cullen Owens, Rosemary, *Smashing Times: A History of the Irish Women's Suffrage Movement 1899–1922* (Dublin, 1984; reprint 1995).

'Louie Bennett (1870–1956)' in Mary Cullen and Maria Luddy (eds), *Female Activists: Irish Women and Change, 1900–1960* (Dublin, 2001), pp 37–60.

Louie Bennett (Cork, 2001).

A Social History of Women in Ireland 1870–1970 (Dublin, 2005).

'"The Machine Will Work Without Them": Kevin O'Higgins and the Jury Bills 1924 and 1927' in Myles Dungan (ed.), *Speaking Ill of the Dead* (Dublin, 2007), pp 41–66.

Curtayne, Alice, *The New Woman* (Dublin, 1934).

Daly, Mary E., *Dublin, the Deposed Capital: A Social and Economic History 1860–1914* (Cork, 1984).

'Women in the Irish Free State, 1922–39: The Interaction Between Economics and Ideology' in Joan Hoff and Moureen Coulter (eds), *Irish Women's Voices: Past and Present* (Bloomington, Ind., 1995), pp 99–116.

Davitt, Cahir, 'The New College (1908–1916) IV' in James Meenan (ed.), *Centenary History of the Literary and Historical Society of University College Dublin 1855–1955* (Dublin, 2005, 2nd ed.), pp 114–26.

Dillon, Thomas, 'The Origin and Early History of the National University: Part I', *University Review*, 1, 5 (1955), pp 43–51; Part II, *University Review*, 1, 6 (Autumn 1955), pp 12–28.

'Early Days in the New University College Dublin', *University Review*, 2, 3/4 (1958), pp 23–32.

Doherty, Martin A., 'Kevin Barry and the Anglo-Irish Propaganda War', *Irish Historical Studies*, 32, 126 (November 2000), pp 217–31.

Downes, Margaret Tierney, *The Case of the Catholic Lady Students of the Royal University Stated* (Dublin, 1888).

Dunleavy, Janet and Gareth Dunleavy, *Douglas Hyde: A Maker of Modern Ireland* (California, 1991).

Dyhouse, Carol, *Feminism and the Family in England 1880–1939* (Oxford, 1989).

No Distinction of Sex: Women in British Universities 1870–1939 (London, 1995).

Edwards, David, 'Salvaging History: Hogan and the Irish Manuscripts Commission' in Donnchadh Ó Corráin (ed.), *James Hogan: Revolutionary, Historian and Political Scientist* (Dublin, 2001), pp 116–32.

Edwards, Robert Dudley, 'An Agenda for Irish History 1978–2018' in Ciaran Brady (ed.), *Interpreting Irish History: The Debate on Historical Revisionism* (Dublin, 1994), pp 54–67.

Edwards, Ruth Dudley, *Patrick Pearse: The Triumph of Failure* (London, 1979, 2nd ed.).

Ellis, Steven, 'Nationalist Historiography and the English and Gaelic Worlds in the late Middle Ages' in Ciaran Brady (ed.), *Interpreting Irish History: The Debate on Historical Revisionism* (Dublin, 1994), pp 161–80.

Evans, Richard J., *The Feminists: Women's Emancipation Movements in Europe, America and Australasia* (London, 1977).

Faithful, L.M., 'Home Science (1911)' in Dale Spender (ed.), *The Education Papers: Women's Quest for Equality in Britain, 1850–1912* (London, 1987), pp 325–7.

Fanning, Ronan, *Independent Ireland* (Dublin, 1983).

'Mr de Valera Drafts a Constitution' in Brian Farrell (ed.), *De Valera's Constitution and Ours* (Dublin, 1988), pp 32–45.

'"The Great Enchantment": Uses and Abuses of Modern Irish History' in Ciaran Brady (ed.), *Interpreting Irish History: The Debate on Historical Revisionism* (Dublin, 1994), pp 146–60.

Fathers of the Society of Jesus, *A Page of Irish History: The Story of University College Dublin 1883–1909* (Dublin and Cork, 1930).

Ferriter, Diarmaid, 'Hayden, Mary Teresa', *Dictionary of Irish Biography* (Cambridge, 2009), vol. 4, pp 531–2.

Fitzpatrick, David, 'The Futility of History: A Failed Experiment in Irish Education' in Ciaran Brady (ed.), *Ideology and the Historian* (Dublin, 1991), pp 254–62 (Historical Studies XVII).

Foster, R.F., *Modern Ireland 1600–1972* (London, 1989).

'History and the Irish Question' in Ciaran Brady (ed.), *Interpreting Irish History: The Debate on Historical Revisionism 1938–1994* (Dublin, 1994), pp 122–45.

W.B. Yeats: A Life. 1. The Apprentice Mage 1865–1914 (Oxford, 1997).

Gaelic League, *Annual Reports* (Dublin, 1905–10).

Garvin, Tom, *1922: The Birth of Irish Democracy* (Dublin, 1996).

Green, Alice Stopford, 'Tradition in Irish History' in her *The Old Irish World* (Dublin, 1912), pp 168–97.

Woman's Place in the World of Letters (London, 1913).

Harford, Judith, *The Opening of University Education to Women in Ireland* (Dublin, 2008).

'The Historiography of the Professoriate: Reflections on the Role and Legacy of Professor Mary Hayden (1862–1942)', *Paedagogica Historica*, 2019, DOI. https://doi.org/10.1080/00309230.2019.166968 1.

Hayden, John J., 'The Diary of John J. Hayden: 25 April–15 June 1878' in Conan Kennedy (ed.), *The Diaries of Mary Hayden* (Killala, 2005), 5 vols, V, pp 2351–62.

Poems: Original and Translated (Dublin, 1938).

Hogan, James, 'Memoir 1913–1937' in Donnchadh Ó Corráin (ed.), *James Hogan: Revolutionary, Historian and Political Scientist* (Dublin, 2001), pp 186–202.

Hogan, J.J., 'The Work of Dr Coffey and Dr Conway' in Michael Tierney (ed.), *Struggle with Fortune* (Dublin, 1954), pp 81–102.

Hogan, Mary J., *University College Dublin Women Graduates' Association 1902–1982*.

Hyde, Douglas, 'My Memories of the Irish Revival' in William G. FitzGerald (ed.), *The Voice of Ireland (Glór na h-Éireann): A Survey of the Race and Nation from all Angles by the Foremost Leaders at Home and Abroad* (Dublin, 1924), pp 454–6.

Irish Dominion League, *Official Report Setting Forth a Summary of the Results Achieved By, Together with the Proceedings on Dissolution* (Dublin, 1921).

Irish Women's Suffrage and Local Government Association, *Reports of the Executive Committee* ([Dublin], 1906–1910).

Kennedy, Conan (ed.), *The Diaries of Mary Hayden, 1878–1903* (Killala, 2005), 5 volumes.

Kennedy, Finola, 'Family Life' in Kieran A. Kennedy (ed.), *From Famine to Feast: Economic and Social Change in Ireland 1847–1997* (Dublin, 1998), pp 123–33.

Cottage to Crèche: Family Change in Ireland (Dublin, 2001).

Keogh, Dermot, *Twentieth Century Ireland: Nation and State* (Dublin, 1994).

Laffan, Michael, *The Resurrection of Ireland: The Sinn Féin Party 1916–1923* (Cambridge, 1999).

Lane, Leeann, *Rosamond Jacob: Third Person Singular* (Dublin, 2010).

Lee, J.J., *Ireland 1912–1985: Politics and Society* (Cambridge, 1989).

Levine, Philippa, *Feminist Lives in Victorian England: Private Roles and Public Commitment* (Oxford, 1990).

Lillis, Mercedes, 'The Ursulines in Thurles: The First Hundred Years 1787–1887' in William Corbett and William Nolan (ed.), *Thurles: The Cathedral Town: Essays in Honour of Archbishop Thomas Morris* (Dublin, 1989), pp191–211.

Luce, John Victor, *Trinity College Dublin: The First 400 Years* (Dublin, 1991).

Luddy, Maria, 'Prostitution and Rescue Work in Nineteenth Century Ireland' in Maria Luddy and Cliona Murphy (eds), *Women Surviving: Studies in Irish Women's History in the 19th and 20th Centuries* (Dublin, 1989), pp 51–84.

Women in Ireland, 1800–1918: A Documentary History (Cork, 1995).

'Isabella M.S. Tod (1836–1896)' in Mary Cullen and Maria Luddy (eds), *Women, Power and Consciousness in 19th Century Ireland: Eight Biographical Studies* (Dublin, 1995), pp 197–230.

Women and Philanthropy in Nineteenth-Century Ireland (Cambridge, 1995).

'Women and Politics in Nineteenth Century Ireland' in Maryann Valiulis and Mary O'Dowd (eds), *Women and Irish History: Essays in Honour of Margaret Mac Curtain* (Dublin, 1997), pp 89–108.

'A "Sinister and Retrospective Proposal", Irish Women's Opposition to the 1937 Draft Constitution', *Transactions of Royal Historical Society*, 15 (2005), pp 175–95.

Prostitution and Irish Society 1800–1940 (Cambridge, 2007).

Lyons, F.S.L., *Ireland Since the Famine* (Glasgow, 1973, 2nd ed.).

Lyons, J.B., *The Enigma of Tom Kettle: Irish Patriot, Essayist, Poet, British Soldier, 1880–1916* (Dublin, 1983).

MacBride, Maud Gonne, *A Servant of the Queen: Reminiscences*, edited by A. Norman Jeffares and Anna MacBride White (Gerrard's Cross, 1994, rev. ed.).

McCartney, Donal, *The National University of Ireland and Eamon de Valera* (Dublin, 1983).

W.E.H. Lecky: Historian and Politician, 1838–1903 (Dublin, 1994).

UCD, A National Idea: The History of University College, Dublin (Dublin, 1999).

'History of UCD at Earlsfort Terrace' in Niamh Puirséil and Ruth Ferguson (eds), Farewell to the Terrace (Dublin, 2007), pp 1–16.

Mac Curtain, Margaret, 'St Mary's University College', University Review, 3, 4 (1963), pp 33–47.

and Donncha O'Corrain (eds), Women in Irish Society: The Historical Dimension (Dublin, 1978), pp 92–102.

Mary O'Dowd and Maria Luddy, 'An Agenda for Women's History in Ireland, 1500–1900, Part 1: 1500–1800; Part 2: 1800–1900', Irish Historical Studies, 28, 109 (1982), pp 1–19, 19–37.

Macken, Mary M., 'The German Catholic Women's League', Studies, 20 (December 1931), pp 555–69.

'Women in the University and the College: A Struggle Within a Struggle' in Michael Tierney (ed.), Struggle with Fortune: A Miscellany for the Centenary of the Catholic University of Ireland (Dublin, [1954]), pp 142–65.

'In Memoriam. Mary T. Hayden', Studies, 31 (September 1942), pp 369–71.

Manning, Maurice, 'Women in Irish National and Local Politics 1922–77' in Margaret Mac Curtain and Donncha O'Corrain (eds), Women in Irish Society: The Historical Dimension (Dublin, 1978), pp 92–102.

Martin, F.X., 'The Vacant Chair at University College, Dublin, 24 May 1916–24 May 1918' in F.X. Martin and F.J. Byrne (eds), The Scholar Revolutionary: Eoin MacNeill 1867–1945 and the Making of the New Ireland (Shannon, 1973), pp 385–90.

Mathews, P.J., Revival: The Abbey Theatre, Sinn Féin, the Gaelic League and the Co-Operative Movement (Cork, 2003).

Maume, Patrick, 'Nationalism and Partition: The Political Thought of Arthur Clery', Irish Historical Studies, 31 (November 1998), pp 222–40.

Meenan, F.O.C., Cecilia Street: The Catholic University School of Medicine 1855–1931 (Dublin, 1987).

Meenan, James (ed.), Centenary History of the Literary and Historical Society of University College Dublin, 1855–1955 (Dublin, 2005, 2nd ed.).

Morrissey, Thomas J., Towards a National University: William Delany (1835–1924): An Era of Initiative in Irish Education (Dublin, 1983).

Thomas A. Finlay SJ, 1848–1940: Educationalist, Editor, Social Reformer (Dublin, 2004).

Mowbray, John, 'Curfew (1916–23)' in James Meenan (ed.), *Centenary History of the Literary and Historical Society of University College Dublin 1855–1955* (Dublin, 2005, 2nd ed.), pp 141–7.

Murphy, Cliona, *The Women's Suffrage Movement and Irish Society in the Early Twentieth Century* (London, 1989).

'"Great Gas" and "Irish Bull"; Humour and the Fight for Irish Women's Suffrage' in Louise Ryan and Margaret Ward (eds), *Irish Women and the Vote: Becoming Citizens* (Dublin, 2007), pp 90–113.

Murphy, John A., *Ireland in the Twentieth Century* (Dublin, 1975).

The College: A History of Queen's/University College Cork 1845–1995 (Cork, 1995).

Nevin, Monica, 'The 1930s' in Anne Macdona (ed.), *From Newman to New Woman: UCD Women Remember* (Dublin, 2001), pp 11–12.

Ní Chinnéide, Máiréad, *Máire de Buitléir: Bean Athbheochana* (Baile Átha Cliath, 1993).

Nic Congáil, Ríona, *Úna Ní Fhaircheallaigh agus an Fhis Útóipeach Ghaelach* (Baile Átha Cliath, 2010).

Ó hÓgartaigh, Margaret, *Kathleen Lynn: Irishwoman, Patriot, Doctor* (Dublin, 2006).

Quiet Revolutionaries: Irish Women in Education, Medicine and Sport, 1861–1964 (Dublin, 2011).

Ó Lúing, Seán, *Kuno Meyer 1858–1919: A Biography* (Dublin, 1991).

O'Connor, Anne V. and Susan M. Parkes, *Gladly Learn and Gladly Teach: Alexandra College and School 1866–1966* (Dublin, 1984).

'The Revolution in Girls' Secondary Education in Ireland, 1860–1910' in Mary Cullen (ed.), *Girls Don't Do Honours: Irish Women in Education in the 19th and 20th Centuries* (Dublin, 1987), pp 31–54.

'Anne Jellicoe 1823–1880' in Mary Cullen and Maria Luddy (eds), *Women, Power and Consciousness in 19th Century Ireland: Eight Biographical Studies* (Dublin, 1995), pp 125–55.

O'Conor, Norreys Jephson, *Changing Ireland: Literary Backgrounds of the Irish Free State 1889–1922* (Cambridge, 1924).

O'Dowd, Mary, 'From Morgan to Mac Curtain: Women Historians in Ireland from the 1790s to the 1990s' in Maryann Valiulis and Mary O'Dowd (eds), *Women and Irish history: Essays in Honour of Margaret Mac Curtain* (Dublin, 1997), pp 38–58.

O'Farrelly, Agnes, 'Mary Hayden', *Alexandra College Magazine* (December 1942), pp 32–5.

O'Flynn, Grainne, 'Augustine Birrell and Archbishop William Walsh's Influence on the Founding of the National University of Ireland', *Capuchin Annual* (1976), pp 145–62.

O'Halpin, Eunan, 'Historical Revisit: Dorothy Macardle *The Irish Republic* (1937)', *Irish Historical Studies*, 31 (May 1999), pp 389–94.

O'Neill, Maire, 'The Dublin Women's Suffrage Association and its Successors', *Dublin Historical Record*, 38 (1985), pp 126–40.

From Parnell to de Valera: A Biography of Jennie Wyse Power 1858–1941 (Dublin, 1991).

Grace Gifford Plunkett and Irish Freedom: Tragic Bride of 1916 (Dublin, 2000).

O'Sullivan, J. M., 'The Congress of Historical Studies', *Studies*, 2 (June 1913), pp 92–8.

Oldham, Alice, 'Women and the Irish University Question', *New Ireland Review*, 6, 5 (January, 1897), pp 257–63.

Padbury, Joyce, 'Mary Hayden (1862–1942): Historian and Feminist', *History Ireland*, 15, 5 (2007), pp 10–11.

'Mary Hayden and Women's Admission to the University: The Establishment of the National University of Ireland in 1908', *Dublin Historical Record*, 61, 1 (2008), pp 78–86.

'Mary Hayden (1862–1942): Feminist', *Studies*, 98 (2009), pp 145–58.

'"A Young Schoolmaster of Great Literary Talent": Mary Hayden's Friend, Patrick Pearse' in Roisín Higgins and Regina Uí Chollatáin (eds), *The Life and After-Life of P.H. Pearse* (Dublin, 2009), pp 33–44.

'A Mixture of Flattery and Insult: Women's Opposition to the 1937 Constitution', *History Ireland*, 26, 3 (2018), pp 38–40.

Parkes, Susan M. (ed.), *A Danger to the Men? A History of Women in Trinity College Dublin, 1904–2004* (Dublin, 2004).

and Judith Harford, 'Women and Higher Education in Ireland' in Deirdre Raftery and Susan M. Parkes (eds), *Female Education in Ireland 1700–1900: Minerva or Madonna* (Dublin, 2007), pp 105–43.

'Intermediate Education for Girls' in Deirdre Raftery and Susan M. Parkes (eds), *Female Education in Ireland 1700–1900: Minerva or Madonna* (Dublin, 2007), pp 69–104.

Pašeta, Senia, *Before the Revolution: Nationalism, Social Change and Ireland's Catholic Elite, 1879–1922* (Cork, 1999).

'Ireland's Last Home Rule Generation: The Decline of Constitutional Nationalism in Ireland 1916–30' in Mike Cronin and John M. Regan (eds), *Ireland: The Politics of Independence 1922–49* (London, 2000), pp13–31.

Thomas Kettle (Historical Association of Ireland, Life and Times, 2008).

'Hayden, Mary Teresa', *Oxford Dictionary of National Biography* (Oxford, 2004), vol. 26, pp 5–6.

Perrot, Michelle, 'Stepping Out' in Genevieve Fraisse and Michelle Perrot (eds), *A History of Women in the West: Vol. 4, Emerging Feminism from Revolution to World War* (Harvard, 1993), pp 449–81.

Pope Hennessy, R., *The Irish Dominion League: A Method of Approach to a Settlement* (London, 1919).

Prunty, Jacinta, 'Margaret Louisa Aylward (1810–1889)' in Mary Cullen and Maria Luddy (eds), *Women, Power and Consciousness in 19th Century Ireland: Eight Biographical Studies* (Dublin, 1995), pp 55–88.

Purvis, June, *A History of Women's Education in England* (Milton Keynes, 1991).

Quinlan, Carmel, *Genteel Revolutionaries: Anna and Thomas Haslam and the Irish Women's Movement* (Cork, 2002).

Raftery, Deirdre, 'Francis Power Cobbe (1822–1904)' in Mary Cullen and Maria Luddy (eds), *Women, Power and Consciousness in 19th Century Ireland: Eight Biographical Studies* (Dublin, 1995), pp 89–123.

'The Higher Education of Women in Ireland 1860–1904' in Susan M. Parkes (ed.), *A Danger to the Men? A History of Women in Trinity College Dublin 1904–2004* (Dublin, 2004), pp 5–18.

Regan, John M. and Mike Cronin, 'Ireland and the Politics of Independence 1922–49: New Perspectives and Reconsiderations' in Mike Cronin and John M. Regan (eds), *Ireland: The Politics of Independence 1922–49* (Basingstoke, 2000), pp 1–12.

Regan, Nell, *Helena Molony: A Radical Life, 1883–1967* (Dublin, 2017).

Reilly, Eileen, 'Women and Voluntary War Work' in Adrian Gregory and Senia Pašeta (eds), *Ireland and the Great War: 'A War to Unite Us All?'* (Manchester, 2002), pp 49–72.

Reynolds, Paige, 'Staging Suffrage: The Events of 1913 Dublin Suffrage Week' in Louise Ryan and Margaret Ward (eds), *Irish Women and the Vote: Becoming Citizens* (Dublin, 2007), pp 60–74

Rice, Joy K. and Annette Hemmings, 'Women's Colleges and Women Achievers: An Update' in Elizabeth Minnich, Jean O'Barr and Rachel Rosenfeld (eds), *Reconstructing the Academy: Women's Education and Women's Studies* (Chicago, 1998), pp 220–33.

Roche, Peig, 'Coffee, Cream Buns and Civil War' in Anne Macdona ed.), *From Newman to New Woman: UCD Women Remember* (Dublin, 2001), pp 31–5.

S.M.R., Convent of St Louis, Monaghan, 'Some Thoughts on Woman and her Rights', *Irish Educational Review*, 2, 11 (August 1909), pp 653–6.

Sacerdos [i.e. Peter Finlay], 'Mr Birrell's University Bill', *New Ireland Review*, 24 (June 1908), pp 210–20.

Scannell, Yvonne, 'The Constitution and the Role of Women' in Brian Farrell (ed.), *De Valera's Constitution and Ours* (Dublin, 1988), pp 123–36.

Semple, Mary, 'Going Hatching' in Anne Macdona (ed.), *From Newman to New Woman: UCD Women Remember* (Dublin, 2001), p. 13.

Smith, Nadia Clare, *A "Manly Study"? Irish Women Historians, 1868–1949* (Basingstoke, 2006).

Dorothy Macardle: A Life (Dublin, 2007).

Solomon, Barbara Miller, *In the Company of Educated Women: A History of Women and Higher Education in America* (New Haven, 1985).

Sullivan, M., 'Co-Education in the National University of Ireland', *Irish Educational Review*, 3, 10 (1909–10), pp 577–83.

Thompson, Lucinda, 'The Campaign for Admission, 1870–1904' in Susan M. Parkes (ed.), *A Danger to the Men? A History of Women in Trinity College Dublin 1904–2004* (Dublin, 2004), pp 19–54.

Tidball, M. Elizabeth, 'Women's Colleges and Women Achievers Revisited' in Elizabeth Minnick, Jean O'Barr and Rachel Rosenfeld (eds), *Reconstructing the Academy: Women's Education and Women's Studies* (Chicago, 1988), pp 206–19.

Tierney, Michael, '"A Weary Task": The Struggle in Retrospect' in Michael Tierney (ed.), *Struggle with Fortune: A Miscellany for the Centenary of the Catholic University of Ireland* (Dublin, [1954]), pp 1–18.

Uí Chollatáin, Regina, *An Claidheamh Soluis agus Fáinne an Lae 1899–1932: Anailís ar Phríomhnuachtán Gaeilge Ré na hAthbheochana* (Baile Átha Cliath, 2004).

Valiulis, Maryann, '"Free Women in a Free Nation": Nationalist Feminist Expectations for Independence' in Brian Farrell (ed.), *The Creation of the Dáil* (Dublin, 1994), pp 75–90.

'Defining their Role in the New State: Irishwomen's Protest Against the Juries Act of 1927', *Canadian Journal of Irish Studies*, 18 (1992), pp 43–60.

'Engendering Citizenship: Women's Relationship to the State in Ireland and the United States in the Post-Suffrage Period' in

Maryann Valiulis and Mary O'Dowd (eds), *Women and Irish History: Essays in Honour of Margaret Mac Curtain* (Dublin, 1997), pp 159–72.

'Neither Feminist Nor Flapper: The Ecclesiastical Construction of the Ideal Irish Woman' in Mary O'Dowd and Sabine Wichert (eds), *Chattel, Servant or Citizen? Women's Status in Church, State and Society* (Belfast, 1995), pp 168–78.

'Power, Gender and Identity in the Irish Free State' in Joan Hoff and Moureen Coulter (eds), *Irish Women's Voices: Past and Present* (Bloomington, Ind., 1995), pp 117–36.

'Toward "The Moral and Material Improvement of the Working Classes": The Founding of the Alexandra College Guild Tenement Company, Dublin 1898', *Journal of Urban History*, 23, 3 (1997), pp 295–315.

Vicinus, Martha, *Independent Women: Work and Community for Single Women 1850–1920* (Chicago, 1985).

Wall, Mervyn, 'New Beginnings 1923–30, IV' in James Meenan (ed.), *Centenary History of the Literary and Historical Society of University College Dublin, 1855–1955* (Dublin, 2005, 2nd ed.), pp 177–83.

Ward, Margaret, *Hanna Sheehy Skeffington: A Life* (Cork, 1997).

In Their Own Voice: Women and Irish Nationalism (Dublin, 1995).

Maud Gonne: Ireland's Joan of Arc (London, 1990).

Unmanageable Revolutionaries: Women and Irish Nationalism (London, 1995 ed.).

Webb, Alfred, *The Autobiography of a Quaker Nationalist*, edited by Marie-Louise Legg (Cork, 1999).

Williams, T. D., 'The College and the Nation' in Michael Tierney (ed.), *Struggle with Fortune: A Miscellany for the Centenary of the Catholic University of Ireland* (Dublin, [1954]), pp 166–192.

Yeates, Padraig, *Lockout: Dublin 1913* (Dublin, 2000).

Orpen, William, 208
Oxford Dictionary of National Biography, 17, 24, 111, 337, 347

Pacifism/Pacifist, 25, 213, 215
Palatine Pact, 38
Palestine, 71
Palles, Chief Baron Christopher, 154, 156, 173
Pankhurst, Emmeline, Christabel and Sylvia, 199, 201, 216
Paris, France, 31, 47, 63, 168
Parliament Act, 1911, 200
Parliamentary franchise, 18, 40, 134, 189, 196, 200, 207, 216, 218, 221, 233, 255–256, 263, 284, 299, 302, 324, 327
Parliamentary politics, 63, 150
Parnell, Anna, 39
Parnell, Charles Stewart, 34, 53, 62–63, 152, 162, 311, 346
Parsons Hill, Tipperary, 26–27
Pašeta, Senia, 17, 24, 53, 82, 115, 162, 225, 256, 279, 346–347
Paternalism/paternalist, 255, 263, 276, 293, 301–302, 308
Patriarchal, 19, 40, 63, 180, 276
Patriotism, 183, 197–198
Patterson, Dr Anne, 42, 55
Pearse, Margaret, 170, 295
Pearse, Mary Brigid, 143, 160, 190, 335
Pearse, Patrick, 12, 23, 76, 105, 114, 126, 139, 141–149, 154, 157–163, 170–171, 190, 204, 206, 215, 219, 226, 253, 255–256, 332, 335–336, 338, 341, 346
Penal Laws, 232, 240
Peter Street School of Medicine, 27

Petrie, George, 75
Philanthropy/ism, 19, 88, 92–96, 111–112, 197–198, 205, 230, 254, 326, 343
Phoblacht, An, 284
Piatt, Donn, 92, 105
Plunkett, Sir Horace, 66, 256
Polin, Abbé G, 43
Power, Eileen, 183, 192, 338
Power, Jennie Wyse, 21, 25, 203–206, 264, 267, 275, 294, 311, 329, 346
Poynings Law, 1570, 237, 252
Proclamation, 1916, 215, 217, 261, 284, 288, 298–299
Propaganda, 199, 211, 279, 340
Prostitution, 40, 93–94, 111, 212–213, 223, 326, 343
Protestant, 26, 36–43, 60, 61, 74, 95, 118–120, 125, 208, 230, 233, 272, 274, 303
Public Record Office, 257, 279
Purser, Sarah, 78

Quaker, 25, 70, 83, 349
Queen's College, Belfast, 118
Queen's College, Cork, 118, 149, 156
Queen's College, Galway, 118, 156
Queen's University, Belfast, 118, 132, 180, 192
Quinn, Stephen and James, 58, 62

Raleigh, Walter, 232–233
Rathmines School of Commerce, 205
Redmond, Bridget, 286, 295
Redmond, John, 200, 211, 215
Redmond, Willie, 201
Reeves, Annie, 314

South Africa, 72, 74, 102–103
109, 152
Spenser, 184
Spiritualism, 77
St Columban, Life of, 181
St Enda's School, Rathfarnham,
157
St Joan's Social Club, 245, 326
St John Gogarty, Oliver, 208
St Mary's Dominican College,
42, 74–75, 80, 98, 119–122,
128, 130, 136, 174, 176–177,
344
Standard, The, 292–293
Stanford, Professor W.B., 213
Starkie, Dr Enid, 67, 92, 321, 332
Starkie, William J.M., 67, 92, 98
Stern, Professor Ludwig, 150,
161–162
Stokes, Professor Whitley, 66
Story, Emma Mary, 65
Strachan, Dr John, 144, 149, 160–
161
Studies, 66, 85, 161, 185, 189–190,
192–193, 240, 249–252, 333–
335, 344, 346
Suffrage, 11–12, 19, 24–25, 40,
73–74, 78–79, 127, 133–134,
158–159, 172, 179, 180, 183,
186, 194–226, 233, 238, 256,
268–270, 274, 280, 291, 293,
299, 319, 324, 326, 329, 339–
340, 345, 347–348
Switzerland, 32, 52

The Catholic Citizen, 208, 225–
226, 250, 337
The Leader, 123, 136, 337
The Nation, 76
The Songs of Buchet's House,
150, 333
The Sphere, 97, 113, 184, 192, 337

Third International Congress of
Historical Studies, 1913, 185,
189, 193, 334, 346
Tod, Isabella, 19, 25, 35, 40–41,
53, 110, 117, 247, 254, 343
Transvaal committee, 152
Trevelyan, Professor G.M., 240,
252
Trinity College/Dublin
University (TCD), 37–38, 43,
45, 54, 59, 66–67, 69, 72, 78,
81, 86, 97, 118–119, 124–125,
128–129, 132–133, 135–137,
155, 160–161, 167, 177, 180,
182, 191, 206, 239, 290, 310–
311, 315, 318, 336–337, 343,
346–348

Unionist, 21–22, 156, 174, 188,
202–203, 216–217, 220, 329
United Kingdom, 155
University College Cork (UCC),
55, 135, 156, 170, 188, 193,
242, 345
University College Dublin
(UCD), 4, 9, 13, 20, 23, 52, 55,
66, 76, 78, 83, 99–100, 113,
126, 132–133, 135–138, 149,
156, 159, 161, 163, 165–166,
169, 170–173, 175–178, 180,
186–187, 189–192, 202, 204,
211, 213, 224–225, 227, 238–
240, 242, 245, 249, 252–254,
265, 273, 281–282, 288, 294,
305, 310, 311, 313, 316, 330,
332, 336–338, 340, 344–345,
347–349
University College Galway
(UCG), 156, 182, 188, 209,
224, 234, 293, 312, 337, 339
University of London, 41
Upper class, 92, 197, 247